PYTHON

QuickStart Guide®

PYTHON

QuickStart Guide®

The Simplified Beginner's Guide to
Python Programming Using Hands-On Projects
and Real-World Applications

Robert Oliver

Editors: Bryan Basamanowicz, Marilyn Burkley
Technical Reviewers: Derik Stiller, Robert Utterback, Michael Wheelock
Cover Illustration and Design: Katie Donnachie, Nicole Daberkow, Copyright © 2023 by ClydeBank Media LLC
Interior Design & Illustrations: Katie Donnachie, Brittney Duquette, Copyright © 2023 by ClydeBank Media LLC

First Edition - Last Updated: June 19, 2023

ISBN: 9781636100357 (paperback) | 9781636100371 (hardcover) | 9781636100395 (audiobook) | 9781636100364 (ebook) | 9781636100388 (spiral bound)

Publisher's Cataloging-In-Publication Data
(Prepared by The Donohue Group, Inc.)

Names: Oliver, Robert, 1980- author.
Title: Python QuickStart guide : the simplified beginner's guide to Python programming using hands-on projects and real-world applications / Robert Oliver.
Other Titles: Python Quick Start guide
Description: [Albany, New York] : ClydeBank Technology, [2023] | Series: QuickStart Guide | Includes bibliographical references and index.
Identifiers: ISBN 9781636100357 (paperback) | ISBN 9781636100371 (hardcover) | ISBN 9781636100364 (ebook)
Subjects: LCSH: Python (Computer program language)
Classification: LCC QA76.73.P98 O45 2022 (print) | LCC QA76.73.P98 (ebook) | DDC 005.133--dc23

Library of Congress Control Number: 2022947452

Author ISNI: 0000 0005 0677 4266

For bulk sales inquiries, please visit www.go.quickstartguides.com/wholesale, email us at orders@clydebankmedia.com, or call 800-340-3069. Special discounts are available on quantity purchases by corporations, associations, and others.

ClydeBank
MEDIA

OVER
850,000
READERS **LOVE** *QuickStart Guides.*

Really well written with lots of practical information. These books have a very concise way of presenting each topic and everything inside is very actionable!

— ALAN F.

The book was a great resource, every page is packed with information, but [the book] never felt overly-wordy or repetitive. Every chapter was filled with very useful information.

— CURTIS W.

I appreciated how accessible and how insightful the material was and look forward to sharing the knowledge that I've learned [from this book].

— SCOTT B.

After reading this book, I must say that it has been one of the best decisions of my life!

— ROHIT R.

This book is one-thousand percent worth every single dollar!

— HUGO C.

The read itself was worth the cost of the book, but the additional tools and materials make this purchase a better value than most books.

— JAMES D.

I finally understand this topic ... this book has really opened doors for me!

— MISTY A.

I dedicate this book to Marsha, my wife.
Only through her steadfast support was this possible.

Contents

PART I – GETTING STARTED WITH PYTHON

PART III – PYTHON IN ACTION

PART IV – ADVANCED PYTHON

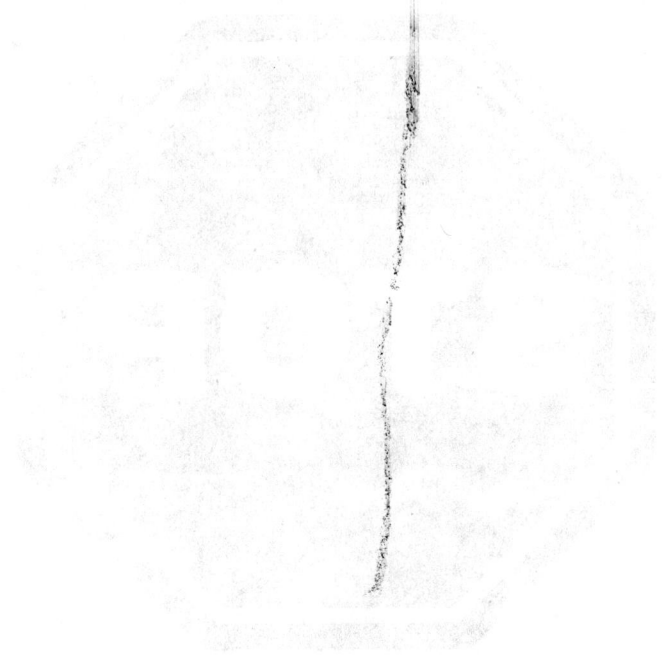

STOP

BEFORE YOU START READING,
DOWNLOAD YOUR FREE DIGITAL ASSETS!

- **All Source Code from Game and Examples**
- **Regular Expression Cheat Sheet**
- **List of Built-in Exceptions Cheat Sheet**

TWO WAYS TO ACCESS YOUR FREE DIGITAL ASSETS

Use the camera app on your mobile phone to scan the QR code
or visit the link below and instantly access your digital assets.

or

go.quickstartguides.com/python

SCAN ME　　　　**VISIT URL**

Introduction

Welcome to Python.

My name is Robert Oliver and I'll be your guide through the exciting, engaging, and challenging endeavor of learning a programming language.

It Was a Dark and Stormy Night

While I now program quite a bit at night, my programming journey started on a bright, sunny early June morning. As a young teenager, I sat in front of my stepmother's Tandy 1000 (an older computer, even in the early 1990s) and enjoyed playing the myriad of video games that had been installed on it. Even though I previously had some computer experience, I was mystified by the possibilities.

It was summer break, and I had all the time in the world, so I started reading the BASIC (Beginner's All-purpose Symbolic Instruction Code) language source code to some of these games. It was a struggle at first, as I really didn't know much about programming, but soon I started to see patterns in the code and how everything fit together to make the video games run.

Armed with several books, I taught myself DOS, BASIC, and even dabbled in a little Pascal, another programming language, as I fully extracted the computing goodness that old Tandy had to offer. Later, I got my own computer, a Tandy 2500, an Intel 386 computer that ran MS-DOS 5 and Windows 3.1. Armed with QBasic, I wrote my own video games and programs. It was fun, but I quickly ran into problems.

Video games take a lot of computing power, and computers back then didn't exactly have that to spare. So, to extract the most performance from the machine and power my games, I wrote critical parts of the games in *assembly language*—a bare-metal language that computers natively understand—to speed things along. Granted, I ran into numerous problems talking back and forth between my BASIC and assembly programs, but I eventually worked out a solution that made me reasonably happy.

I poked and prodded into every corner of that machine's memory, and by the time I had moved to Windows 98 (I largely skipped Windows 95), I could tell you everything about that computer you could possibly want to know, down to the basic hardware level. My immense love of systems programming came from this era, and it hasn't left me.

My dad bought me Visual Basic 6 and some great manuals in the Windows 98 years, and from this I really started to formalize my programming knowledge, learning about classes, objects, and all the things I'd need to know to program professionally. From there, I went into web programming, but I continued to write scripts and programs—first with Perl, then with Python from 2006 onward.

Despite having learned so much since then, nothing can replace the joy I felt when I mastered the mystical world of computing by telling my computer exactly what I wanted it to do. I want you to feel that same joy, too.

By the end of this book, you'll have a good understanding of Python and will have written a fair number of lines of code. In addition, we'll be building a coffee shop game that will be both fun to write and fun to play. You'll not only have experience coding in Python, but you'll have a project to show for it, and the knowledge to create your own programs.

What Is Python?

There are two ways to answer that question. First, here's the technical explanation with computer science terminology kept to a minimum.

Python is a multipurpose programming language. It is flexible enough to allow several different programming approaches and comes with a large array of functionality right out of the box. It enforces a strict code formatting style that places a high emphasis on readability.

Now, what is Python in everyday terms? It's an awesome programming language that lets you do a wide variety of tasks—everything from system utilities to business programs to games to website backends and even artificial intelligence. Many Fortune 500 companies use Python, including household names like Google, IBM, Intel, Netflix, and Spotify. And Python is very popular in scientific circles. In fact, NASA uses Python heavily.

What Is Programming?

This might seem like an unusual question to ask in a programming book, but it's a question I've been asked more than once by people who are considering getting into the field. If you aren't a programmer, the definition can seem a bit nebulous.

Programming is the act of defining instructions that tell a computer how to solve a problem or perform some tasks. It differs from merely *using* a computer in that running a program like a word processor, spreadsheet, or video editor might create content (for instance, a balance sheet, a YouTube video, or a book), but it doesn't tell the computer how to solve a specific problem. To continue with this analogy, using a word processing program to write a book is not programming, but programming would describe the creation of the word processor.

I have a friend who's a very talented web designer who doesn't really consider himself a programmer. He's made the argument that someone who just copies and pastes code, modifying it to suit their purposes, is more of a hacker than a programmer. Whenever he mentions this, I tell him it's pure hogwash. A programmer is anyone who writes programs, and writing a program includes modifying an existing program to do what you want it to do.

In a rapidly changing field like computer science, feeling like an impostor in a highly technical and competitive industry like this is a very real thing. In fact, many programmers, myself included, sometimes feel inadequate for the challenges we face. I remind my humble friend of that, and in doing so bolster my own self-esteem a bit. Anyone who wants to become more than a user of computers is already well on their way toward joining an elite and dedicated group of people who are willing to sacrifice sleep, sunshine, and physical activity for the sake of getting a computer to do what they tell it to do.

What We'll Cover in This Book

First, we'll learn the nuts and bolts of the Python programming language. Once we have a firm foundation, we'll look at more complex data structures and logic. We'll explore functions and object-oriented design, then dive deep into aspects of Python you'll use daily, like handling text, numbers, input and output, website functionality, debugging, and even Git source code management.

How to Use This Book

We'll learn as we go, working through sample exercises and building the ClydeBank Coffee Shop game with each chapter. This way, you won't have to learn everything up front before doing something useful. By the time you finish your first chapter, you'll have written a very simple program.

Rather than present you with a dry, boring reference book, I want to keep things interesting by giving you practical knowledge that you can use right away. I'd rather focus first on writing programs, then explore the theory behind it. I find it much easier to understand example code after I've seen it run.

Example Code

Most of the examples and all the game code are available on GitHub at https://github.com/clydebankmedia/python-quickstartguide. While the code is provided as a handy digital reference, I recommend typing each code example as we go, either in the Python interpreter or Visual Studio Code, because doing so will strengthen your understanding of the concepts we're learning.

I'll explain the differences between these two methods in chapter 1, but for now, *the important thing is that you start writing Python code as you read the book*. Simply reading the content will help, but it won't give you the hands-on experience involved in writing Python.

What You'll Need

First, you'll need a computer. A phone or tablet won't work for this exercise, unfortunately. However, if you have the e-book version of this title, you'll find it handy to have it beside your computer as you work through the exercises. I've been known to use my iPad to reference material while I code.

As for the computer, it can be any modern Windows, macOS, or Linux computer. For Windows, that would mean a computer running Windows 10 or 11. There isn't anything stopping you from running an older version of Windows, but using an out-of-date version means you could be missing important security updates. Additionally, newer versions of Python might not run on very old versions of Windows.

For macOS: I wrote these exercises on macOS Monterey, but any recent, supported version of macOS should be fine. Fortunately, Python comes preinstalled on macOS, so that part of the setup will be easy. However, if your version of macOS is older, it may come with Python 2 rather than 3. If updating to a modern version of macOS isn't possible, consider installing Homebrew (commonly called "brew", available at https://brew.sh) and running "brew install python" to install Python 3.

Any modern Linux distribution should be fine. Debian, Ubuntu, Linux Mint, Pop!_OS, Fedora, Arch, and Manjaro all make it super easy to install Python (and some even have it preinstalled).

A Google Chromebook® can technically run the Python interpreter in its Linux terminal, but you won't be able to run Visual Studio Code (the editor we'll be using in this book), so your experience will be severely hampered. We don't recommend that type of computer for use with this book.

Operating System and Python Version Notes

There have been many individual versions of Python released since version 0.9 in 1991, but two major branches, versions 2 and 3, have dominated the Python landscape for nearly fifteen years.

Python 3 introduced a lot of new concepts into the language, but also created some incompatibility issues with version 2. Since Python 2 had a large ecosystem of modules, there was a split in the community between versions 2 and 3, with developers (especially in the early days) having to choose between version 2 compatibility and version 3 features.

In 2022, this isn't really a concern. Python 3 was released in 2008, and Python 2 has been unsupported (end of life) since 2020. Thus we'll be focusing entirely on version 3 in this book.

> **NOTE**
> When I talk about the "ecosystem" of a project or version, I am referring to not only the software itself but the documentation, third-party modules and support, and community that is engaged in that particular version.

Getting Ready

Installing Python

First, we need to install Python. The instructions for this vary a bit depending on your operating system.

Windows

If you're on Windows, you have two choices: install Python from the Microsoft Store or go to https://python.org and click *Downloads*. If you use the store version, please select version 3.10 or higher.

If you choose to download it from the website, it should automatically detect that you're on Windows and offer the download link. Once you've downloaded the installer, run it, and accept the default options. Once that's done, Python should be installed.

macOS

If you're on macOS, it's already installed, so there's no need to do anything else.

Linux

If you're on Linux, you probably already have Python installed. To check, open a terminal / command shell and type:

```
python3 --version
```

If that doesn't work, try:

```
python --version
```

If the `python` command works but `python3` doesn't, and the version shown begins with a 2, then you need to specifically install Python 3. One of these commands should do the trick:

```
sudo apt install python3
sudo yum install python3
sudo dnf install python3
sudo pacman -S python
```

If these don't work, consult the documentation for your version of Linux for instructions on installing Python 3.

QUICKCLIP

I've put together a quick video on installing Python on Windows, macOS, and Linux.

To watch the QuickClip, use the camera on your mobile phone to scan the QR code or visit the link below.

or

www.quickclips.io/python-1

SCAN ME

VISIT URL

Installing Visual Studio Code

There are many code editors on the market, many of them free/open-source. Here is a list of commonly used code editors with Python support, including their operating system support and license:

» Visual Studio Code (Windows, macOS, Linux; free, mostly open source)
» Notepad++ (Windows only; free, open source)
» Sublime (Windows, macOS, Linux; paid software with free trial)
» PyCharm (Windows, macOS, Linux; paid software with free trial)
» Vim (Windows, macOS, Linux; free, open source)
» Emacs (Windows, macOS, Linux; free, open source)

In this book, we'll be using Visual Studio Code because it's well supported on all operating systems and it's free/open source. It's an excellent code editor and development environment. That said, if you're fond of another editor, please feel free to use it—just know that the instructions here will center around Visual Studio Code.

The simplest way to install Visual Studio Code on Windows is to use the Microsoft Store.

For macOS or Linux, go to https://code.visualstudio.com and download it for your platform. On macOS, the disk image can be mounted by double-clicking it. Then drag Visual Studio Code to your Applications folder. Linux users will need to download either a `.deb` (Debian, Ubuntu, Linux Mint, MX Linux) package or a `.rpm` (Fedora, openSUSE, Red Hat Enterprise Linux) package and install it on their system.

We'll configure it in the next section, after creating a place for our code.

DETOUR

Other than Visual Studio Code for this book's exercises, I'm not particularly recommending one editor over another. Code editor choice is a question of personal preference and workflow, and everyone has their own opinions on the subject. Nevertheless, if you're looking for an alternative to Visual Studio Code, here are a few thoughts I have on each:

Notepad++ is an excellent code editor but is only available for Windows. If you only use Windows, this might be just fine, but its lack of multi-platform support creates issues for my workflow.

I haven't had much experience with Sublime, but I know several colleagues who really like it. The price is reasonable and has some unique features you might find appealing.

I quite like the JetBrains products, including PyCharm, but this is a paid solution, so I didn't want to focus on it in the book. Since I use other JetBrains products like DataGrid and RubyMine, PyCharm fits in well.

Vim and Emacs are more advanced editors. I use Vim quite a bit in my day-to-day programming and system administration work, and it has a lot of advantages, but I wouldn't necessarily recommend it or Emacs to someone new to programming, as they both have a steep learning curve.

Creating a Folder for Your Code

I recommend making a folder in which to save all your Python code files. Where this is on your disk is entirely up to you, but I'll share my approach, for inspiration.

Regardless of my operating system (macOS, Windows, Linux—I use them all), I create a folder called `Source` in my home directory. On macOS, you can access your home directory in Finder by clicking the *Go* menu, then clicking Home. On Windows, press the Windows key and R together, then type `%USERPROFILE%` in the box and click OK, or navigate to `C:\Users\You` (where `You` is your username). On Linux, most file managers open to this folder by default, but you can find it at `/home/you` (where `you` is your username).

Once in the home folder, I create a folder inside of that for each project I make. If you're unsure how you want to proceed, just save it to a new folder called `PythonQSG` in your `Source` folder. You can always move it later if you like.

NOTE

Even though the screenshots in this book are mostly taken from macOS, this doesn't mean Windows and Linux users will be left out in the cold. As I said, I use all three platforms and love all of them for their strengths and weaknesses alike. Since Python is cross-platform, there are few instances where platform-specific instructions are necessary. However, any time there is a difference I'll explain it on all three systems, so you'll be able to enjoy Python no matter what computer you have.

Visual Studio Code Walk-Through

Visual Studio Code is a powerful open-source editor that makes it easy to manage programming projects both large and small. It supports many different programming languages, but we'll be focused on Python.

NOTE

Technically, the core of Visual Studio Code is open-source and is available at https://github.com/Microsoft/vscode; however, the Visual Studio Code product we'll use that's accessible through your Digital Assets contains proprietary Microsoft technology. Nevertheless, the bulk of the editor is open-source.

When you first start Visual Studio Code, you should see a link on the page to install support for Python. If so, click it and the necessary extensions will be installed. If you don't see a link, that's fine—there's a way to get to the extensions from the left-hand pane (figure 1).

IMAGE

fig. 1

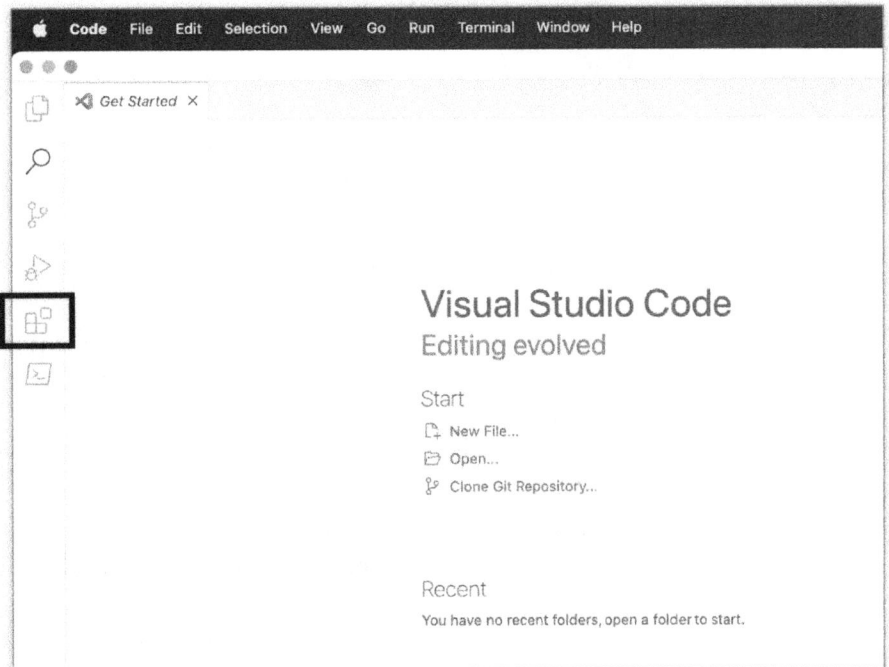

The Visual Studio Code welcome screen.
The Extensions icon is highlighted in this figure on the left-hand pane.

When you click the Extensions icon, a list of common extensions will appear. Type "Python" in the search box and you'll see the official Python extension from Microsoft in the list. You'll know it's the official extension because it says "IntelliSense (Pylance), Linting ... " etc., and has Microsoft as the publisher with a blue check mark next to it. If it doesn't have a green *Install* button beside it, it's already installed. If it does, go ahead and click the button to install it (figure 2).

fig. 2

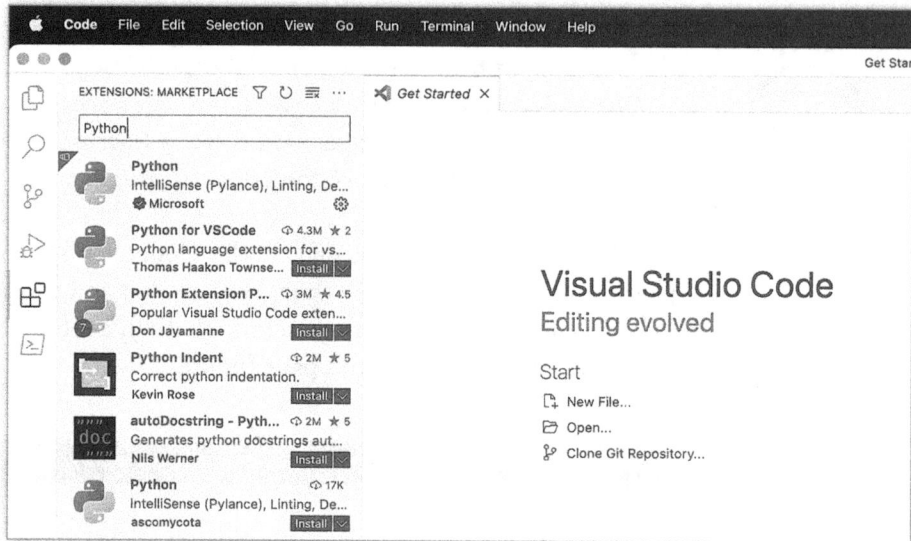

Searching for the Python extension in the extensions list of Visual Studio Code.
In this figure, the official Python extension is shown with a check mark badge and the publisher, Microsoft, beneath the listing.

While you're here, you can install other extensions if you like. If you're new to programming in general, I don't recommend you install anything else, except perhaps a theme. A theme in Visual Studio Code changes the colors of the editor to help with readability or simply to allow you to make adjustments according to your own preferences. To see the available themes, click on the funnel icon above the *Extensions* search box, click the *Category* menu, then select *Themes*.

This will show a list of themes available in Visual Studio Code. You have a lot to choose from. If you aren't sure which you like, click one that interests you and it will generally display screenshots. Click *Install* next to the one you want to install, and it will automatically switch to it once downloaded.

If you're looking for suggestions, I would recommend the Dracula Official theme or One Dark Pro. If you prefer lighter themes, GitHub Theme is quite nice. Filtering by theme (as shown in figure 3), then typing the name of the theme you'd like to install, will filter the available options to show only those for the name you type.

The GitHub Theme has several variations, so you'll need to switch to it if you want the light variety. To switch themes at any time, click the *Code* menu at the top (or click the *File* menu on Windows and Linux), click *Preferences*, then *Color Theme* (figure 4).

fig. 3

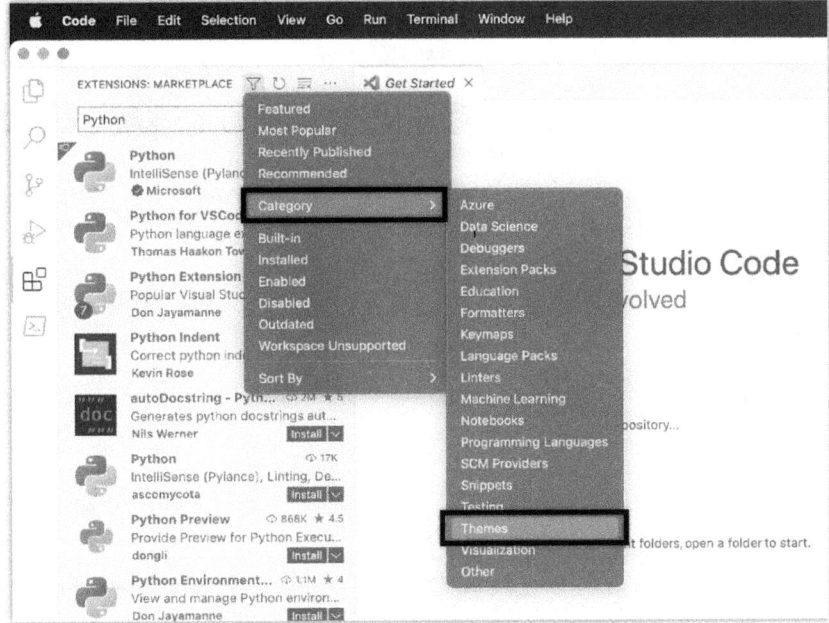

Accessing the Themes category filter in the extension viewer.

fig. 4

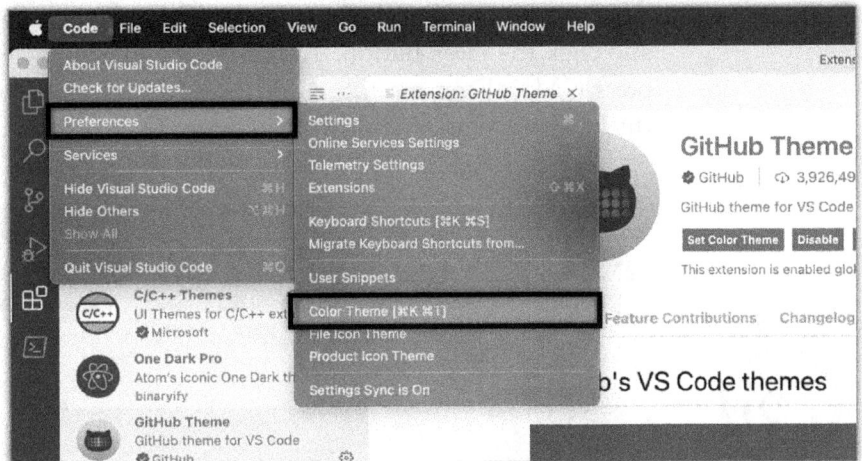

The Color Theme menu item in the *Code > Preferences* menu.

Alternatively, you can use CTRL+K then CTRL+T on Windows and Linux, or CMD+K then CMT+T on macOS. A selection box will be displayed where you can change the theme (figure 5).

fig. 5

Extension: GitHub Theme

Select Color Theme (Up/Down Keys to Preview)

+ Browse Additional Color Themes...

GitHub Light	light themes
GitHub Light Colorblind (Beta)	
GitHub Light Default	
Light (Visual Studio)	⚙
Light+ (default light)	
PowerShell ISE	
Quiet Light	
Solarized Light	
Abyss	dark themes
Dark (Visual Studio)	
Dark+ (default dark)	
Dracula	
Dracula Soft	
GitHub Dark	
GitHub Dark Colorblind (Beta)	
GitHub Dark Default	
GitHub Dark Dimmed	

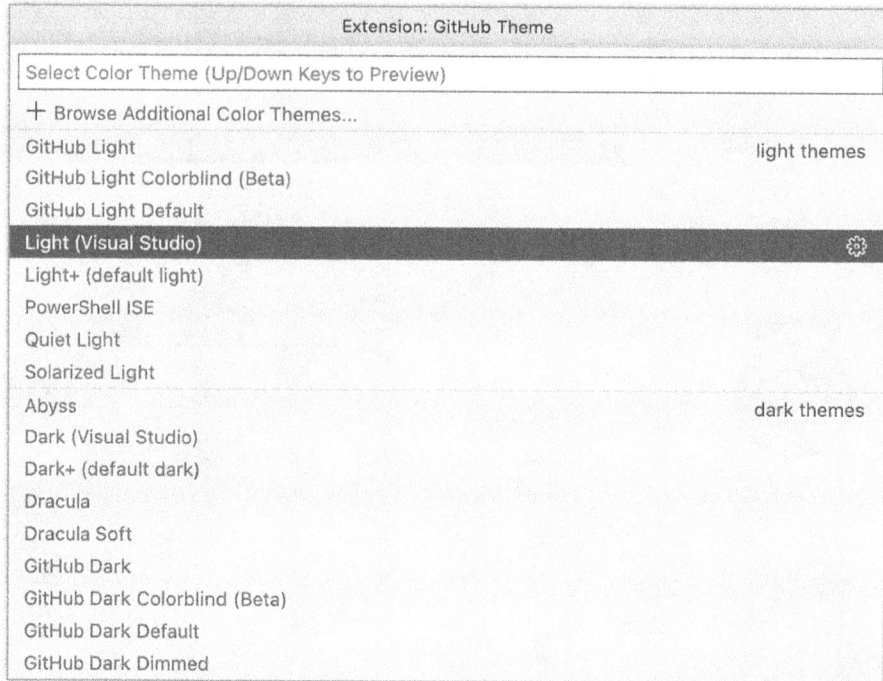

The color theme selector.

Now that we have Python support installed and our preferred color theme selected, let's open the folder we created for our Python code. Click on the *File* menu and click *Open Folder*. Then navigate to the folder you chose and click the *Open* button. To browse the folder, click the Explorer icon (or press CMD+E on macOS, CTRL+SHIFT+E on Windows and Linux) in the left-hand pane (highlighted in figure 6).

fig. 6

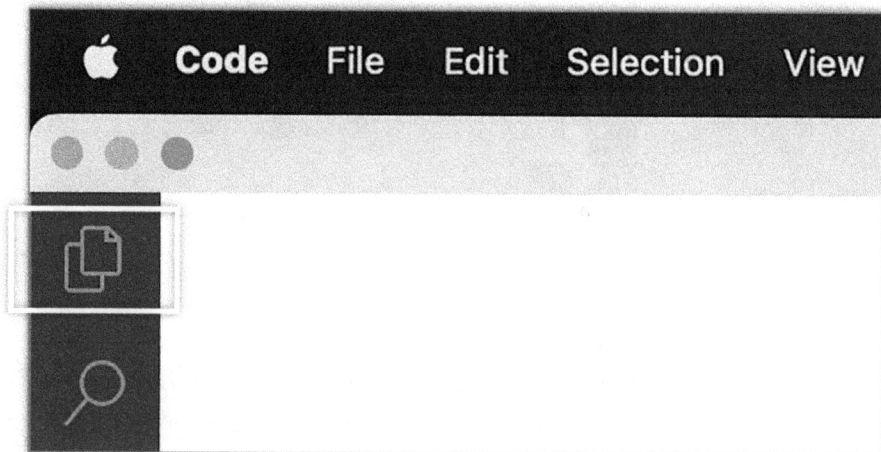

The Explorer icon is in the box.

When you create new Python code files in the folder you selected for your code, they will show in the Explorer pane of Visual Studio Code.

That's all you need to know about Visual Studio Code for now. We'll pick up the actual coding workflow in chapter 1.

IMPORTANT

Code that should appear on a single line but must be broken due to page constraints is indicated using arrows. A straight arrow (↦) at the end of a line and and a curved arrow (↪) at the beginning of the next line indicate that those lines should be combined to make one continuous line.

Chapter by Chapter

» **Part I: Getting Started with Python**

» In part I, we'll learn the basics of Python, from a tour of the Python interpreter (the core of the language) to understanding variables and working with conditionals and loops. We'll also cover how to handle errors.

» In chapter 1, we'll get our feet wet with Python, learning about the interpreter and how to run a program in Visual Studio Code, and we'll talk about strings and numbers.

» In chapter 2, Python data structures are covered, including lists, tuples, sets, and dictionaries. We also explore working with multiple sets of data.

» In chapter 3, program flow is discussed, including `if` statements and their variants, as well as loops.

» In chapter 4, we'll learn how to handle errors (called exceptions in Python) in our program.

» **Part II: Functions and Classes**

» In part II, we explore functions and classes and introduce the object-oriented programming paradigm, which will empower you to solve complex problems with simple yet logically organized code.

We'll also cover inheritance, modules, and packages.

» In chapter 5, we explore the world of functions and learn how to pass arguments to them. Functions let us avoid repeating ourselves and modularize our code.

» In chapter 6, object-oriented programming and classes are introduced. Classes are structures that contain both data and code, letting us organize our application's functionality.

» In chapter 7, we dive deep into inheritance and common design patterns.

» In chapter 8, a survey of dataclasses shows how to save time by helping us prototype our classes.

» In chapter 9, we modularize and reuse our code files and logic with modules and packages.

» **Part III: Python in Action**

» In part III, we'll delve into advanced Python functionality, like math, statistics, input/output, and interacting with the internet. We'll also tour several popular website frameworks and learn about debugging techniques.

» In chapter 10, advanced strings, input validation, and compression are covered. We also delve into the immensely powerful world of regular expressions.

» In chapter 11, we explore the wealth of Python's math and statistics functionality.

» In chapter 12, input and output functionality is covered, and we discuss how to serialize our classes.

» In chapter 13, we'll interact with the internet, send email, and fetch web pages.

» In chapter 14, we learn how to debug our Python applications.

» **Part IV: Advanced Python**

» In part IV, we'll finish our journey by learning about interfacing with databases, test-driven development, managing source code with Git, and optimization. And we cover a cornucopia of additional functionality you'll use in your everyday Python work.

» In chapter 15, the focus turns to web development frameworks like `web.py`, Flask, and Django.

» In chapter 16, the SQLite database system is explored with a practical example database.

» In chapter 17, test-driven development is covered.

» In chapter 18, the basics of the Git source code management system are discussed.

» In chapter 19, we pull out the junk drawer and go over several smaller topics that didn't quite deserve an entire chapter but are important for Python developers.

» In chapter 20, profiling and optimizing Python code are discussed, both for absolute performance and apparent speed.

» In chapter 21, I suggest some next steps in your Python journey.

I'm excited to teach you Python. Let's get started!

PART I

GETTING STARTED WITH PYTHON

| 1 |

Getting to Know Python

Chapter Overview

> » The Python interpreter runs Python code
> » Python programs are text files ending in `.py`
> » Variables store data, including strings and numbers

The Python interpreter is the heart of the Python programming language. True to its name, it interprets and runs the commands we give it, either interactively or, most commonly, from a file. Just as a text file generally ends in `.txt` and an image file in `.jpg`, a Python program is essentially nothing more than a text file with a `.py` extension that contains instructions for the Python interpreter. In the simplest of terms, writing a Python program is like writing a text file with special commands that the Python interpreter understands.

Before Our First Line of Code

Programming is an art and not an exact science. Many beginning programmers feel intimidated about making a mistake or not making the right choices. That's perfectly natural. If you're concerned about starting what you fear is a daunting task, let me say right now that you will make mistakes and things will go wrong.

Perhaps that doesn't sound very reassuring, but take comfort in the fact that this happens to every programmer all the time. I have been frustrated for days over something not working right, only to discover that one simple letter had broken my code and the fix for it took less than half a second. Programming can be frustrating, but it can also be wildly rewarding. As you learn more about Python and write programs, you will feel more comfortable with the language.

So get comfortable, take a deep breath, and let's dive in!

Hello, World!

The very first thing most programmers learn to write is the classic "Hello, World!" program. This was popularized in the 1978 book *The C Programming Language* by Brian Kernighan and Dennis Ritchie. The first example in the book was a simple program that wrote "Hello, World!" to the screen and exited. Carrying on with this fine tradition, let's write our first program.

Since Python programs can be entered interactively in the *interpreter* or in a text file ending in `.py`, we're going to use both methods so you can get a feel for each. In most of the examples in this book, we'll be using Python files, but entering commands in the interpreter can be an excellent way to test small snippets of code and get immediate results.

NOTE

If you haven't set up Python or Visual Studio Code, please refer to the introduction.

In the Interpreter

Let's launch Python. If you're on Windows and used the Microsoft Store to install Python, you can find it in the Start menu. Just search for Python and then run the program. If you used the website installer, double-click the Python icon on the desktop. In either case, you can type `python3` on the command prompt in Windows (accessible via the Start menu) and that will load Python.

On macOS and Linux, launch a terminal (on macOS, press CMD and SPACE and type `terminal` and on Linux, find *Terminal* in your application menu). In the terminal window, type `python3` at the prompt. You're now running Python. You'll see something like what's shown in figure 7:

GRAPHIC

```
Python 3.9.9 (main, Nov 21 2021, 03:16:13)
[Clang 13.0.0 (clang-1300.0.29.3)] on darwin
Type "help", "copyright", "credits" or "license" for more information.
>>>
```

fig. 7

The Python interpreter prompt.

The interpreter is awaiting your input directly after the `>>>` mark. This is called the *prompt*. To get Python to tell us hello, type the following and hit ENTER:

```
print("Hello, World!")
```

When you do so, you'll be pleasantly greeted, as in figure 8.

NOTE

In the previous code, there is no space between `print` and the opening parenthesis. In fact, in this command, there is only one space—between the comma and the capital W in World.

GRAPHIC

```
Python 3.9.9 (main, Nov 21 2021, 03:16:13)
[Clang 13.0.0 (clang-1300.0.29.3)] on darwin
Type "help", "copyright", "credits" or "license" for more information.
>>> print("Hello, World!")
Hello, World!
>>>
```

fig. 8

The Python interpreter after running the "Hello World!" print statement

As a Python Program File

Let's do the exact same thing, but this time put it in a text file. This method has many advantages, but the primary reason for using it is that it's impractical to input all our Python commands in the interpreter each time we want to run a program we wrote.

Start Visual Studio Code and click the *File* menu, then choose *New Text File*. A new tab inside the editor will appear with text like the following:

Select a language to get started. Start typing to dismiss, or don't show this again.

Select *Python* from the list.

NOTE

You might find it odd that Visual Studio Code is asking you to choose a language, but this editor is used for many different programming languages. You can even edit plain text in it if you like.

The introductory text will appear, and you'll see an empty tab waiting for your input. Type the following line:

```
print("Hello, World!")
```

Then click the *File* menu and click *Save*. You'll be prompted for a location. Choose the code folder you created in the introduction (see "Creating a Folder for Your Code"). I recommend naming this file `hello.py`.

Once you've saved the file, click the *Run* menu, and click *Start Debugging*. Alternatively, you can press the F5 key on your keyboard. You may be prompted again to select which kind of file it is, and if so, select *Python*. When you do this, Visual Studio Code runs the `python3` interpreter on the `hello.py` file. After that, a *Terminal* tab will open in the lower third of the Visual Studio Code screen and display the output (figure 9). It should show "Hello, World!"

IMAGE

fig. 9

```
hello.py
⬥ hello.py   ✕
Users > rwoliver2 > Source > python-book > ⬥ hello.py
    1   print("Hello, World!")
    2
    3

PROBLEMS    OUTPUT    DEBUG CONSOLE    TERMINAL
rwoliver2 in ~/Source/python-book on master λ /usr/bin/env /opt/homebrew/bin/python3 /Users/rwoliver2/.vscode/extensions/ms-python.python-2022.2.1924887327/pythonFiles/lib/p
ython/debugpy/launcher 56752 -- /Users/rwoliver2/Source/python-book/hello.py
Hello, World!
rwoliver2 in ~/Source/python-book on master λ
```

The Visual Studio Code display after running your Python program.
Note the "Hello World!" output in the bottom pane of the window.

CAUTION

If you run into any errors, recheck the text file you created to ensure that it contains only the line above. The word `print` must be all lowercase, with no spaces before or after, but it's fine to press ENTER after the entire command to create a new line, if you like.

Congratulations, you just wrote your first program!

What Happened

In Python, `print` is a ***function***. We'll expand on functions in chapter 5, but for now, consider a function as a predefined set of commands. The `print` function handles the work of taking the text we supply between the parentheses and quotation marks and displaying it on the screen. That might seem a simple task, but there's a lot going on behind the scenes to make it happen.

We can change "Hello World!" to any text we like. In fact, to demonstrate this point, let's have it display our names.

```
print("Hello, Robert!")
```

Unless your name is Robert (and bonus points if so), change it to your name, save the modification to your file by clicking the *File* menu and clicking *Save* (or pressing CTRL+S on Windows and Linux and CMD+S on macOS) and then choosing *Start Debugging* (F5) from the *Run* menu. Your greeting will now be a lot more personal.

Working with Variables

Displaying text like "Hello, World!" is certainly fun but not particularly useful. To do real work in our programs, we'll need to collect information, process it, and then produce some output. A practical example of this might be accepting a name, email address, and comment on a website, validating it, storing it, and then telling the user their request was submitted successfully.

For now, we'll focus on the first part of that chain of events—collecting information. But before we ask the user for input, we need a place to put that information. Fortunately, Python gives us a very powerful tool for the job: *variables*.

You probably first heard of variables in algebra class. Don't worry, though—this is the last time we'll use the A-word in this book. You don't need to know any kind of higher math to use them, but if you did learn about variables in math, you'll likely recall that they are places where a number is stored. This holds true for Python, except we can store much more than a number—we can also store text and lists.

Let's look at a quick example that will illustrate collecting input into a variable. Create a new file in Visual Studio Code (CTRL+N or CMD+N, depending on your operating system—or via the *File* menu). Select the Python language, then enter the following text:

NOTE

```
name = input("What is your name? ")
```

In this example, the space after the question mark is deliberate.

Save the file as `hello2.py` and run the program (F5, or click the *Run* menu then *Start Debugging*). When you do, the program will run as usual and print "What is your name?" in the *Terminal* tab at the bottom of Visual Studio Code. However, the program will not finish as it did before.

The input function works similarly to the print function in that it prints text (in this case, "What is your name?"). However, it also waits for you to type something and press ENTER. Whatever you type is then stored in the variable specified at the beginning of the line. In this case, the variable is called name.

In Visual Studio Code, click on the bottom *Terminal* tab and then type your name and press ENTER. Once you do, the program will end. We stored whatever you typed in the variable name, but since that's all we did, it wasn't used before the program ended. Let's change that.

Right after the first line, let's add a print function.

```
name = input("What is your name? ")
print("Hello, " + name)
```

Add this to your file and save it (CTRL+S, CMD+S, or click the *File* menu and click *Save*). Now let's run it again. Once it starts, click the *Terminal* tab in the bottom pane of Visual Studio Code and enter your name when prompted.

fig. 10

```
                                              hello2.py — python-book
 hello2.py  ✕

 hello2.py > ...
    1    name = input("What is your name? ")
    2    print("Hello, " + name)
    3

PROBLEMS    OUTPUT    DEBUG CONSOLE    TERMINAL

"Hello, Robert"
```

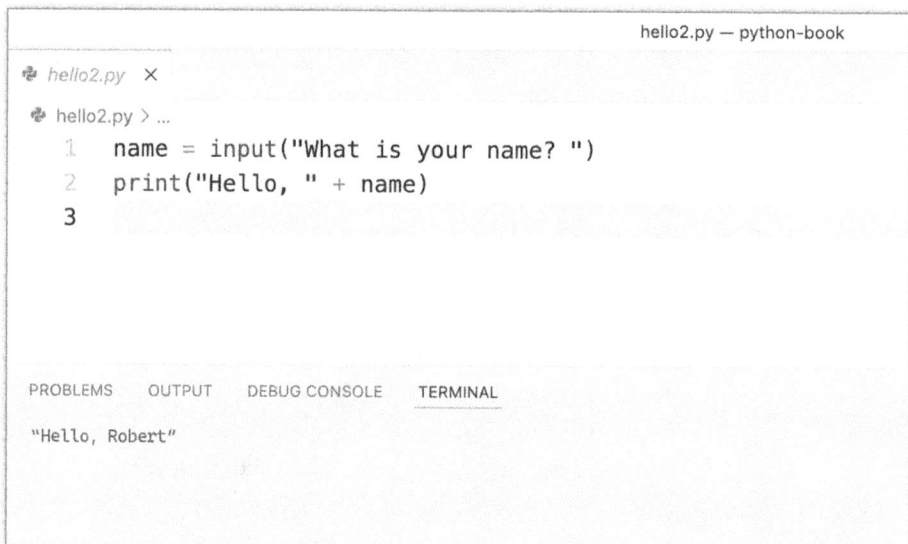

The Visual Studio Code display after running hello2.py.
Note the "Hello, Robert" output in the bottom pane of the window.

Several things happened here, as we can see in figure 10, so let's step through them one by one. First, the input statement collected your input (the text you typed after the prompt) and then stored that text in a variable called name. Then, on the next line, the `print` function displayed the text "Hello, " and *added* the text in the variable `name`.

That last part might seem a bit odd. How do you add text? When I say add, I don't mean mathematically, though we use the plus symbol in Python to combine, or ***concatenate***, variables with text. "Concatenate" is a technical way of saying that we're linking multiple pieces of text together in a series. And, in this case, we're concatenating "Hello, " with the text inside of the `name` variable.

When we put text in a variable, that variable is then known as a ***string***. A string is still a variable, but when we say "string," we know that the variable has text stored in it. That might seem an unnecessary distinction, but it's important because variables can be more than just text—they can be numbers and other types of data as well.

Variable names, and in fact nearly all other things in Python, are case-sensitive. The variable name cannot be referenced using `Name` or any other variation—it must be entirely lowercase in this instance. And, by convention, variable names are lowercase.

Strings

There are a few other types of variables in Python, but for now, let's focus on strings and how they interact with code. You already know how to use a string to gather input from the user, but you can also assign a value to a string in your code. Start a new file in Visual Studio Code and type the following:

```
word1 = "Hello"
word2 = "World!"
print(word1 + word2)
```

In this code, the variable `word1` is assigned the text "Hello". The variable `word2` is assigned the text "World!" The third line uses `print` to display the values within the parentheses—in this case, the strings `word1` and `word2`. Save the file as `hello3.py` and, before you run it, try to predict the result.

When you run the code, you'll get this output:

```
HelloWorld!
```

That's a bit off. When you pass a string to `print`, it will display exactly what is in the string—nothing more, nothing less. We have at least three different ways to fix this. I want to show each to you so you'll see how flexible Python programming can be.

Adding a Space to the String

Perhaps the simplest solution is to add a space to the end of word1.

```
word1 = "Hello "
word2 = "World!"
print(word1 + word2)
```

This certainly does the job:

```
Hello World!
```

Adding a Space to Print

The second option is to add a space *inline* within the print function. Doing something inline means that we perform an operation within another line of code. In the example below, we've added a space (specified by " ") inline (in the print line) between word1 and word2.

```
word1 = "Hello"
word2 = "World!"
print(word1 + " " + word2)
```

This works as well:

```
Hello World!
```

fig. 11

```
word1 = "Hello"
word2 = "World!"
print(word1 + " " + word2)
```

The inline string operation is circled in figure 11.

Using a Third Variable

Let's try something different. Instead of appending the space to the word1 variable or adding a space inline with the print function, we'll assign a third string and pass it to print.

```
word1 = "Hello"
word2 = "World!"
space = " "
print(word1 + space + word2)
```

This works but is a bit more cumbersome.

```
Hello World!
```

So which approach is best? The unfortunate truth is that there is no simple answer. In a small program like this, it largely comes down to personal choice. All other things being equal, I prefer to use the simplest approach, and this generally means the fewest lines of code.

But that isn't always the best method. If you are going to have to insert spaces between strings often in your program, having a predefined string named space with the contents of exactly one space in it, and then using it whenever you need it, makes sense. Remember what we said at the beginning of the chapter: programming is an art and not an exact science.

Slicing

Now that we've combined strings together, let's break them apart again. Python lets us slice strings—that is, take a portion of a string for use in another string.

```
greeting = "Well, hello there!"
hello = greeting[6:11]
print(hello)
```

When we run this, we see:

```
hello
```

In this example, we define the string greeting that contains Well, hello there! Then we create a new string called hello that is made up of the characters starting after character position 6 and going up to and including position 11. The numbers in the brackets, 6 and 11, define the range of characters to use. Then, on the third line, we display the new string hello.

If we won't need the hello string again and only mean to display it, we can reduce this code to two lines by making `hello` inline in the `print` function.

```
greeting = "Well, hello there!"
print(greeting[6:11])
```

If we omit the second number after the colon, we can have it finish the rest of the string (starting after position 6).

```
greeting = "Well, hello there!"
print(greeting[6:])
```

This code displays:

```
hello there!
```

And if we omit the first number and change the 11 to a 4, we see the beginning of the string up to (and including) position 4.

```
greeting = "Well, hello there!"
print(greeting[:4])
```

This modification displays:

```
Well
```

String slicing can be very useful for extracting certain parts of strings and storing them in other strings, or for doing something with the result inline.

Numbers

Now let's focus on numbers. Numbers in Python are largely divided into two groups: *integers* and *floating-point numbers* (or floats, for short). An integer is a whole number, be it negative or positive. A floating-point number is a number that has a decimal. When we define a number in Python, we don't put quotes around it like we do with strings (unless we want it to be a string with numbers).

Let's look at some examples of integers in Python.

```
apples = 4
pears = 8
attendees = 3042
zip_code = 12345
```

In this random assortment of variables, we assign the value 4 to the variable named `apples`, 8 to `pears`, 3042 to `attendees`, and 12345 to the variable `zip_code`. Note that the `zip_code` variable name has an underscore; this is a common way to give a variable a name that consists of multiple words, because you can't use spaces in your variable names. The underscore provides a visual reference that it's two separate words yet doesn't confuse the interpreter with a stray word in your line of code.

Now let's look at some floating-point numbers:

```
price = 4.95
gpa = 3.74
pi = 3.14159
```

These are still number variables, but since they contain a decimal, Python treats them as floating-point numbers. It may seem strange that there's a distinction, because even whole numbers can be represented as decimals (e.g., 4.00), but computers treat integers and floating-point numbers differently at the hardware level, and this difference is passed up through the Python interpreter.

FUN FACT

In general, integers are simpler to work with and are a bit faster, though on today's computers the difference is barely noticeable unless you're doing an extremely large number of calculations. In the early days of computing, processors didn't even work with floating-point numbers natively. Floating-point units became common on processors starting in the early 1990s and today are standard issue in every computer.

Let's create a new file in Visual Studio Code and enter the following:

SNIPPET

```
price = input("What is the price of a cup of coffee? ")
cups = input("How many cups do you want? ")
total = price * cups
print("Your total is $" + total + " for " + cups + " cups.")
```

01-01.py

Before we proceed further, I should mention that the star (asterisk) symbol on the line where we calculate the total is Python's way of multiplying two numbers.

Save the file as `cups.py` and run it. Just for testing purposes, enter the floating-point 3.99 for the coffee and 3 for the number of cups (we have a lot to do today). Don't forget to press ENTER after you enter both values. If you've entered everything correctly, it won't work! The code probably seems correct, but there's a flaw. Visual Studio Code points out our error, but its meaning is not entirely clear (figure 12).

GRAPHIC

fig. 12

```
1      price = input("What is the price of a cup of coffee? ")
2      cups = input("How many cups do you want? ")
3      total = price * cups

       Exception has occurred: TypeError x
       can't multiply sequence by non-int of type 'str'
           File "/Users/rwoliver2/Source/cups.py", line 3, in <module>
               total = price * cups

4      print("Your total is $" + total + " for " + cups + " cups.")
5
```

Something went wrong! A TypeError has occurred.

Visual Studio Code highlights the exact line in which the problem occurred and raises a `TypeError`, which is a particular kind of error that occurs when we try to do something with a variable that isn't supported for that kind of variable.

That likely doesn't clear anything up at this point because, from the user's perspective, they entered a number. Why can't they multiply 3.99 (`price`) by 3 (`cups`)?

NOTE

A string is a text variable, so that's why it can't be used (directly) in math.

The problem lies in the fact that the `input` function fills the variables with strings and not numbers. When a function fills, or provides a value, it is said to *return* that value, meaning it does its work and, upon return to our code, fills the variable on the left side of the equals sign with whatever input it collected. So the `price` and `cups` variables contain the strings 3.99 and 3, respectively, as if they were text and not numbers.

Python can add strings with the plus sign, but when it does, it won't perform math—instead, it will combine the two strings. Nevertheless, Python can't multiply strings, so it generates an error. To fix this, we need to convert the variables we collect into numbers.

Converting Strings to Numbers

Assuming a string contains the text of a number (for example, the string is "3"), Python can convert that into an actual number, one on which we can perform math operations. To do this, use the built-in function `int`, like this:

```
total = price * int(cups)
```

Now the string `cups` will be converted into an integer. Go ahead and make that change to your file and save, but we're not quite done. We need to convert the string `price` into a number, but not just any number. Since `price` has decimals (in this case, 3.99), we'll need to convert it to a float instead. Let's use the `float` function in Python to do just that.

```
total = float(price) * int(cups)
```

This will convert the `price` string to a `float` and the `cups` string to an `int` (integer), and since both are numbers, they can be multiplied with the `*` symbol. Now our calculation of the total is fixed, but there's one more step before our program will work correctly.

Converting Numbers to Strings

On the last line, we print the value of the variables `total` and `cups`. The `cups` variable will display correctly with `print` because `print` expects strings and `cups` is a string. But `total` is a number (specifically a `float`, because a `float` was used as one of the values in the multiplication). We'll need to convert that to a string to feed it to the `print` function. In Python, we do that with the `str` function.

```
print("Your total is $" + str(total) + " for " + cups + " cups.")
```

Save your file and run the program. If you supply 3.99 as the price and 3 as the cups, you'll get the correct answer.

```
What is the price of a cup of coffee? 3.99
How many cups do you want? 3
Your total is $11.97 for 3 cups.
```

When we convert variables from one type to another, we are *casting*. In the previous example, we are casting the cups variable as an integer, the price variable as a float, and the total as a string.

One additional note about casting variables into other types. We can store the result of our cast operation in another variable. In the example we've been using, we're casting inline, meaning we are using the `int`, `float`, and `str` functions to convert those values instantly so they can be supplied to the `print` function or so we can perform math with those values.

But if we did this . . .

```
number_of_cups = int(cups)
actual_price = float(price)
```

. . . the `cups` variable would still be a string with the number "3" and the `number_of_cups` would become exactly the value of 3. Also, the `actual_price` variable would become the number 3.99, while leaving the original `price` variable intact as a string. We can print `actual_price` and use `price` in a calculation.

```
total = actual_price * number_of_cups
```

While this is a perfectly acceptable way to handle this issue, it uses more lines and is more complex, so I opted to perform the casting inline. However, if you were going to use the numbers frequently over many calculations, casting them once and storing the result in another variable like `number_of_cups` would be not only easier but faster for the Python interpreter because it doesn't have to convert it repeatedly. Since our example was a simple one-time calculation, the inline approach is best.

A Few Comments

Our code samples so far have been short, but we're about to create a larger file. It would be nice to be able to include some text before certain parts of our code to remind ourselves (and others who will see or edit the file) what we're doing. Comments are not run or processed by the interpreter in Python. As far as Python is concerned, they might as well not be there.

To create a comment, simply insert a hash symbol (#), and anything else you type after that on the same line will be ignored.

```
# This code prints Hello, World!
print("Hello, World!")
```

Comments are incredibly helpful, and I highly encourage you to use them as often as necessary. Even experienced programmers forget the reason for writing certain parts of a program. I've done it countless times. The best way to prevent this is to document your code with comments.

Newlines

There's one last thing we need to discuss before we're ready to start our game. You might think the heading of this section is a typo—but it isn't. A *newline* is a special code that instructs the `print` function to stop displaying text on the current line and move to the next line. `print` automatically inserts one of these when it finishes displaying the string(s) we provide.

If we want to move down to the next line in the middle of our string, we simply insert a backslash and the letter n (styled as `\n`) in our string. Go ahead and start a new file in Visual Studio Code. Save the file as `scratch.py`, as this will be our scratch pad for trying new ideas.

```
print("Hello,\nWorld")
```

When you run the code, you'll see this output:

```
Hello,
World
```

You'll note that it isn't necessary to insert a space after the comma, because the newline character simply moves the remaining text to the next line. We *could* insert a space before it if we wanted to, but it wouldn't show. We can also insert newlines (represented by two `\n`) before and after the greeting.

```
print("Hello, World!\n\nHello, World!")
```

This will give the following result:

```
Hello, World!

Hello, World!
```

What's in a Name?

I have a simple exercise for you. Let's say we want to collect a person's name and then return to them the first letter of their name. What code could you write to do this?

Try this on your own. I have confidence you'll be able to do it. If you get stuck, consult the appendix. You can use your `scratch.py` file or create a new one if you like. (Hint: String slicing is your friend in this exercise).

ClydeBank Coffee Shop: Our First Cup

We have now gathered enough beans of wisdom to pour our first cup in the ClydeBank Coffee Shop game. Since this is our first step in writing our game, we'll keep things simple and use what we've learned so far to set up the game's parameters.

Let's create a new file and save it as `coffee.py`. A blank Python code file, just like a blank screen on a word processor, can be a bit intimidating. That's all right, though—we'll start small and build from there. Also, code isn't etched in stone. By the time we're finished, we'll have changed things around quite a bit, and that's perfectly fine.

I'll list the code first and then explain it line by line.

SNIPPET

CCS-01.py

```python
# ClydeBank Coffee Shop Simulator 4000
# Copyright (C) 2023 ClydeBank Media, All Rights Reserved.

print("ClydeBank Coffee Shop Simulator 4000, Version 1.00")
print("Copyright (C) 2023 ClydeBank Media, All Rights Reserved.\n")
print("Let's collect some information before we start the game.\n")

# Get name and shop name
name = input("What is your name? ")
shop_name = input("What do you want to name your coffee shop? ")

print("\nThanks, " + name + ". Let's set some initial pricing.\n")

# Get initial price of a cup of coffee
cup_price = input("What do you want to charge per cup of coffee? ")
```

```
# Display what we have
print("\nGreat. Here's what we've collected so far.\n")
print("Your name is " + name + " and you're opening " + shop_name + "!")
print("Your first cup of coffee will sell for $" + cup_price + ".\n")
```

First, we display the name of the game. Why 4000 in the title? Remember when everything had 2000 in the title right around the start of the new millennium? If you don't, then I just aged in that last sentence. Using 3000 seemed a bit silly, but 4000 seemed just right. You don't have to name it that, though. It's your game, and you can name it whatever you like. But I think it'd be awesome if you included 4000 after it.

After that, we ask for the player's name via the `input` function and store the result in the `name` variable. We do the same for the name of the coffee shop, storing it in the `shop_name` variable. We then print a notice with their name to customize it. We technically don't have to do that, but it's a nice personal touch.

Next, we ask how much they want to charge per cup. In this line, the input will return a string if the player inputs a decimal value. After that, we display the `cup_price` variable to confirm with the user what they entered. We'll need to convert this to a float to make use of `cup_price` in a mathematical way, but we'll worry about that later.

Want to look over my shoulder as I code the first bit of our ClydeBank Coffee Shop Simulator 4000 game?

To watch the QuickClip, use the camera on your mobile phone to scan the QR code or visit the link below.

SCAN ME   or   www.quickclips.io/python-2   **VISIT URL**

There's a lot that can go wrong with this code, but most of it revolves around the user not inputting the values we expect. Don't worry about that for now, though—we'll get to error handling in chapter 4. And, admittedly, this is a small start to a coffee shop simulator video game. However, it's a start. Your first program in Python. I encourage you to take a moment and be proud of your accomplishment. You've earned it!

Chapter Recap

» The Python interpreter runs our Python code.

» Variables are places to store data. Strings are a type of variable that stores text, and integers store whole numbers. Floats store numbers with decimals.

» We can convert between strings, integers, and floats.

| 2 |
Understanding Python Data Structures

Chapter Overview
>> Data in Python can be organized into data structures
>> Data structures include lists, tuples, sets, and dictionaries
>> You can combine and nest data structures to represent complex data

The variables we used in chapter 1 are containers for storing strings and numbers. They work well for simple pieces of data, but often we need to assemble and manage data in a more organized manner. Fortunately, Python gives us far more powerful ways to arrange our data. At the end of this chapter, we're going to apply our new knowledge by storing data for our coffee shop simulator game.

Lists

Lists in Python are data structures that can contain other variables. Think of a list as a basket, except there isn't a limit to the number of items you can store (other than the available amount of memory on your computer). Let's look at a few examples.

```
grocery_list = ["eggs", "milk", "cheese", "pasta"]

planets = ["Mercury", "Venus", "Earth", "Mars", "Jupiter", "Saturn",
"Uranus", "Neptune"]

odd_numbers = [1, 3, 5, 7, 9]
```

REMEMBER

When using numbers, don't put quotes around them—unless you want them to be a string with a number inside it.

In the previous examples, `grocery_list`, `planets`, and `odd_numbers` act like variables, except they contain individual strings and numbers.

You might wonder why you can't just store the grocery list, or any list, in a big string, like this:

```
grocery_list_string = "eggs, milk, cheese, pasta"
```

You can, of course. There's nothing stopping you, and this is a viable strategy in some cases. But lists have many powerful tricks up their sleeves—the most useful of which is the ability to instantly reference one of the elements of that list.

```
grocery_list = ["eggs", "milk", "cheese", "pasta"]

print("The first item on the list is " + grocery_list[0])
print("The second item on the list is " + grocery_list[1])
```

I encourage you to run this code in the interpreter or via your `scratch.py` file. If you do, you'll see this:

```
The first item on the list is eggs
The second item on the list is milk
```

Using the name of the list followed by square brackets enclosing a numerical position lets us fetch any item we want off the list. That number in brackets is called the *index* because it points to the item on the list we want to access. Pretty neat, huh?

You may have noticed that I used position numbers 0 and 1 instead of 1 and 2. In programming, we start counting from 0 due to the way the interpreter internally references a list of values. When we create a list, the interpreter assigns a memory address (a position in memory) for it so that it can be accessed later in your code. If you supply an index position, like 1 in `grocery_list[1]`, it adds this number to the memory address to get the location in memory that contains the specific item we want.

So let's pretend the address of the list is 8000. That's a completely made-up memory address, but it's simple enough for our example. Item number 0 is simply the first item in the list, which is at 8000. The second item (referenced by `grocery_list[1]`) is derived by taking the index number (1) and then calculating the position based on that with the math operation 8000 + (index × length), yielding 8008 in our simplified example. The interpreter looks at this location in memory and gets the specific item we wanted.

THE GROCERY LIST IN MEMORY

	0	1	2	3	4	5	6	7	
8000	E	g	g	s					
8008	M	i	l	k					
8016	W	a	t	e	r				
8024	A	p	p	l	e	s			
8032	S	o	a	p					
8040	C	r	a	c	k	e	r	s	
8048	B	r	e	a	d				
8056	G	i	n	g	e	r			

The grocery list in memory. The vertical column headings are the absolute position in memory, and the numbers in the horizontal top row denote the length of the string.

fig. 13

I stress that this example is contrived. Normally, a lot of complicated memory management is going on behind the scenes, as each item on the list can be a different size and the interpreter tries to be as efficient as possible. Also, the interpreter reserves space for additional items. Given that the list items are of varying lengths (the number of letters in each word), realistically 8000 would be the first entry, and perhaps 8032 would be the second, in case the first item on the list is changed to a longer string. Don't worry too much about the actual numbers; the concept is the important part of this detour.

I spent a bit of time with this little detour on starting your indexes with 0 instead of 1 because it is a common mistake for beginner programmers. Also, indexes with zero let you perform interesting and useful math on the index position.

Lists can have different kinds of data. For example, it's perfectly permissible to mix strings and numbers.

```
random_assortment = ["egg", "tree", 3, "green", 94, "pluto", 3.14]
```

In this case, we have strings, integers, and floats.

Tuples

Tuples act much like lists except they can't be changed, thus they are *immutable*. In programming terminology, an immutable variable or data type is read-only, whereas *mutable* data is editable. At first, you may wonder why you'd want a list that couldn't be changed. But if your program is going to be using a predefined set of data, a tuple is not only safer, it's faster.

By safer, I mean that if you accidentally try to modify a tuple, an error will be generated. Also, since the Python interpreter can create the tuple in memory without having to make space for potential future edits, it won't have to be reshuffled and rearranged in memory as much as a regular list, thus allowing your code to access the contents of the tuple much faster. Additionally, tuples use less memory.

In our code so far, we haven't needed to use a tuple, but our planet example is an excellent use case for tuples. To make a tuple, instead of enclosing the list of elements in square brackets, use parentheses.

```
planets = ("Mercury", "Venus", "Earth", "Mars", "Jupiter", "Saturn",
"Uranus", "Neptune")
```

The list of planets in our solar system isn't going to change unless astronomers decide Pluto really is a planet. Nevertheless, this list won't change during the execution of a program, so it's safe to put it under lock and key.

There's one more benefit to making a list of values read-only: security. Having a value defined at the start of program execution and not available for editing within the code means that malicious commands injected into the interpreter cannot modify values relied upon by security or authentication functionality.

For the most part, we use tuples just like we do lists. Accessing an element of the tuple is simple:

SNIPPET

02-02.py

```
planets = ("Mercury", "Venus", "Earth", "Mars", "Jupiter", "Saturn",
"Uranus", "Neptune")

print(planets[3])
```

If we enter this code into our scratch file, or in the interpreter directly, we will find out what is the true third rock from the sun.

```
Mars
```

In programming terms, Earth is the second planet, and Mercury is planet zero! If you're confused by this statement, recall from the "Detour" in the Lists section of this chapter that indexes in Python start with 0, not 1.

Sets

A set is very similar to a list except that it contains only unique values. If we add a duplicate value to our set, it will be ignored.

This can be very useful if we want to *deduplicate* our data. Data deduplication means that we store only unique data, not redundant information. This results in less memory and disk space consumed, as well as improved performance of our code in some situations.

Let's consider an example where this might be beneficial. In this code, we'll create a set with customer names. We collected the data from a variety of sources and simply copied and pasted the names into the set. Since this will be a master customer list, we don't want to store duplicates.

A set is surrounded not by square brackets as in lists or parentheses as in tuples, but by braces (otherwise called curly brackets).

```
customers = {"James Smith", "Andrea Richards", "Sam Sharp", "Brenda
Longmire", "Veronica March", "Sylvia Smith", "James Smith", "Vanessa
Bush", "Steve Hammersmith", "Brenda Longmire", "Sylvia Smith", "Steve
Hammersmith", "Walt Hawkins"}
```

If we enter this code in our scratch file and then print it, like this ...

```
print(customers)
```

... we'll see that the actual data stored in `customers` has been deduplicated for us.

```
{'Sam Sharp', 'Brenda Longmire', 'Veronica March', 'Sylvia Smith',
'Walt Hawkins', 'Steve Hammersmith', 'Andrea Richards', 'James Smith',
'Vanessa Bush'}
```

Your results may not look exactly like the previous example, because sets are unordered—that is, Python doesn't guarantee to present items in a particular order when you access them from an existing set. Regardless, you won't find any duplicate entries in a set.

By the way, the code listing for creating this customer list was kind of messy. Data wrapped to the next line, and that can be a bit distracting to read and more cumbersome to edit. Fortunately, Python gives us an elegant way to solve this problem:

```python
customers = {
        "James Smith",
        "Andrea Richards",
        "Sam Sharp",
        "Brenda Longmire",
        "Veronica March",
        "Sylvia Smith",
        "James Smith",
        "Vanessa Bush",
        "Steve Hammersmith",
        "Brenda Longmire",
        "Sylvia Smith",
        "Steve Hammersmith",
        "Walt Hawkins"
}
```

Not only is this easier on the eyes but it allows us to quickly add or edit elements. Just remember to add a comma after each line (except for the last) and to indent each item by pressing the TAB key.

You can format lists and tuples this way, too; just replace the braces (curly brackets) with square brackets for lists and parentheses for tuples.

NOTE Since sets can contain only unique values, this data structure may not be ideal for actual lists of customers. It was used here simply for illustrative purposes. When choosing which data structure to use, the fact that sets contain unique values is an important consideration.

Dictionaries

Dictionaries are indexed lists of values. Like sets, they are surrounded by braces and don't allow duplicates, and they are mutable (that is, editable). Each piece of data in a dictionary is referenced by a string or number. The easiest way to explain dictionaries is to show a few simple examples.

```python
customer1 = {
        "name": "James Smith",
        "age": 24,
        "phone": "555-555-1941",
        "email": "james@xyzinternet.net"
}
customer2 = {
        "name": "Andrea Richards",
        "age": 33,
        "phone": "555-555-4928",
        "email": "andrea@coffeeloversunite.us"
}
```

There's a lot going on here, so let's step through each line one by one. In this example, there are two separate dictionary variables—one titled `customer1` and the other titled `customer2`. In each dictionary, there are four values, each referenced by a key. This is called a ***key-value pair***, often styled as key:value pair. A key:value pair is simply a way to reference a piece of data that has a key, or index, attached to it.

The keys are name, age, phone, and email, and the values for `customer1` are "James Smith", 24, 555-555-1941, and james@xyzinternet.net. To access one of these values by its key, we would use the name of the dictionary followed by the key name in brackets.

```python
print(customer1["name"])
```

As mentioned at the beginning of this section, keys are unique, so you cannot have more than one name, age, phone, or email key in a dictionary in this example. If you assign another key with the same name in a dictionary, like this:

```python
customer3 = {
        "name": "Robert"
        "name": "John"
}
```

Python simply replaces the first value with the second, so ...

```python
print(customer3)
```

... shows this:

```
{'name': 'John'}
```

Using the `print` function on a list, set, tuple, or dictionary displays the entire contents of that data structure. I've prepared a chart to remind you which characters to use for which data structure (figure 14).

GRAPHIC

fig. 14

PYTHON DATA STRUCTURE		
STRUCTURE	**FORMAT**	**EXAMPLE**
List	`["item1", "item2"]`	`planets = ["Venus", "Earth", "Mars"]`
Tuple	`("item1","item2")`	`flavors = ("grape", "cherry", "lemon")`
Set	`{"item1", "item2"}`	`grades = {"A", "B", "C", "D", "F"}`
Dictionary	`{"key": "value"}`	`names = {"name": "Robert", "age": 42}`

Boolean Variables

There are many times when we need to express whether something is true or false. We could use an integer and set 0 as false and 1 as true or use a string with "True" as a value of true and "False" as a value of false. To be more efficient, we could say "T" is true and "F" is false. But there's no need to do any of that because Python has a built-in solution—a Boolean.

Booleans can have only two values—`True` or `False`. I capitalize the first letters because those are the actual values. Python treats these two words with capital letters as special values.

```
walking = False
running = True
```

In this example, the value of `walking` is `False`, and the value of `running` is `True`. We could set these variables to either `True` or `False`; it just so happens that those are the values I initially set in this example.

The utility of Booleans will become even more apparent when we talk about comparisons in chapter 3. Regardless, I wanted to mention this type of data so you'll know how to handle these on/off, true/false kinds of values in your code.

Combining Data Structures

Now that you know the basic Python data structures, let's explore how to combine them to form innovative and convenient ways to store data.

Multidimensional Lists

Lists don't have to be simply a flat listing of values. We can have lists of lists, or what are commonly called multidimensional lists. Let's consider an example.

```
# Daily high and low temperature (in Fahrenheit)
temps = [
    [ 66, 34 ],
    [ 57, 25 ],
    [ 49, 45 ]
]
```

In this structure, we're storing three days' worth of high and low temperatures. Essentially, it's a list of three lists. We can easily access the data, no matter where it's stored in the structure, by specifying, in brackets, the position (index) in the first (outer) group, and then in a second set of brackets the position in the inner group.

REMEMBER

Before I explain this with an example, recall that in Python, the first element in an array is position 0, not 1.

Here's an example:

SNIPPET

02-05.py

```
# Day 1 temps
print(temps[0])

# Day 2 temps
print(temps[1])

# Day 3 temps
```

```
print(temps[2])

# Day 1 high
print(temps[0][0])

# Day 1 low
print(temps[0][1])
```

Running this code produces the following:

```
[66, 34]
[57, 25]
[49, 45]
66
34
```

The first three `print` functions simply display the contents of lists 1, 2, and 3 in the multidimensional list. The last two `print` functions use a second set of brackets to specify the first and second elements in the first list.

If we wanted to access the low temperature for day three, what notation would we use? If you said `temps[2][1]` (the second element in the third list, counting from zero), then you would be correct.

You aren't limited to two dimensions either. You can continue nesting lists as much as you like.

SNIPPET

02-06.py

```
# Weekly (then daily) high and low temperature (in Fahrenheit)
temps = [
    [
        [ 66, 34 ],
        [ 57, 25 ],
        [ 49, 45 ],
        [ 45, 19 ],
        [ 33, 7  ],
        [ 32, 14 ],
        [ 49, 37 ]
    ],
    [
```

```
        [ 52, 39 ],
        [ 61, 51 ],
        [ 64, 51 ],
        [ 67, 57 ],
        [ 69, 42 ],
        [ 32, 14 ],
        [ 49, 37 ]
    ]
]
```

In this example, we have two weeks of high and low temperatures stored in the temps list. To access the third day in the second week's low, we'd use this:

```
print(temps[1][2][1])
```

Remembering that the counting starts at zero in indexes, this finds us the second (index 1) element of the third (index 2) list in the second (index 1) week of data.

Lists of Sets, Tuples, and Dictionaries

We've already seen how lists can be multidimensional—essentially containing lists of lists. However, this property isn't restricted to lists. Lists can contain sets, tuples, and dictionaries, and those data structures can often contain other structures as needed.

There is a caveat, though. Each data structure, no matter in which position it sits in a Russian doll-esque collection of other data structures, retains its properties. For example, sets contain only unique values, tuples are immutable (read-only), and dictionaries are still key:value stores. If you stick to those rules and use the data structure type that best suits your needs, you won't run into any problems.

Picking the Right Data Structure

Remember when I said programming is an art and not an exact science? This is one of those situations. In some cases, the choice of which data structure you should use is clear. I'll list some basic guidelines to follow, but note that there are few absolute rules. It is fair to say that a working program runs circles around one that doesn't, but if programming is indeed an art, we can't be complete pragmatists.

In high-performance, business-critical applications, these choices can be pivotal. That said, I don't want to scare you into second-guessing yourself as you code. That perpetual self-doubt should come much later in your Python career (just kidding). In all seriousness, though, I want you to consider the idea that there are multiple ways to solve problems in programming. I believe that having this kind of flexibility in your thinking makes you a better programmer.

» Lists are going to be your go-to solution for storing collections of data. If in doubt, this is the safest bet.

» Sets are faster than lists in some cases, but running many calculations on the data contained in a set can be slower overall. We'll address performance tuning in chapter 20.

» If your data won't change and you're performing many calculations on that data in situations where performance is critical, tuples are a great solution.

» If your data is complex or you think you'll add additional parts to a structure, a dictionary is often a good choice.

ClydeBank Coffee Shop: Starting the Grind

We need to get our new coffee shop off the ground. We're already storing some variables, like our player's name and the name of the player's coffee shop, but we need to go a step further. In chapter 3, we'll build the main game loop—that is, the repeating code that walks the player through each day of their operations. But before we do that, we need a place to store data about each day's pricing, advertising budget, sales, and even weather.

We could store these in individual variables, but that would get problematic when we needed to store the results of each day's progress. So let's construct a data structure to collect this information. Since we don't have the loop yet, all we can really do is create an empty list and a day counter, but in comments we can model the data we anticipate storing. I often use comments to plan out what I'm going to do. Comments also have the side benefit of providing insight for future developers on a project. In the following code, I added the `day` variable (we start at 1), and the empty sales list.

The list is a list of dictionaries, and it's formatted in a way that allows us to avoid cramming everything on one line. There are two good reasons for this. First, formatting dictionaries in this manner makes them more readable.

The second reason is entirely practical, if not a bit self-serving. Pages don't have infinite width and we simply can't print the sample dictionary structure all in one line—unless we make the font impossibly small and unreadable. But we're not just trying to save paper here. If your lines are too wide, they'll run off the edge of the screen. This isn't technically an issue, but from an aesthetic and usability perspective it's quite problematic.

In the sales list of dictionaries, I'm logging the day, the end-of-day coffee inventory (abbreviated `coffee_inv`), the advertising budget, the temperature, and the number of cups sold. But since this is just sample data to illustrate the point, we still must create an empty sales list to have a place to store our sales data. Additionally, the new code comes before the welcome message, by tradition. Generally, global variables (that is, variables that are used throughout the program) are stored near the top of the code.

CCS-02.py

```
# ClydeBank Coffee Shop Simulator 4000
# Copyright 2022 (C) ClydeBank Media, All Rights Reserved.
# Current day number
day = 1
# Sales list of dictionaries
# sales = [
#       {
#               "day": 1,
#               "coffee_inv": 100,
#               "advertising": "10",
#               "temp": 68,
#               "cups_sold": 16
#       },
#       {
#               "day": 2,
#               "coffee_inv": 84,
#               "advertising": "15",
#               "temp": 72,
#               "cups_sold": 20
#       },
#       {
#               "day": 3,
#               "coffee_inv": 64,
#               "advertising": "5",
#               "temp": 78,
#               "cups_sold": 10
```

```
#           },
# ]
# Create an empty sales list
sales = []

# Print welcome message
print("ClydeBank Coffee Shop Simulator 4000, Version 1.00")
print("Copyright (C) 2022 ClydeBank Media, All Rights Reserved.\n")
print("Let's collect some information before we start the game.\n")

# Get name and shop name
name = input("What is your name? ")
shop_name = input("What do you want to name your coffee shop? ")

print("\nThanks, " + name + ". Let's set some initial pricing.\n")

# Get initial price of a cup of coffee
cup_price = input("What do you want to charge per cup of coffee? ")

# Display what we have
print("\nGreat. Here's what we've collected so far.\n")
print("Your name is " + name + " and you're opening " + shop_name + "!")

print("Your first cup of coffee will sell for $" + str(cup_price) + ".\n")
```

If you run our game, you'll see that it does the same thing it did in chapter 1, because most of what we added was comments. It may seem like we haven't done much, but that couldn't be further from the truth. The thinking ahead and planning we do in a project is just as important as the lines of code we write. We've got a plan to store our data, and that's a huge step forward.

In the next chapter, we'll learn how to direct the flow of our code and loop through days of gameplay in our coffee shop simulator.

Chapter Recap

» Data structures allow the logical organization of data in Python.

» Lists are collections of individual variables.

» Tuples are essentially immutable (read-only) lists.

» Sets are like lists but can only contain unique values.

» Dictionaries can contain key:value pairs of indexed data.

| 3 |
Controlling Program Flow

Chapter Overview
» Logical comparisons and loops allow control of program flow
» The `if` statement compares values and executes code accordingly
» A loop lets you execute the same code multiple times

Until this point, our Python programs have been executed in only one direction. This works fine for extremely simple programs, but most of the time we'll need to collect input and then make decisions based on that input. Python is a powerful Swiss Army knife that is capable of so much more than simple top-to-bottom scripting. With logical comparisons, we can control the flow of the program. Our code can make decisions and adjust for as many conditions as we choose.

Logical Comparisons

Comparisons are at the heart of every decision in programming. Recall what I said in chapter 1: programs collect information, process it, then produce a result. We've collected input with the input function, and we've displayed output with the `print` function. But we really haven't processed it in any meaningful way. Python provides a variety of ways to compare data.

If
With the `if` evaluation, we're asking Python to say, "Do something if this condition is met." Oftentimes the comparison will go something like this:

SNIPPET

```python
a = "Yes"
b = "Yes"


if a == b:
    print("a is equal to b")
```

03-01.py

Note that when we assign a value to a variable, as in `a = "Yes"`, we use one equals sign, and when we make a comparison, like `if a == b`, we use two. This tells the interpreter we want to compare the two values, not take the value of variable `b` and place it in variable `a`. At the end of our `if` statement, we use a colon.

Before you type this code into the interpreter or add it to your `scratch.py` file, let's address a few things. First, you'll notice that the `print` function is indented. Some programming languages are not so picky about this type of formatting, but Python is strict and requires indentation in this and other instances, which we'll cover in later chapters.

I simply hit the TAB key on the keyboard and Visual Studio Code will indent the code for me.

MY TAKE

While you can use spaces instead of tabs to indent in Python, I strongly recommend using tabs. You have fewer keystrokes with tabs, they're consistent, and if you want to change the indent size at some point, you can adjust the size of a tab in your editor rather than going through your file and adjusting indents to match your new preference.

Before reading any further, try to predict what will happen when you run the code. Then run the previous Python code and see if you were right.

When you do, you'll see this:

```
a is equal to b
```

Let's change things a bit.

SNIPPET

03-02.py

```
a = "Yes"
b = "No"

if a == b:
    print("a is equal to b")
```

What will happen now? If you run this code, you should see nothing. The condition tested by the `if` statement wasn't met, so the `print` function won't run.

You can do several things when a condition is met—you aren't limited to just one command.

```
a = "Yes"
b = "Yes"
if a == b:
    print("a is equal to b")
    print("Really, it is, I promise!")
else:
    print("a is not equal to b")
```

When you run this, here's what you'll see:

```
a is equal to b
Really, it is, I promise!
```

You can enter as many lines as you wish—just be sure they're indented with the TAB key.

You aren't limited to checking for equality. You can also check a variety of conditions, like "less than" (using the < sign), "greater than" (using the > sign), and more. For now, we'll stick to equals, less than, and greater than, but in future chapters we'll explore how to make more complex comparisons.

Here are some examples using less than and greater than comparisons.

```
a = 1
b = 2

if a < b:
    print("a is less than b")
```

Else

What if we want to do one thing if the condition is true and another if the condition is false? The `else` statement lets us do just that.

```
a = "Yes"
b = "No"
```

```
if a == b:
    print("a is equal to b")
else:
    print("a is not equal to b")
```

When we run this code, the second `print` statement ("a is not equal to b") will run because the condition wasn't met.

Elif (else if)

Sometimes we want to compare conditions in a chain, starting with a base assumption and then asking the logical equivalent of "If something isn't true, perhaps this next comparison will be true." Let's look at an example.

03-06.py

```
a = 1
b = 2
c = 3

if a > b:
    print("a is greater than b")
elif b < c:
    print("b is less than c")
```

When you run this code in the interpreter, you'll see this:

```
b is less than c
```

This is displayed because the first comparison, `a > b`, was unsuccessful, so `elif` asked another question of the interpreter—is `b` less than `c`? Since it is, the second `print` statement was processed.

If you use an `else`, it must appear after all `elif`s.

The symbols used for comparison are called *operators*. For example, the double equals sign is an operator that means "if one variable is equal to another." Here is a list of comparison operators we can use in Python (figure 15).

ESSENTIAL COMPARISON OPERATORS IN PYTHON	
==	Equals
!=	Not equals
>	Greater than
<	Less than
>=	Greater than or equal to
<=	Less than or equal to

Nested Comparisons

Comparisons don't have to be one-dimensional—we can nest them together to perform complex logical comparisons. Here is an example:

```python
a = 1
b = 2
c = 3

if a  b:
        print("a is greater than b")
        if b != c:
            print("but b is not equal to c")
        else:
            print("b is equal c")
else:
        print("a is less than b")
```

Q: Can you predict how this code will run?

Pretend you are the Python interpreter and you're tasked with running this code. Step through each line in your head and see if you can follow the flow. Now try changing the values of a, b, and c and predict again.

There is no practical limit to how many layers deep your nested comparisons can go, but you must pay special attention to indentation. When you start the lines of code that are to be run for the next comparison, they must be tabbed over until you come out of that part of the code. It may be helpful to think of these indented sections as blocks of code, and, indeed, they are often called "code blocks." Visual Studio Code will help you with the formatting and show red underlines (figure 16) so you can alter the formatting (figure 17).

GRAPHIC

fig. 16

```
1    a = 1
2    b = 2
3    c = 3
4
5    if a > b:
6        print("a is greater than b")
7        if b != c:
8        print("but b is not equal to c")
9        else:
10           print("b is equal to c")
11   else:
12       print("a is less than b")
13
```

Visual Studio Code marks improperly formatted code
with red squiggly underlines, as in line 8.

GRAPHIC

fig. 17

```
1    a = 1
2    b = 2
3    c = 3
4
5 ∨  if a > b:
6        print("a is greater than b")
7 ∨      if b ≠ c:
8            print("but b is not equal to c")
9 ∨      else:
10           print("b is equal to c")
11 ∨ else:
12       print("a is less than b")
13
```

Properly formatted code is not marked. (Note that Visual Studio Code replaces the != that we typed with an equals sign with a slash through it, which better conveys the meaning. We use the != only because we can't make this symbol with our keyboard.)

I would caution against too many nested comparisons. It makes your code harder to follow and can make it easier to miss an error. For now, you probably don't have to worry about this, but it will become more important as your programs become more complex.

Loops

You may not realize it, but your computer is currently running a multitude of operations inside several running program loops. A program loop is simply a piece of code that is executed repeatedly for a fixed number of times, until a certain condition is met, or until you turn your computer off.

Some of these loops, executed by the operating system, tell the program you're running (e.g., Visual Studio Code) whether you've pressed any keys or moved your mouse. Another loop is checking your input to see if you have made a syntax error or to provide help with a particular function. Still another is keeping your internet connection alive, checking mail, displaying notifications, and doing literally thousands of other tasks. When a computer is "sitting there doing nothing," it is really processing many things constantly in loops.

Loops are quite important in programming because they let us repeat functionality. If loops didn't exist, we would have to write code that handled every possible input and output in our program over and over. It would be tedious and extremely counterproductive. Loops are a tremendous timesaver and extremely powerful.

Loops let us use the programming concept of *iteration*; that is, stepping through variables or parts of data, running code that interacts with that data, then moving to the next piece. When we move through a collection of data like this in a loop, we are said to be iterating over it.

For

A `for` loop is extremely versatile, allowing us to perform operations on a data structure. We can also use it to repeat code for a number of times specified by a supplied number (via a variable or a range or inserted directly into the code). Let's look at some examples.

03-08.py

```
# Display the planets

planets = ["Mercury", "Venus", "Earth", "Mars", "Jupiter", "Saturn",
"Uranus", "Neptune"]
```

```
for planet in planets:
    print(planet)
```

This code displays:

```
Mercury
Venus
Earth
Mars
Jupiter
Saturn
Uranus
Neptune
```

Before we examine what's happening in this code, I'd like to point out that this is different than merely using `print(planets)`. When we print the contents of a list, it displays just as we entered it into our code. Using the previous `for` statement, we're iterating over the planet list and running the `print` statement on each entry.

Now let's step through the code line by line. First, the planet list is defined with the list of currently named planets in our solar system. Then we use the `for` statement to say, "For each `planet` in planets, run the following code."

A `for` statement contains two major parts: the data structure or range to iterate through, and the temporary variable we'll use (in this case, `planet`). The indented text after the `for` statement is the `for` loop itself, in this case, the `print` function. At the end of the `for` statement is a colon to let the interpreter know that the code to be repeated starts on the next line, and the subsequent lines of code that make up the loop are indented. The code to run inside the `for` loop can consist of as many lines as we like, but that code must be indented (figure 18).

> **NOTE**
>
> Why did I name the temporary variable `planet` in this code? Does it matter what I named it? Technically, no—I could use any name. However, I like to follow the convention of giving a list of items a plural name, like planets, customers, students, etc., and the temporary variable used in a loop a singular name, like planet, customer, or student. You don't have to follow this pattern, but I find it helpful and encourage you to use it.

LOOPING THROUGH THE PLANETS

fig. 18

REMEMBER

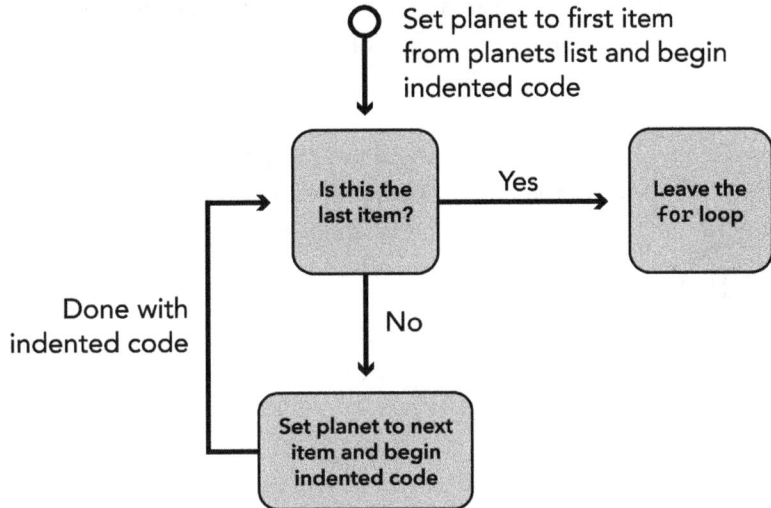

Indentation is critical in Python. If you don't use the indent for the code inside the `for` loop, you'll get an error.

Even though we've covered the basic concept of `for` loops, they're extremely flexible and useful, so let's look at various ways to use them.

SNIPPET

```python
# Iterate through a string
a = "Hello, World!"
for c in a:
    print(c)
```

03-09.py

This code displays as follows:

```
H
e
l
l
o
,

W
o
r
l
d
!
```

In this case, the string, `a`, was iterated as though the letters in it were part of a list. A `for` loop treats strings as lists of individual characters, so the temporary variable `c` is set to the value of each letter in the string with each pass.

NOTE

Why did I name the temporary variable `c`? As I mentioned before, the name doesn't matter, but I used `c` as a short form of "character." If it's not part of a plural named set (e.g., customers, students, etc.), I prefer to give the temporary variable a one-letter abbreviation of what the singular form will be. In this case, each part of a string is a character, thus a `c`. Use whatever naming scheme works for you, but be consistent. This way you, and others who might read your code, will be able to follow along with ease.

Here's an example in which we modify the temporary variable.

SNIPPET

```
singular_words = ["student", "teacher", "room"]
for word in singular_words:
    word = word + "s"
    print(word)
```

03-10.py

In this case, we created a list with three singular nouns, then iterated over that three-word list with a `for` statement, setting `word` as the temporary, in-loop variable. We then modified the temporary variable by setting it equal to itself plus the letter "s" at the end, then displayed the result.

However, I could have made this code simpler. Instead of modifying the temporary variable word, I could have saved a line and used this:

SNIPPET

```
singular_words = ["student", "teacher", "room"]
for word in singular_words:
    print(word + "s")
```

03-11.py

This code produces the same result but without modifying the temporary variable named `word`. In this simple situation, this optimization is desirable, but if I was going to use the variable `word` later in the loop (especially with an "s" at the end), setting that once and using it afterwards is preferable, like in the first example.

If we want to run code after the `for` loop is finished, the `else` statement can be used.

```
singular_words = ["student", "teacher", "room"]
for word in singular_words:
    print(word + "s")
else:
    print("Done!")
```

In this case, the three plural words will be displayed, followed by "Done!"

You might wonder why you would use `else` when you can simply put the code that you want to execute directly after the `for` loop. Good question! Code in the `else` portion will not run if the `for` loop has been exited by `break`, which we'll cover shortly. This strategy will let you run code with `else` that you want to run only if the `for` loop is successfully completed.

Range

`For` loops can work over ranges of numbers. To accomplish this, we supply the `range` function in place of the data structure normally used in the `for` loop.

```
# Display the first ten numbers
for i in range(10):
    print(i)
This produces:
0
1
2
3
4
5
6
7
8
9
```

If you expected the digits shown to be 1 through 10, recall that Python starts counting at zero.

The `range` function returns the equivalent of a list. So, in this example, `for` is iterating over a list like [0, 1, 2, 3, 4, 5, 6, 7, 8, 9]. The range function is far more concise.

In this example, the `for` loop iterates over the result from the `range` function supplied with the **argument** `10`. An argument is a value that we supply to a function (like the text we provide to the `print` function). The `range` function is executed with 10 as its argument. Just as the `print` function performs action, the `range` function does work too, but instead of displaying a result itself, it simply returns a value to the `for` statement, so it knows how many times to execute the loop.

FUN FACT

I used the variable `i` in this example because it is a variable name often used in loops across many programming languages. This has historical precedent: FORTRAN, a programming language originally developed by IBM in the 1950s, used the letters `i` through `n` to denote integers. This tradition stuck with early programmers and has persisted until now. Of course, you don't have to use `i`; you can use `x`, `z`, `purple`, or `rhinoceros`, but following these kinds of traditional patterns makes it easier for the people who will examine and work with your code to follow what you're doing.

Enumerate

`range` is extremely helpful for iterating over a list, but what if we need to track the position in the list? We could maintain a separate variable and increment it by 1 in each pass of the loop, but that's not necessary. `enumerate` to the rescue!

SNIPPET

03-14.py

```
# The planets
planets = ["Mercury", "Venus", "Earth", "Mars", "Jupiter", "Saturn",
"Uranus", "Neptune"]

# Display the planet and its number
for index, value in enumerate(planets):
    print("Planet " + str(index) + ": " + value)
```

With this code, we'll get this:

```
Planet 0: Mercury
Planet 1: Venus
Planet 2: Earth
Planet 3: Mars
Planet 4: Jupiter
Planet 5: Saturn
```

```
Planet 6: Uranus
Planet 7: Neptune
```

But that's not quite what we want. The index starts at zero, so let's add 1 to what we display.

```
# The planets
planets = ["Mercury", "Venus", "Earth", "Mars", "Jupiter", "Saturn",
"Uranus", "Neptune"]

# Display the planet and its number
for index, value in enumerate(planets):
    print("Planet " + str(index + 1) + ": " + value)
```

That does the trick!

```
Planet 1: Mercury
Planet 2: Venus
Planet 3: Earth
Planet 4: Mars
Planet 5: Jupiter
Planet 6: Saturn
Planet 7: Uranus
Planet 8: Neptune
```

enumerate provides us with both the index and the value. You don't have to name them index and value like I did in this example. You can name them i and v, or whatever you like.

While

A while loop runs commands as long as a comparison *evaluates* to be true. Evaluation in Python is the act of running a statement and obtaining a value. When comparing values, an evaluation will be true or false (figure 19). Let's look at an example and go through it in detail.

```
# While i is less than 10, display i
i = 0
while i < 10:
    print(i)
    i += 1
```

In this example, we first set the variable `i` to zero. Then we use the `while` statement to execute two commands as long as the comparison `i < 10` (`i` is less than 10) evaluates to be true. The comparison will initially be true because 0 is less than 10, so the first command, the `print` function, is executed. Then the second command is executed: a statement that is a shortcut for adding one digit to `i` (or, said in a more programming-specific way, *incrementing* the `i` variable by 1).

PYTHON WHILE LOOPS

fig. 19

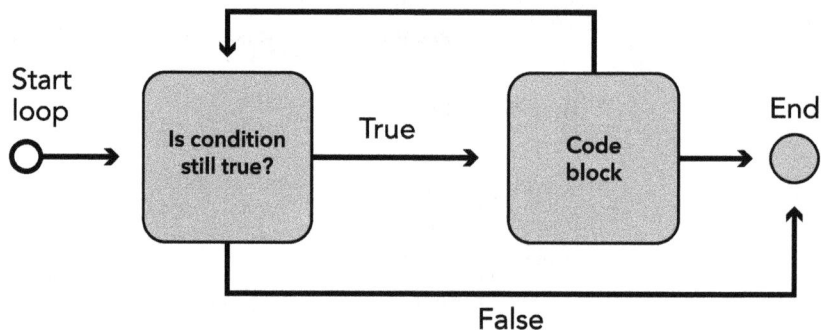

The `i += 1` is shorthand for the following:

```
i = i + 1
```

Both `i += 1` and `i = i + 1` will give the same result, but `i += 1` is easier to type and is very commonly used.

When we run the code, the numbers 0 through 9 are displayed.

```
0
1
2
3
4
5
6
7
8
9
```

If we want to display the numbers 1 through 10, we can simply change the starting value of i.

```
# While i is less than or equal to 10, display i
i = 1
while i <= 10:
    print(i)
    i += 1
```

In this case, we're setting the initial value of i to 1 instead of 0 and then using the <= comparison, meaning less than or equal to, instead of <. So the count will go from 1 to 10.

```
1
2
3
4
5
6
7
8
9
10
```

Remember how I said that Boolean variables would become useful in this chapter? They're incredibly useful in loops—specifically while loops. A while loop executes if the comparison in it is true, and as such, we don't have to specifically compare two values. For example, Python contains several built-in constants—that is, predefined values that are immutable (read-only). Two that are especially useful are True and False (styled with capital first letters).

This code will run indefinitely (also called an *infinite loop*):

```
while True:
    print("It's true!")
```

You can run this code if you want, but if you do, you'll have to either hit CTRL+C in the interpreter or click on the *Run* menu and click *Stop Debugging* to interrupt the program. If you don't, it will continue forever, because True is always true.

On the other hand, this code ...

```
while False:
    print("It's true!")
```

... will run and immediately finish without displaying anything, because the `False` constant is never true and thus the `while` loop is never executed.

Let's go through one more example with `while` loops. Say we want Python to sing the old "99 Bottles of Beer" drinking song. An everyday scenario in programming, to be sure! The `while` loop is perfect for this.

SNIPPET

03-17.py

```
bottles = 99
while bottles > 0:
    print(str(bottles) + " bottles of beer on the wall.")
    print(str(bottles) + " bottles of beer.")
    bottles -= 1
    print("Take one down, pass it around,")
    print(str(bottles) + " bottles of beer on the wall.")
```

Put this in your scratch file and run it. If all goes well, you'll see the old tune's lyrics written out for you in the results window. Let's step through this code and see what it does.

First, we set the `bottles` variable to 99. Then we start a `while` loop and say, "run the following code while `bottles` is greater than zero." Then we print the first and second lines, inserting the `bottles` variable (integer) into the `print` statement when necessary, converting it inline to a string. On the next line, we subtract 1 from the `bottles` variable, then run `print` again, twice, using the same integer-to-string conversion via `str`, but this time on the `bottles` variable that has now had 1 subtracted from it. The code will loop until the expression `bottles > 0` is no longer true (that is, when `bottles` becomes 0).

ON YOUR OWN

Try writing the previous example using a `for` loop instead of a `while` loop.

Break

A `while` or a `for` doesn't have to run its full course. By using the `break` statement, we can conditionally exit a loop before it's finished.

```
while True:
    print("Hello, World!")
    break
```

Without the `break`, this would be an infinite loop. But instead, the loop starts, displays "Hello, World!", then exits the loop.

```
Hello, World!
```

Instead of immediately breaking, we can conditionally break.

```
for i in range(10):
    print(i)
    if i > 5: break
```

If we run this code, here is what we'll see:

```
0
1
2
3
4
5
6
```

In this case, we loop through a range of 10 with `i` as our temporary variable. For each iteration, we display the value, then on the next line we check to see if it's greater than 5. If so, we break, exiting the loop before it's finished.

MY TAKE

I put the `break` statement on the same line as the `comparison` statement, so that if `i > 5: break` forms one line. This is permissible in Python if the code to be executed for the conditional (if `i > 5` in this case) can fit on one line. I'm generally not a fan of trying to make everything fit on one line, as I believe code looks neater when given room to breathe, but in this case, since the next line indented would simply contain the word `break`, it looks better and is more concise.

If you expected numbers 0 through 5 to be displayed, don't worry—this is a common mistake. "Greater than" simply asks the question, "Is `i` greater than 5?" This is not true until `i` is actually 6, A while loop executes if the comparison in it is true because we ask that question *after* we display the number, and each new start of the loop increments the counter (`i`).

If we want to display the numbers 0 through 5, we have two choices. First, we can change the `>` (greater than) comparison operator to `>=` (greater than or equal to). Or we can keep the comparison just as it is and move the print function after it, like this:

```
for i in range(10):
    if i > 5: break
    print(i)
```

Either way works fine. Sometimes there are two (or more) equally valid approaches to solving a problem in programming.

Continue

The `continue` statement allows us to skip the current iteration and move to the next without exiting the loop. Let's look at an example.

```
for i in range(10):
    if i % 2: continue
    print(i)
```

If we run this code, we'll see the following output:

```
0
2
4
6
8
```

The `%` operator is called the *modulo* operator, or mod for short. Mod performs a division operation on the variable by the number you provide (in this case, it divides `i` by 2) and returns only the remainder. Using this technique, we can tell if a number is odd because if you divide a number by 2 and it has a remainder, it's odd.

It might seem odd (OK, I admit it, pun intended) that a number can provide a true or false comparison. But in Python, 0 is false and any non-zero integer is true. So when `i` is odd, the `i` mod (`%`) 2 is not zero, so it evaluates as true, and the code for the conditional is run—in this case, `continue`. When that happens, the next line(s) is skipped, and the interpreter returns to the next step in the loop. Therefore, only even numbers are displayed.

Let's walk through what Python does with this evaluation when `i` is 3:

» Substitute `i` with `3`
» Evaluate: `3 % 2`
» Evaluate: `if 3 % 2: continue`
» Evaluate: `if 1: continue`
» Evaluate `if True: continue` (since Python considers any non-zero integer as `True`)
» Since evaluation becomes `True`, continue

Nested Loops

Loops can exist within themselves, just like nested comparisons.

```python
for i in range(10):
    for j in range(10):
        print(str(i) + str(j))
```

When you run this code in Visual Studio Code via your `scratch.py` file, you'll see the numbers 00 through 99 displayed. Let's take this nested loop step by step.

First, a `for` loop is established with a range of 10 using `i` as the temporary variable. With each pass through the loop, `i` goes from 0 to 9. With each iteration of `i`, a new loop is started using `j` with a range of 10. Since we're in the loop of both `i` and `j` at this point, both variables are accessible to us, so we display them both using the `print` statement.

Before displaying them, we convert both to strings via the `str` function. If we didn't do this, we'd add both numbers (using math, not joining strings), and the results would be very different.

As with nested comparisons, you can go as deep as you want with nested loops, but I advise keeping them as short as possible so that your code is fast, easily read, and simple to maintain.

Take an interactive tour of how nested loops work.

To watch the QuickClip, use the camera on your mobile phone to scan the QR code or visit the link below.

or

www.quickclips.io/python-3

SCAN ME **VISIT URL**

Number-Guessing Game

You now have most of the pieces you need to create an extremely simple game. I'm not referring to the coffee shop game, but rather a simple number-guessing game. You undoubtedly played it as a kid. You think of a number between one and ten, or perhaps one and a hundred, and someone else tries to guess what it is. Here's the basic outline of how a game like this would work:

1. Generate a random number between 1 and 10.
2. Ask the player for their guess.
3. Compare the guess and report the result.

The only thing missing here is how to generate random numbers. Fortunately, Python makes that simple. At the top of your code, you'll include these lines:

```
from random import seed
from random import randint
```

We'll get into the specifics of importing modules in chapter 9, but for now, just know that it includes the random number functionality we'll need for this exercise. Now we can simply use the `randint` function to generate a number between 1 and 10:

```
number = randint(1, 10)
```

Armed with this knowledge, you possess the last piece of the puzzle needed for making this game. Rather than showing you the source code for the game, I am challenging you to create it on your own. Writing code that you create in your head is the best way to learn to program. I know you can do it!

Try this on your own first, but if you do run into problems and need a hint, don't feel bad. You can refer to the appendix for a solution.

Notice that I said *a* solution rather than *the* solution. There are multiple approaches to take here, and none of them is wrong. Let's see which one you use. By the way, feel free to expand the game beyond just guessing 1 through 10. Here are some suggested enhancements:

> » Expand the random digits from 10 to 100.
> » Display whether the guess is higher or lower than the number.
> » Loop until they get the correct answer.
> » Show how far away the number is from their guess.

ClydeBank Coffee Shop Simulator: The Circle of Life

The life of a video game is eternal—well, at least as long as it's running. In game design, there is the concept of a core gameplay loop. In the gameplay loop, a player makes choices, implements them, and then sees the outcome. In our game, that will be a straightforward series of events.

> » The player is shown the day of the month (day number) and weather forecast.
> » The player is asked how much they want to spend on advertising and if they want to buy more coffee.
> » A simulation of the day's events occurs.
> » The sales results are shown to the player.
> » Return to step 1.

Typically, in a semi-infinite loop like this, we have a running flag, that is, a variable (often named `running`) that is initially set to `True`. To exit the gameplay loop (i.e., if the player wants to quit the game), the `running` variable is set to `False`. The simplest example might look like this:

```
running = True
while running:
        # Do things
```

Unless those "things" alluded to in the comment set the running variable to `False` at some point, this will continue forever.

Let's look at the code for the coffee shop simulator game so far. There are a few new concepts, which we'll explain after the code.

CCS-03.py

```python
# ClydeBank Coffee Shop Simulator 4000
# Copyright 2022 (C) ClydeBank Media, All Rights Reserved.

# Import items from the random module to generate weather
from random import seed
from random import randint

# Current day number
day = 1

# Starting cash on hand
cash = 100.00

# Coffee on hand (cups)
coffee = 100

# Sales list of dictionaries
# sales = [
#       {
#               "day": 1,
#               "coffee_inv": 100,
#               "advertising": "10",
#               "temp": 68,
#               "cups_sold": 16
#       },
#       {
#               "day": 2,
#               "coffee_inv": 84,
#               "advertising": "15",
#               "temp": 72,
#               "cups_sold": 20
#       },
#       {
#               "day": 3,
#               "coffee_inv": 64,
#               "advertising": "5",
```

```
#              "temp": 78,
#              "cups_sold": 10
#          },
# ]


# Create an empty sales list
sales = []


# Print welcome message
print("ClydeBank Coffee Shop Simulator 4000, Version 1.00")
print("Copyright (C) 2022 ClydeBank Media, All Rights Reserved.\n")
print("Let's collect some information before we start the game.\n")


# Get name and shop name
name = input("What is your name? ")
shop_name = input("What do you want to name your coffee shop? ")


print("\nOk, let's get started. Have fun!")


# The main game loop
running = True
while running:
        # Display the day and add a "fancy" text effect
        print("\n-----| Day " + str(day) + " @ " + shop_name + " |-----")


        # Generate a random temperature between 20 and 90
        # We'll consider seasons later on, but this is good enough for now
        temperature = randint(20, 90)


        # Display the cash and weather
        print("You have $" + str(cash) + " cash and it's " + str(temperature) + " degrees.")
        print("You have coffee on hand to make " + str(coffee) + " cups.\n")


        # Get price of a cup of coffee
        cup_price = input("What do you want to charge per cup of coffee? ")


        # Get price of a cup of coffee
        print("\nYou can buy advertising to help promote sales.")
        advertising = input("How much advertising do you want to buy? (0 for none)? ")


        # Convert advertising into a float
```

```
advertising = float(advertising)


# Deduct advertising from cash on hand
cash -= advertising


# TODO: Calculate today's performance
# TODO: Display today's performance


# Before we loop around, add a day
day += 1
```

You may recall these two lines from our number-guessing game:

```
from random import seed
from random import randint
```

About midway through the code, we start the main game loop. We display the day, weather, and how much cash and coffee they have. Then we deduct the advertising from the cash on hand, and before we leave the loop, we add 1 to the day.

The focus of this chapter was on the loop, so we put in a # TODO comment to note the lack of game processing and displaying the results of the day. This TODO comment isn't specific to Python, and it's not really an official standard, but quite a few editors and most programmers will know that seeing TODO in a comment means that you (or someone else) will finish the feature described in the comment later. It's a great way to keep a placeholder and describe your thoughts at the time. Once you've completed the feature, just remove the comment. The best part is that this scheme requires no other software—it's simply a way to put a to-do list in your code.

If you run this code several times, you'll notice there are some bugs—especially if you don't enter a value for certain input statements. Don't worry. We'll address that in the next chapter.

NOTE

Feel free to modify the game in any way you see fit. We're only providing a template, but you can take it as far as you'd like to go. Want to change some text, or even the name of the game? Go for it! Just remember that if you change any of the functionality, you'll need to adjust for it in future additions as we continue learning about Python.

Chapter Recap

» To compare one value to another and run code based on the result, use the `if` statement.

» The `for` loop can iterate over a data structure like a list or run code a certain number of times with the `range` statement.

» A `while` loop allows you to run code until a certain condition is met.

» The `break` statement allows you to prematurely exit a loop.

| 4 |
Handling Errors

Chapter Overview
» Errors happen, but they can be addressed with exception handlers
» Wrapping code in `try` provides a safety harness against failure
» The `finally` statement ensures that code is run even if an error occurs

Things will go wrong. Count on it. Fortunately, Python lets us construct an excellent safety net for when the unexpected happens.

As you may have discovered, Python stops running your program if an error occurs. While you're learning, or testing a concept, this is fine. However, if you're going to use your program for serious work (or fun) or plan to distribute it to others, you'll want to handle unexpected issues with grace, rather than simply exiting the program.

When I wrote video games as a teenager, I didn't really understand error handling. And the languages I used at the time didn't have the robust error-handling techniques that we have now with Python and other modern languages. If anything went wrong—perhaps even just moving my character a bit too far off-screen—the game would crash.

One other aspect to consider when it comes to error handling: if you are going to perform critical work, an error and abrupt termination of your program could cause data or financial loss. Handling errors with care can be of vital importance. This task may seem daunting, but don't worry, Python makes it easy to save the day.

Exceptions

When an error happens, it causes an *exception*. You may also hear it said than an error "throws" an exception. This expression is commonly used to describe code that executes in some abnormal way. Either way, it's the same situation—something happened, and we need to deal with it in our code. You can visualize how exceptions are handled with the chart in figure 20.

fig. 20

```
try:
    → Try to run this code.

except:
    → Run this code when something goes wrong.

else:
    → Everything went fine, so run this.

finally:
    → No matter what happens, run this code.
```

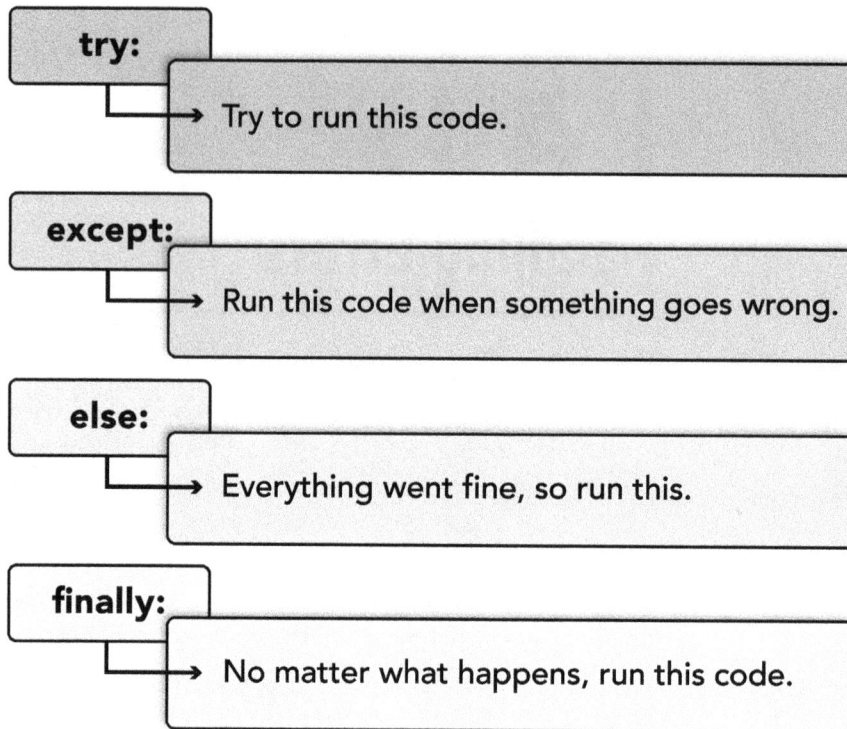

The Python exception-handling process.

We'll get to `try`, `except`, `else`, and `finally`, but first, let's set the stage. To explore this topic, we'll need to write some code that purposely generates an error. I know that sounds weird, but the best way to see how to handle errors is to create some. One of the simplest errors that can occur is when we try to divide a number by zero. When Python encounters this issue, it generates an exception (technically a `ZeroDivisionError`, but we'll get into specific exceptions shortly).

You might wonder why Python can't continue from such a seemingly simple issue, but if an exception occurs, the state of the program's flow is suddenly in question, and to prevent further problems, the interpreter stops execution.

04-01.py

```python
# Divide a number by zero
a = 7
b = 0

print(str(a) + " divided by " + str(b) + " is " + str(a / b))
print("All done!")
```

If you run this in the interpreter or put it in your scratch file in Python, you'll see this:

```
Traceback (most recent call last):
      File "scratch.py", line 1, in <module>
ZeroDivisionError: division by zero
```

The best way to avoid this error would be to check that the variables are not zero before you try to divide them. However, sometimes it is difficult or inconvenient to check for invalid data up front. So, for the purposes of our example, we'll assume the worst case and try to cope with the fact we've been given incorrect data.

If we think an operation might generate an error, we can wrap it in a `try` statement.

04-02.py

```
# Divide a number by zero
a = 7
b = 0

try:
      print(str(a) + " divided by " + str(b) + " is " + str(a / b))
except:
      print("Sorry, a problem occurred dividing the numbers.")

print("All done!")
```

The indentation on `try` and `except` is much like that of `if/else` and `for/else`, so we must press TAB on the code after `try:` and its companion, `except:`.

Any code in the `try:` block is executed as normal but with one key difference—any error that occurs is processed by the code in the indented lines after `except:`. If we run the previous code, we'll see this:

```
Sorry, a problem occurred dividing the numbers.
All done!
```

The variables were set, and the `print` statement was executed just as before, but this time, since an error occurred, `try` shifted execution of the code to the `except` statement, and it printed the apology phrase. Then, execution continued outside of the `try` block, printing the message "All done!"

If I had used `try` blocks in my early video-game days, I could have handled the errors a lot more gracefully and not had games crashing on anything unexpected. Divide-by-zero was an error I ran into quite often, and to avoid it, I'd add extra conditionals around my calculations. However, you can't catch every bug before it happens, so it's good to have a safety net for when things go wrong.

Speaking of safety nets, if you use `except` as shown previously, with nothing else specified on that line, you'll catch all exceptions. This is generally not recommended. Catching all exceptions doesn't allow much specificity in the way you handle the error. Sometimes I'll catch all exceptions in a piece of code first and then note which exceptions are fired during extensive testing. Then I can handle those specific errors in the way best suited for the situation.

```
# Divide a number by zero
a = 7
b = 0

try:
        print(str(a) + " divided by " + str(b) + " is " + str(a / b))
except ZeroDivisionError as e:
        print("Sorry, a problem occurred dividing the numbers.")

print("All done!")
```

By specifying `ZeroDivisionError`, we're telling Python we're only interested in handling that particular type of exception. Everything else will be unhandled and thus cause the program to fail should a problem arise. If we run the previous code, it will display the apology just as before. But let's throw a wrench into the works.

```
# Divide a number by zero
a = 7
b = 0

try:
        print(str(a) + " divided by " + str(b) + " is " + str(a / b))
except OverflowError as e:
        print("Sorry, a problem occurred dividing the numbers.")

print("All done!")
```

Here, we're telling Python we'll handle the `OverflowError` exception—an error that occurs when the resulting answer to a math problem is too large to store. That doesn't happen here, so the `ZeroDivisionError: division by zero` error occurs and the program terminates early, not showing the "All done!" message.

If we're not sure which exception might happen, we can use the generic `Exception`, like this:

```
except Exception as e:
```

This will do the trick, but if we can narrow down what could occur (or more specifically, which exception error we can realistically recover from), it's best to specify that exception.

You probably noticed the `e` in the `except` line. This is the temporary variable (much like `i` is the temporary variable in `for i in range(10)`) that contains details about the exception error. Let's change the code back to what it is in the previous snippet and add a line to print the contents of the `e` variable.

SNIPPET

04-03.py

```
# Divide a number by zero
a = 7
b = 0

try:
        print(str(a) + " divided by " + str(b) + " is " + str(a / b))
except Exception as e:
        print("Sorry, a problem occurred dividing the numbers.")
        print("Error details: " + str(e))

print("All done!")
```

When we run this code, we'll see this:

```
Sorry, a problem occurred dividing the numbers.
Error details: integer division or modulo by zero
All done!
```

You might find it odd that I used `str` on the temporary variable named `e` within the `except` code block. If we don't include it, an error will be generated, because `e` isn't technically a string. It's an exception, which is a type of data called a *class*. We'll get into those in chapter 6, but for now, consider it a special data structure. When we use the `str` function on `e`, we convert it into a string so its contents can be displayed on-screen.

DIGITAL ASSETS

Please see "List of Built-in Exceptions" included with your Digital Assets at go.quickstartguides.com/python.

Mopping Up the Mess with Finally

When an exception happens, things can get messy. With the help of the `finally` clause, we can restore sanity to the execution of our program. Code in the `finally` block is executed even if an exception is raised in the code protected by `try`.

SNIPPET

04-04.py

```python
# Divide a number by zero
a = 7
b = 0

try:
        print(str(a) + " divided by " + str(b) + " is " + str(a / b))
except Exception as e:
        print("Sorry, a problem occurred dividing the numbers.")
        print("Error details: " + str(e))
finally:
        print("But still, we tried!")

print("All done!")
```

If we run this code, here's what we'll see:

```
Sorry, a problem occurred dividing the numbers.
Error details: integer division or modulo by zero
But still, we tried!
All done!
```

Here, the exception occurred when the divide-by-zero operation was attempted, then the exception handler—that is, the code in the `except` block—ran and printed the error details. Then the `finally` code ran and displayed "But still, we tried!" before returning control outside of the `try` statement and back to the main program, which displays "All done!" before it ends.

It's important to note that the `finally` code will always run, exception or not. This makes it ideal for placing code that cleans up the messes that could potentially be made in the `try` loop. In a more complex program, this would do more than print a message; it would use conditionals to restore sanity to the execution of the program. When we get into file and network access in chapters 12 and 13, you'll find the `finally` block extremely useful for ensuring that *resources* (i.e., open files, network connections, etc.) are closed properly to prevent problems if something goes wrong.

ClydeBank Coffee Shop: Spilt Milk

Our game is coming along nicely, but there's a problem we'll run into with any prolonged amount of testing. If the user doesn't input the correct values when prompted, or just hits ENTER, it can cause an exception. Let's fix that!

Here's the corrected code, and I'll explain the fixes below.

SNIPPET

CCS-04.py

```
# ClydeBank Coffee Shop Simulator 4000
# Copyright 2022 (C) ClydeBank Media, All Rights Reserved.


# Import items from the random module to generate weather
from random import seed
from random import randint


# Current day number
day = 1


# Starting cash on hand
cash = 100.00


# Coffee on hand (cups)
coffee = 100


# Sales list of dictionaries
# sales = [
#     {
#         "day": 1,
#         "coffee_inv": 100,
#         "advertising": "10",
```

```python
#        "temp": 68,
#        "cups_sold": 16
#    },
#    {
#        "day": 2,
#        "coffee_inv": 84,
#        "advertising": "15",
#        "temp": 72,
#        "cups_sold": 20
#    },
#    {
#        "day": 3,
#        "coffee_inv": 64,
#        "advertising": "5",
#        "temp": 78,
#        "cups_sold": 10
#    },
# ]
# Create an empty sales list
sales = []


# Print welcome message
print("ClydeBank Coffee Shop Simulator 4000, Version 1.00")
print("Copyright (C) 2022 ClydeBank Media, All Rights Reserved.\n")
print("Let's collect some information before we start the game.\n")


# Get name and shop name using the following approach:
# 1. Set name and shop_name to False
# 2. Use while not name and shop_name to continue to prompt for a non-empty string

name = False
while not name:
    name = input("What is your name? ")


shop_name = False
while not shop_name:
    shop_name = input("What do you want to name your coffee shop? ")


# We have what we need, so let's get started!
```

```python
print("\nOk, let's get started. Have fun!")


# The main game loop
running = True
while running:
    # Display the day and add a "fancy" text effect
    print("\n-----| Day " + str(day) + " @ " + shop_name + " |-----")


    # Generate a random temperature between 20 and 90
    # We'll consider seasons later on, but this is good enough for now
    temperature = randint(20, 90)


    # Display the cash and weather
    print("You have $" + str(cash) + " cash on hand and the temperature is " + str(temperature) + ".")
    print("You have enough coffee on hand to make " + str(coffee) + " cups.\n")


    # Get price of a cup of coffee
    cup_price = input("What do you want to charge per cup of coffee? ")


    # Get price of a cup of coffee
    print("\nYou can buy advertising to help promote sales.")
    advertising = input("How much do you want to spend on advertising (0 for none)? ")


    # Convert advertising into a float
    # If it fails, assign it to 0
    try:
        advertising = float(advertising)
    except ValueError:
        advertising = 0


    # Deduct advertising from cash on hand
    cash -= advertising


    # TODO: Calculate today's performance
    # TODO: Display today's performance


    # Before we loop around, add a day
    day += 1
```

Not every error-handling scheme has to be an exception handler. We see this in the `while not` loop I use to get the `name` and `shop _ name` variable. We didn't cover adding `not` into the equation, but as its name suggests, it simply negates the comparison. So, if we say `while not name`, and `name` was set to `False`, it will loop until name evaluates to True, or, in the case of a string, has content. If a string is empty, it evaluates to `False`.

At the conversion of `advertising` to a float, we don't have to prompt the user for another value. If something goes wrong—say they enter a letter or something similar—it's safe to assume that we can fall back to the value 0. Because of this, our exception block for this function is simple.

We've taken the game about as far as we can go without some more advanced functionality. I'm eager to introduce functions and classes to you. This will make a huge difference in how we structure our code and make things easier to navigate and understand.

Chapter Recap

» An exception occurs when an error happens. We can handle exceptions with the `try` statement.

» Whenever a problem occurs in the `try` block, code in the `except` block is run.

» If no error occurs, code in the `else` block is run, but this block is skipped if something goes wrong.

» The `finally` block is executed in either case and is commonly used to restore the program's execution to a sane state.

PART II

FUNCTIONS AND CLASSES

| 5 |
Creating Reusable Tasks with Functions

Chapter Overview
- » Functions allow us to reuse code
- » We can pass arguments (parameters) to functions
- » Keyword arguments make it easy to pass arguments

Up until now, we've provided instructions, line by line, to the Python interpreter and it's carried them out for us in the exact order given. This is fine in simple programs, but in more complex applications, we'll need to repeat lines or series of lines of code over and over—sometimes with different input. It's impractical to simply copy and paste these lines repeatedly. That's where functions come into play.

By bundling lines of code together in a function, we avoid repeating ourselves (thus adhering to a programming principle called DRY—Don't Repeat Yourself). When we keep our code DRY, we can start thinking about our program in terms of building blocks rather than one long recitation. We move from writing a simple script to an application. And what's more, we can reuse the functions in other programs, saving ourselves tremendous time in the future.

Our First Function
Let's start with a simple yet immediately useful example so we can see how functions can benefit us in Python programming. But before we do, consider this—you've been using functions already and didn't know it. We've used `print`, `input`, `str`, `int`, `float`, and more. Keep this in the back of your mind for now; we'll get back to it in a moment. For now, let's look at our first custom function.

SNIPPET

05-01.py

```python
# Define the ask function
def ask(prompt):
    return input(prompt + " ")
```

```
# Use the ask function to find out how many cups we want
question = ask("How many cups do you want?")
print(question)
```

Try running the previous code in your `scratch.py` file and see what happens. It should prompt you to enter a value (in this case, "How many cups do you want?") and then display what you entered.

Before we get into a line-by-line analysis, I want to note a quick housekeeping item. There is an unnecessary line in this program. We're saving the result of `ask` in a variable called `question`. Instead, we can eliminate the `question` variable and supply the result of the `ask` function directly to `print`.

```
# Define the ask function
def ask(prompt):
        return input(prompt + " ")

# Use the ask function to find out how many cups we want
print(ask("How many cups do you want?"))
```

Next, it's important to know what parts of this code constitute the function itself. Here, I've relisted the code, but this time I bolded the function (figure 21).

```
# Define the ask function
def ask(prompt):
    return input(prompt + " ")

# Use the ask function to find out how many cups we want
print(ask("How many cups do you want?"))
```

The last line, `print`, is part of the main program. The lines before that (excluding the comment directly above it) are the function definition.

When we define a function with the `def` statement, we aren't running the function at that point. Instead, we're telling the interpreter, "Here's some code I will run later." A function definition is like a lesson we teach Python. We give the lesson a name (in this case, `ask`), we provide instructions (the indented code inside that block), and then the "lesson," or function, is available for use in the rest of our code.

When we continue execution to the print statement, it then runs the ask function, filling the variable prompt with whatever we provide it in the parentheses. The same thing happens when we use the print function, or any other built-in function in Python. The text we supply to the print statement becomes a temporary variable that is used within the function's code itself (the indented portion after the def ask(prompt): line). After it displays the text, it returns control to the main program so Python can run our next line of code.

When I say, "returns control to the main program," I mean that the main program is essentially our Python code file. The function is a subset of that code (everything contained in the indent after def), and when the function is being executed, the code that called it (in our previous example, the print function with its inline use of ask), stops running and waits on the function to finish before it can proceed. The print statement doesn't know what to display until ask returns, and when it does, it then has text supplied to it via the return statement in the ask function. To illustrate this flow, see figure 22.

fig. 22

```
# Define the ask function
def ask(prompt):
    return input(prompt + " ")

# Use the ask function to find out how many cups we want
print(ask("How many cups do you want?"))
```

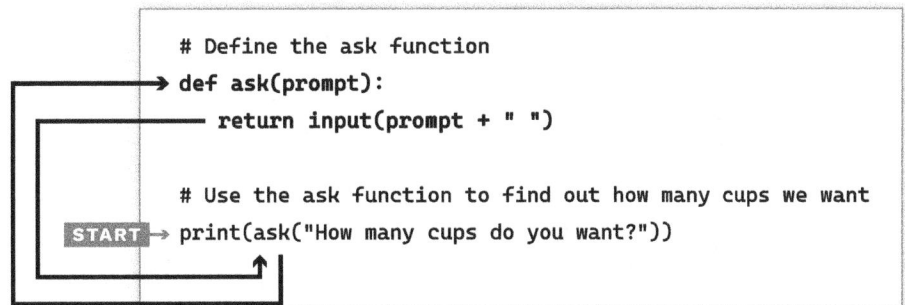

The flow of program execution in our example.

Running a function is a temporary diversion, and then we're back to the top-to-bottom execution we've been using so far.

Passing Values and Returning a Result

In chapter 3, we briefly discussed arguments. Recall that an argument is a value we pass to a function. But did you know you've already been using them since chapter 1? That might seem hard to believe, but remember that when your program uses print, it's calling the print function. Granted, the print function is built in to Python, but nevertheless it's still a function, running code behind the scenes to display text on the screen.

Then, in chapter 3 when we discussed for loops, we had this example:

```
# Display the first ten numbers
for i in range(10):
        print(i)
```

In this case, we have two uses of functions: `range` and `print`. In this example, the value `10` in the `for` loop and the value represented by the variable `i` are arguments. These arguments provide information to the function for use only inside its code.

Armed with this knowledge, let's take another look at our `ask` function.

```
def ask(prompt):
        return input(prompt + " ")
```

In our `ask` function, the `prompt` in the first line is the name of the temporary variable that will be available for use inside the function. It doesn't have to be named `prompt`, but in keeping with the scheme of giving variables meaningful names, I called it `prompt` because that is in fact what it will supply—a prompt to the user. In the next line, this value is then used as an argument for the `input` function after a space is appended to it. The space is added purely for cosmetic reasons, so that when the user types there is a space between the prompt and their input. This space is added inline (as opposed to modifying the `prompt` variable or creating a new variable), and the `input` function will receive the value of `prompt` with a space at the end.

The `return` statement is the line of code responsible for returning a value to the code that called the function. Now that the function is defined, we can (outside of the function) call `ask` again.

```
name = ask("What is your name?")
```

In this line of code, the `ask` function is called with the argument as a string with the text "What is your name?" This is then used in the function, with a space added to the end, to get the user's input. Then, when the user provides a value, the `return` statement delivers that response back to the line that called the `ask` function. This is then stored in the `name` variable. There's some back-and-forth going on with this function (and my explanation), so if it doesn't immediately click with you, don't worry. We'll work through plenty more examples of this.

We aren't limited to passing one value to a function. The function can ask for as many as it needs.

```
# Define the function full_name
def full_name(first, middle, last, display):
        name = first + " " + middle + " " + last
        if display:
            print(name)
        return name

# Use our newly created function
full_name("Robert", "W", "Oliver", True)
complete_name = full_name("Robert", "W", "Oliver", False)
print(complete_name)
```

If we run this code in our `scratch.py` file in Visual Studio Code, we'll see my name printed twice. To understand why this happened, let's go line by line.

First, we create a new function that accepts four arguments—`first`, `middle`, `last`, and `display`. The first three arguments are the first, middle, and last name of a person, and the last argument is `True` or `False`. The function first creates the combined name (stored in the `name` variable) by combining all the variables with a space between them. Then an `if` statement checks to see if `display` is `True` or `False`. If true, it prints the `name` variable. If not, it simply skips this conditional code block. Either way, the `full_name` function returns the value stored in the `name` variable.

The first time we use the `full_name` function, we specify `True` for display, so it prints the name it creates. However, the second time it is run, since we provided `False` for the display argument, it doesn't print the name. It assigns the value it creates to the `complete_name` variable but otherwise displays nothing. On the third line, we print the `complete_name` variable. So it's only shown twice. If we had specified `True` for display on the second line, it would have printed three times.

You might have noticed that we use

```
if display:
```

instead of

```
if display == True:
```

There is essentially no difference between these versions. If we use the if statement to evaluate only a variable, it will test whether that variable is true or false. This means it's literally `True` or `False` (the values) as in this case. Additionally, as you may recall from chapter 3 where `continue` in loops was discussed, an integer variable is true in a conditional if it is anything other than zero. If it's zero, it will be false.

IMPORTANT

We must supply a value for each argument when calling the function. If our function takes one argument, we must provide one argument (like our `ask` function). However, if our function takes four, as in our `full_name` function, we must provide four arguments while using it. If we don't, Python will generate an error explaining how many arguments it expects for the function. There is one exception for the function— except when you use default arguments. We'll address those soon.

Modifying Arguments

I strongly advise against modifying arguments that we pass to our functions.

```
x = 5

def double(x):
        x = x * 2

double(x)
print(x)
```

When we run this code, x will remain 5. You might expect 10, but this function doesn't return a value, and the multiplication that's done within this function stays within this function. The following would be a better way to handle this situation:

```
x = 5

def double(n):
        return n * 2

x = double(x)
print(x)
```

In this case, x is now 10. This wasn't fixed by my swapping x for n. I did that to make the function a bit more generic and to avoid using the same variable name twice. Otherwise, there is nothing special about these variable names. The difference is that the function `double` now returns a value rather than just performing multiplication inside the function. This `return` statement passes the result of `n * 2` outside the function—to the calling code. In this case, the calling code is `double(x)`, and this return value ends up in the x variable.

There are situations where we can modify arguments, but going down that road will surely lead us to dragons. They can be slain, but we must be careful. In general, unless there's a specific need, I recommend against this practice.

Default Arguments

It's possible to tell Python to provide a default value for an argument in case the code that calls it doesn't specify an argument. Let's modify our `ask` function to have a default `prompt` value.

```python
def ask(prompt = "Please enter a value: "):
        return input(prompt + " ")
```

In this code, we define the `ask` function just as we did before, except we change `prompt` to include a default value. Now we can call `ask` without a prompt at all and the `prompt` argument will be filled with a temporary value.

SNIPPET

05-04.py

```python
def ask(prompt = "Please enter a value: "):
        return input(prompt + " ")


a = ask()
print(a)
```

When it's run, we'll see this:

```
Please enter a value:
```

We can type anything, and then we'll see the program display what we typed in the input field. When a default argument value is specified, we don't have to provide a value, but we can if we want to. If we do, our value will be used and not the default.

```
a = ask()
b = ask("What do you want for b?")
```

This produces two different prompts:

```
Please enter a value:
What do you want for b?
```

In the first, the default prompt is used, and in the second, we provide an argument that overrides this default and uses what we specified.

You may notice something about the space after the default value. Let's look at our modified function again.

```
def ask(prompt = "Please enter a value: "):
    return input(prompt + " ")
```

Note that the default value, `Please enter a value: `, has a space after it. This means that Python will add two spaces when asking for the input, because the default value has a space after it and we add a space inline with `prompt + " "` for the argument for input. If we enter a prompt without a space it will be correct, but otherwise we'll get two. Fortunately, we can fix this with a conditional.

```
def ask(prompt = "Please enter a value: "):
    if prompt.endswith(" "):
        return input(prompt)
    else:
        return input(prompt + " ")
```

In this enhanced `ask` function, we provide a default argument value for `prompt` in the first line. Then we check whether `prompt` ends with a space. If it does, we return whatever `input` returns for us, supplying the `prompt` variable unmodified to `input`. If not, then we do the same, but this time appending a space at the end of the `prompt`.

It may seem strange that we check to see if the string ends in a space by putting a dot between `prompt` and the `endswith` function. This dot notation is something we use when dealing with classes, and we'll cover those in chapter 6, but for now just think of this line as "If the prompt ends with whatever string is in the parentheses (in this case, a space), run this code."

You can use a default argument for multiple arguments in your function. For example, let's provide defaults for our `full _ name` function.

```
def full_name(first = "First", middle = "Middle", last = "Last", display = False):
    name = first + " " + middle + " " + last
    if display:
        print(name)
    return name
```

In this case, we're providing defaults for all arguments. If we run `full_name()` it will return "First Middle Last". Note that the last argument, `display`, is set to `False`, and `False` doesn't have quotes around it because it isn't a string, it's a value built into Python.

> We can think of arguments that don't have a default value as required arguments because if we don't specify a value for them, Python will generate an error.

Even though we can provide as many default arguments as we want, we must specify any default arguments after any other argument that requires a value. Let's consider two examples. For brevity's sake, I've omitted the code block of the function.

```
# This works because the last variable provides a default value
def full_name(first, middle, last, display = False):


# This also works because the last two variables provide a default value
def full_name(first, middle, last = "Last", display = False):


# This doesn't work because a required variable
# comes after one with a default value
def full_name(first = "First", middle, last, display = False):
```

I know this may seem a bit confusing, but a helpful way to look at it is from the interpreter's point of view. If we don't provide a value for the first variable but provide a value for the middle two, how does it know which value should go into each argument? By keeping our default argument(s) at the end of our function definition lines, we will help Python understand which value goes with what variable.

Keyword Arguments

Keyword arguments act much like regular arguments but with a twist—the order in which we provide them to the function doesn't matter. This is especially helpful when we want to expand a function's capability but don't want to go back and edit every call to rearrange the order of the functions.

To demonstrate this, let's look at our `full_name` function again. I've set the `display` argument to a default value of `False`, but otherwise the first three arguments are required.

```
def full_name(first, middle, last, display = False):
    name = first + " " + middle + " " + last
    if display:
        print(name)
    return name
```

If we want to use keyword arguments, we don't have to change a thing with the function definition itself. Instead, we simply change the way we call the function.

```
print(full_name(first = "Robert", middle = "W", last = "Oliver"))
```

Here, we provide the values for `first`, `middle`, and `last`, but instead of relying on their position in the function definition, we name each argument and specify the value we wish to provide for it. We omitted the `display` value because its default is `False`. Besides, we're printing the output anyway, because when `full_name` returns the fully computed name, it will take that value inline and supply it as the argument to the `print` function.

In this example, nothing much has changed because we're still providing them in the right order. But now, let's mix things up a bit.

```
print(full_name(last = "Oliver", first = "Robert", middle = "W"))
```

When we run this code, we'll still see the same result—my name displayed on the screen, with each value being in the right argument. By supplying the name for each argument, we're telling Python where to place them. We can even specify `display` too, if we like.

```
# This passes the display value as a keyword argument
print(full_name(last = "Oliver", first = "Robert", middle = "W", display = False))
```

MY TAKE

If we use keyword arguments while calling a function, we should use them for each argument. Technically, we can mix and match keyword arguments with regular arguments if keyword arguments come last. But for clarity's sake, I advise against it.

The general rule of thumb is that keyword arguments are useful when a function takes more than one or two parameters and it's difficult to remember the order. Additionally, if we think the function will expand later with more arguments, it's a good idea to use keyword arguments now rather than make lots of edits to the rest of our code. There isn't a performance penalty for using keyword arguments, so if you like the concept (especially for more complex functions with multiple arguments), go ahead and use them as much as you wish.

Arbitrary Arguments

Arbitrary arguments provide a way to specify that a function can receive one or many arguments. We don't have to specify each individual argument name with this method; instead, we merely provide the name of a tuple, and that will be accessible within the function and contain all the values passed to it.

REMEMBER

A tuple acts much like a list (that is, it contains a list of strings or numbers), but it cannot be modified and is therefore read-only, or immutable. Please refer to chapter 2 for details.

SNIPPET

05-06.py

```
# Define the average function
def average(*numbers):
        sum = 0
        for n in numbers:
            # Add n to sum
            # (+= means add n to sum and store in sum)
            sum += n
        return sum / len(numbers)

# Use our newly minted function
print(average(10, 40, 80, 74, 16, 42, 12, 6))
```

If we run this code, we'll see that the average is calculated as 35. Specifically, it shows 35.0 because the result of a division operation is a float, even if it is a whole number. Let's step through this code line by line to examine what it does.

First, we define the average function. For the argument, we specify one—numbers. However, we put an asterisk (star) in front of it to indicate it will be an arbitrary argument. We set the variable sum to zero, then loop through the tuple numbers, which was provided to the code inside the function. Inside the `for` loop, `n` is our temporary variable, and with each iteration (pass-through), we add the value `n`, which is one of the numbers provided to the function, to the `sum`. The `sum` value grows throughout the `for` loop, and at the end of the loop, we return the `sum` divided by (represented with a forward slash) the total count of items in the `numbers`.

Aside from the arbitrary arguments, we're introducing something else—the `len` function. This is a built-in function in Python that gives us the total number of items (length) in a variable. I say variable and not specifically list or tuple because `len` is incredibly versatile. While we can get the length of lists, sets, tuples, and dictionaries, we can also use it to get the number of characters in a string.

```
print(len("Hello, World!"))
```

When we run this code, we'll see the length displayed as 13.

> **NOTE**
>
> Why is a tuple provided by Python to store the arguments provided in an arbitrary argument function? Recall that tuples are immutable (read-only). Since modifying function arguments doesn't affect their values outside of the function, making them immutable makes sense because it prevents you from modifying them and mistakenly thinking that will have an effect outside the function.

Scope

When we discuss *scope* in programming, we are generally referring to the place where data structures and functions can be accessed. That might sound a bit confusing, and, admittedly, scoping was a difficult concept for me to learn. But you have a huge advantage—you have already been using scope.

The arguments in a function definition (that is, `def ask(prompt):`, where `prompt` is the argument) become variables for use inside the function. They aren't accessible outside the function, and thus they are scoped to that function. To get a variable out of the function for use in other functions or code, we use `return` to deliver that value back to the original scope.

We'll be expanding on the topic of scope as we continue through the book, but I wanted to introduce this term now—both to explain what you've already been using and to lay a foundation for your understanding of how variables live within more complex programs that we'll explore in future chapters.

Generator Functions

A typical function in Python runs until it ends with a `return` statement, but a Python *generator* runs until it reaches a `yield` statement, which returns control of the program back to whatever code called the generator. But that's not the end of the story. Just like the song that never ends, we can keep on calling the generator function and it will pick up right where it left off and continue until it reaches the next `yield` statement.

You might be wondering just how many `yield` statements a generator needs if it might be called many times. It's true that we can include multiple yields in a statement, but in most cases, a generator function, just like a real generator (the kind that produces electricity), runs until we don't need it anymore. Therefore, `for` or `while` loops are generally used in generators to keep the engine (i.e., the function) running.

To illustrate this, let's look at a simple example.

```
def infinity():
    i = 0
    while True:
        yield i
        i += 1
```

This is similar to the `range()` function, except `range` requires us to supply a number limit. In this case, we have essentially an infinite loop. Let's use this generator:

```
for i in infinity():
    print(i)
```

This code will run forever if we let it, but let's hit the *stop* button that appears near the top of Visual Studio (or click inside the terminal window and press CTRL+C). Each time we go through the `for` loop, the infinity generator is used, resuming at the yield point and incrementing the integer returned.

Remember the "99 Bottles of Beer" song from chapter 3? It's time to *refactor* it. Refactoring is the process of restructuring or refining code (generally without changing its overall behavior). It's usually done when we find a better way of doing something, and it usually hides behind statements like "Bug fixes and performance improvements" that are seen in app store change notes.

That's a lot of theoretical talk. Let's see a generator in action. First, let's look at the original code.

```
bottles = 99
while bottles > 0:
        print(str(bottles) + " bottles of beer on the wall.")
        print(str(bottles) + " bottles of beer.")
        bottles -= 1
        print("Take one down, pass it around,")
        print(str(bottles) + " bottles of beer on the wall.")
print("Take one down, pass it around,")
print(str(bottles) + " bottles of beer on the wall.")
```

This is serviceable, but the code is crying out for a generator since it repeats an action over and over.

SNIPPET

05-07.py

```
# Define the generator function
# with the start argument defaulting to 99
def bottles_song(start = 99):
        # Set the initial number of bottles to the start argument
        bottles = start
        # Loop through until bottles are gone
        while bottles > 0:
                # Display the song
                print(str(bottles) + " bottles of beer on the wall.")
                print(str(bottles) + " bottles of beer.")
                print("Take one down, pass it around, ")
                # Subtract a bottle
                bottles -= 1
                print(str(bottles) + " bottles of beer on the wall.")
                # Yield to the calling function
                yield
                # Pick back up here when we return
        return True

# Loop through the generator
for i in bottles_song():
        # Don't do anything as the generator does the printing
        pass
```

First, we define the generator function. It starts out just like any other function, with a default argument of start set to 99. The song typically starts with one hundred bottles (at least as I've heard it), so it makes sense to provide that value if none is specified. Inside the function we set the bottles variable to whatever our starting value is, then start a `while` loop that runs as long as there is more than one bottle (that is, `bottles` is greater than 0).

In the `while` loop, we use `print` to display the song as before, converting the `bottles` integer to a string inline. Then we subtract 1 from the `bottles` variable and then `yield`. Once all the bottles are gone (i.e., the `while` loop condition is no longer true because `bottles` isn't greater than 0), we return `True`. In a generator, returning instead of yielding stops the generator, as we've reached the end of all possible paths of execution inside the function.

In the `for` loop outside the function, we iterate `bottles_song()`, which instructs Python to call our iterator as often as it can until it finishes (reaches the `return` statement). Then, in our `for` loop, we do something unusual—we call `pass`. In Python, `pass` does absolutely nothing. We don't need the loop to do anything because each time `for` calls `bottles_song`, our generator does the heavy lifting (displaying the contents of the song).

If we wanted the `for` loop to do the printing, we would create a temporary string called `verse` (it could be any name, but this matches our intent) inside the `while` loop, then supply `verse` to the `yield` function.

SNIPPET

05-08.py

```
# Define the bottles_song function
# with the start argument defaulting to 99
def bottles_song(start = 99):
    # Set the initial number of bottles to the start argument
    bottles = start
    # Loop through until bottles are gone
    while bottles > 0:
        # Display the song
        verse = str(bottles) + " bottles of beer on the wall. "
        verse += str(bottles) + " bottles of beer. "
        verse += "Take one down, pass it around, "
        # Subtract a bottle
        bottles -= 1
        verse += str(bottles) + " bottles of beer on the wall."
        # Yield to the calling function
        yield verse
        # Pick back up here when we return
    return True

# Loop through the generator
for v in bottles_song():
    print(v)
```

In this version, `verse` becomes our ***buffer*** (a place to temporarily store data) where we construct the song rather than displaying it with `print`. We then use `yield verse` to yield just as before, but this time we send back the value of `verse` to the caller, in this case, the `for` loop at the bottom of the code.

This verse is passed to the code block inside the loop in the variable `v`. I named it `v` because it's short for verse and temporary variables in loops are often given single-character names for simplicity. The verse is printed, and then the `bottles_song` generator is returned to service, returning to the `while` loop until there are no more bottles of beer on the wall.

Python's `pass` statement serves several purposes. Most importantly, loops must have code in them, and `pass` satisfies this requirement without taking any action.

However, the `pass` statement inspires a detour that's worth pursuing in your programming journey. Actions like this are considered a ***NOP*** (no-operation) statement, meaning it does nothing. I say "considered" because Python technically just skips over `pass`, but I want to introduce the concept of NOP to provide a behind-the-scenes peek at how the Python code you enter is represented at a lower level in the computer.

You might wonder why you'd want to do such a thing. Isn't the point of programming to tell the computer to do something, not nothing? An excellent point! But there is a reason for operations like `pass`. The very first software programs used NOP instructions to increase the timing between certain events. Processors would take a small amount of time to process the NOP instruction, and when several were executed in sequence, especially in a loop, they would insert a time buffer between actions. One thing this time spacing was used for was to set the pace of video games. A character walking across the screen would walk slower if more NOPs were added to the loop that animated their movement, and faster if fewer NOPs were executed.

As processors became faster, these timing loops became almost nonsensical. Games designed for slower computers would be too fast to play on faster ones, which created huge problems for players. Soon, games started to rely on ticks from the computer's internal clock to time actions, bringing predictable pauses.

These NOPs weren't just used in games. Operations like NOPs were used by operating systems to reduce power usage or processor temperature. In some early multitasking systems, programs that needed to wait for something to complete but didn't want to freeze the computer could use operations like NOP in loops to yield control to the system.

NOPs have many other purposes and are still in use today. Strategic use of them in a program can provide a smoother user experience, and they can serve as a placeholder for future expansion by the developer. Even though computers are known for executing an astonishing number of operations per second, sometimes the best thing you can instruct a computer to do is to merely do nothing and wait.

We need to make an optimization to our bottle song. On each pass, a new string named verse is created, because Python strings are immutable. Internally, Python is moving around a lot of memory to make this happen, and that can slow things down—especially in loops with a lot of elements. One hundred verses probably isn't enough to cause a problem that's noticeable, but nevertheless, we should always strive to be reasonably frugal with system resources, as they aren't unlimited. To fix this, we can create a list of verses and then join them at the end.

SNIPPET

05-09.py

```python
# Define the bottles_song function with the start argument defaulting to 99
def bottles_song(start = 99):
    # Set the initial number of bottles to the start argument
    bottles = start
    # Loop through until bottles are gone
    while bottles > 0:
        # Display the song
        this_verse = []
        this_verse.append(str(bottles) + " bottles of beer on the wall. ")
        this_verse.append(str(bottles) + " bottles of beer. ")
        this_verse.append("Take one down, pass it around, ")
        # Subtract a bottle
        bottles -= 1
        this_verse.append(str(bottles) + " bottles of beer on the wall. ")
        # Yield to the calling function
        yield "".join(this_verse)
        # Pick back up here when we return
    return True
```

```
# Loop through the generator
for v in bottles _ song():
    print(v)
```

In this code, we create an empty list called `this _ verse` and append each created string. Then we take an empty string (i.e., `""`) and use `join` to combine each item on the list (each verse, in this case) into a string and then `yield` that value. This does the same work as before but uses less memory and CPU power. This approach might seem a bit strange at first, but it touches on a concept we'll explore in chapter 6. For now, just note that all strings have this functionality.

One final note about generators. In our example, the song isn't long (and defaults to 100 verses), but what if we wanted our song to be the longest drinking song in the history of drinking songs? Perhaps one trillion verses? A generator makes that possible because it constructs the song from scratch, verse by verse. If our generator created Fibonacci sequence numbers (i.e., 1, 1, 2, 3, 5, 8, 13, etc.), then we could use it to propagate a seemingly infinite number of values.

But if we stored a trillion verses of our song in long form (as though we had typed them in a text editor), it would take at least 80 terabytes of memory. That's a preposterous amount and would most certainly exceed the capacity of computers (especially laptops and desktops) for the next few years. Even when technology does reach a point where 80 terabytes is a seemingly insignificant amount, why use the resources when we don't have to? Our generator function contains a simple bit of reusable code that can keep us singing silly tunes until the heat death of the universe. Now that's true, scalable power!

MORE BOTTLES! Here's a fun exercise to try. Take the bottle song code (preferably the last version, using the generator) and reverse it, causing it to start from 1 and work up to 99. I highly encourage you to try this on your own. You can do it! If you get stuck, though, consult the appendix for a solution.

ClydeBank Coffee Shop: Our First Major Refactor

First, we should define the term refactor. To refactor code means to refine it generally without changing its overall behavior.

By introducing functions, we can eliminate a lot of duplicate code and make things easier to understand—yet preserve the original functionality. Also, as we expand the game with future functionality, the functions we've created will save us time because we'll have to modify only them, not the loop or other critical game code. For example, our `get_weather` function can become a lot more sophisticated than simply generating a random number. The code that calls `get_weather` doesn't have to know what is going in within that function; it could query an internet resource for the current temperature or connect to a Raspberry Pi device with a thermometer sensor attached. Whatever it does, our code only cares about the result it returns.

IMPORTANT

Code that should appear on a single line but must be broken due to page constraints is indicated using arrows. A straight arrow (↦) at the end of a line and and a curved arrow (↪) at the beginning of the next line indicate that those lines should be combined to make one continuous line.

SNIPPET

CCS-05.py

```
# ClydeBank Coffee Shop Simulator 4000
# Copyright 2022 (C) ClydeBank Media, All Rights Reserved.

# Import items from the random module to generate weather
from random import seed
from random import randint

# Current day number
day = 1

# Starting cash on hand
cash = 100.00

# Coffee on hand (cups)
coffee = 100

# Sales list of dictionaries
# sales = [
#     {
#         "day": 1,
#         "coffee_inv": 100,
#         "advertising": "10",
#         "temp": 68,
#         "cups_sold": 16
#     },
#     {
```

```
#        "day": 2,
#        "coffee_inv": 84,
#        "advertising": "15",
#        "temp": 72,
#        "cups_sold": 20
#    },
#    {
#        "day": 3,
#        "coffee_inv": 64,
#        "advertising": "5",
#        "temp": 78,
#        "cups_sold": 10
#    },
# ]
# Create an empty sales list
sales = []
def welcome():
    print("ClydeBank Coffee Shop Simulator 4000, Version 1.00")
    print("Copyright (C) 2022 ClydeBank Media, All Rights Reserved.\n")
    print("Let's collect some information before we start the game.\n")


def prompt(display="Please input a string", require=True):
    if require:
        s = False
        while not s:
            s = input(display + " ")
    else:
        s = input(display + " ")
    return s


def daily_stats(cash_on_hand, weather_temp, coffee_inventory):
    print("You have $" + str(cash_on_hand) + " cash on hand and the temperature is ↦
    ↳ " + str(weather_temp) + ".")
    print("You have enough coffee on hand to make " + str(coffee_inventory) + " ↦
    ↳ cups.\n")


def convert_to_float(s):
    # If conversion fails, assign 0 to it
    try:
        f = float(s)
```

```
        except ValueError:
            f = 0
        return f

def get_weather():
    # Generate a random temperature between 20 and 90
    # We'll consider seasons later on, but this is good enough for now
    return randint(20, 90)


# Print welcome message
welcome()


# Get name and store name
name = prompt("What is your name?", True)
shop_name = prompt("What do you want to name your coffee shop?", True)


# We have what we need, so let's get started!
print("\nOk, let's get started. Have fun!")


# The main game loop
running = True
while running:
    # Display the day and add a "fancy" text effect
    print("\n-----| Day " + str(day) + " @ " + shop_name + " |-----")


    temperature = get_weather()


    # Display the cash and weather
    daily_stats(cash, temperature, coffee)


    # Get price of a cup of coffee
    cup_price = prompt("What do you want to charge per cup of coffee?")


    # Get price of a cup of coffee
    print("\nYou can buy advertising to help promote sales.")
    advertising = prompt("How much do you want to spend on advertising ↦
    ↪ (0 for none)?", False)


    # Convert advertising into a float
    advertising = convert_to_float(advertising)
```

```
# Deduct advertising from cash on hand
cash -= advertising


# TODO: Calculate today's performance
# TODO: Display today's performance


# Before we loop around, add a day
day += 1
```

Chapter Recap

» Functions allow us to organize our code into reusable portions. This not only saves us time but makes it easier to debug, test, and optimize our code.

» When we provide a value (or values) to a function, it's called passing arguments. Arguments are values that are provided to the function for use within its code.

» Default arguments provide initial values to arguments, making them optional to the calling code.

» Keyword arguments allow us to provide arguments in an easier way by labeling them.

| 6 |
Classes

Chapter Overview

» Classes allow us to organize data and logic into a single container
» Objects are instances of classes
» Classes can have instance and class variables

In chapter 2, we learned about how to structure our data in Python. In chapter 5, we learned how to organize our logic into functions. Now it's time to combine all that into one incredibly useful package—classes. This paradigm of classes and the objects they produce is part of a broader scheme in Python (and programming in general) called *object-oriented programming*.

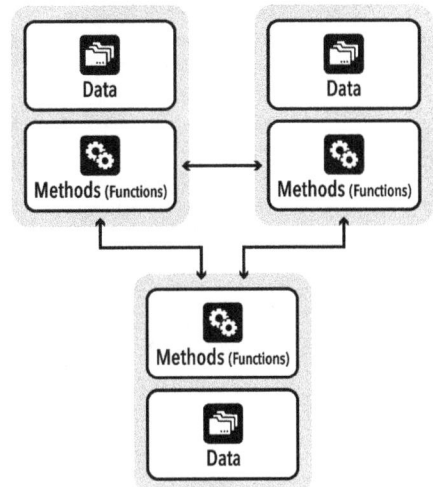

The term "object-oriented programming" is just a fancy way of describing an approach to programming that involves objects. These objects contain code and data and are modeled from classes. That's a lot to unpack, so let's break down each part of this paradigm.

PROCEDURAL PROGRAMMING

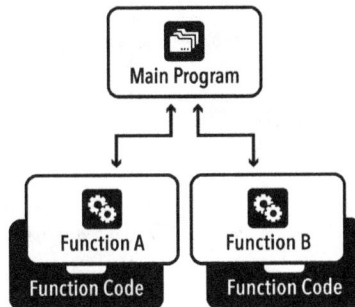

OBJECT-ORIENTED PROGRAMMING

GRAPHIC

fig. 23

Main Program

Function A
Function Code

Function B
Function Code

Data

Methods (Functions)

Data

Methods (Functions)

Methods (Functions)

Data

Until now, we've been writing our programs in a very procedural way, that is, mostly sequentially with our code only taking detours into functions and then returning to the main program flow. With object-oriented programming, we go beyond this paradigm by clustering our logic (i.e., functions) alongside our data, better defining our goals (figure 23).

A *class* in Python defines a structure that can contain both data (variables) and logic (functions) in a single, reusable container. A class is like a cookie cutter, defining a collection of functions and variables.

Classes don't do anything by themselves, though, just like you can't (or shouldn't) eat a cookie cutter. When you want to make use of a class, you create an *object* from it. Following our delicious dessert metaphor, if classes are the cookie cutter, objects that you create from them are the cookies.

When a function (logic) is added to a class, it's called a *method*. I'll call them methods in reference to classes from now on, but whenever you see that word, just think *function*.

Now that we've defined the terms and applied our cheesy food metaphors, let's get our aprons dirty and start baking!

The Hello World Class

Let's dust off our favorite introductory phrase and jump right into an example.

SNIPPET

06-01.py

```python
# Define the World class
class World:
        # Define our greeting
        greeting = "Hello, World!"

        # Run this whenever the object is created
        def __init__(self):
            # Print the greeting
            print(self.greeting)

# Use the class World to create a world object named w
w = World()
```

Copy and paste this code into your `scratch.py` file and run it. The result is fairly straightforward:

```
Hello World!
```

World Class Data

```
# Define the World class
class World:
    # Define our greeting
    greeting =  "Hello, World!"
```

World Class __init__ Method

```
    # Run this whenever the object is created
    def __init__(self):
        # Print the greeting
        print(self.greeting)
```

Main Program

```
# Use the class World to create a world object named w
w = World()
```

Example code, highlighting the class data, the __init__ method, and the main program.

There's a lot of new syntax here, so let's unpack this example. In the first line, we create the `World` class. Class names in Python, by convention, start with a capital letter. Inside the class block, we create a string called `greeting` and assign it the text `"Hello, World!"` Then we create a method (function) *inside* the class called `__init__` (note the two underscores, the word `init`, then two more underscores).

This method has an argument called `self`. It's a special argument that Python automatically uses to reference the object created by the class—in other words, itself. Then it uses the `print` function to print the contents of the string `greeting`, but since `greeting` is not inside the scope of the `__init__` method, it uses the reference `self` that was passed to act as a pointer to the scope above it, giving it access to the `greeting` string.

Let's dive a bit deeper into some of these concepts. First, I said that the `__init__` method is inside the class. Just as the code of a function is contained in the indented code after it, the entire method `__init__` belongs to the `World` class. The variable `greeting` is also contained within the `World` class. Although this example class contains only one method and one variable, classes can have as many variables and methods as needed.

One additional thing: the method name `__init__` sticks out like a sore thumb. You may be wondering why it has two underscores on either side. Most of your methods will be named just like other functions you've created before, with lowercase letters and no special characters before or after them. But the `__init__` method is special. It is automatically called when an object is created from a class (such as when we created the object named `w` from the class `World` in the last line of our example).

Instance Variables

The best way to explain instance variables is to start with an example of a different kind of variable within a class. I know that may seem counterintuitive, but bear with me.

In this example, we create several new objects from the Customer class.

```python
# Define a new class
class Customer:
        def __ init __ (self):
            name = "Robert"


# Create three objects based on the Customer class
c1 = Customer()
c2 = Customer()
c3 = Customer()
```

Next, we create three objects from the `Customer` class. I've given them the names `c1`, `c2`, and `c3`, signifying customers 1, 2, and 3. I didn't have to name them that, but since I had previously named a customer object `c`, I wanted a way to easily distinguish between them.

But there's a problem with this approach. Each customer will have the same variable called `name` with the value "Robert". Surely we want each object from the `Customer` class to have its own `name`. To do that, we use an ***instance variable***, which is a variable defined within a class that is specific to that instance (in other words, specific to that object).

Each object (`c1`, `c2`, and `c3`) has its own unique copy of the `name` variable, but since we set the variable in the `__init__` method, it's the same in all three cases. Let's change that and, while we're at it, provide another detail for our customer list.

SNIPPET

06-02.py

```python
# Define a new class
class Customer:
        def __ init __ (self, name, city):
            self.name = name
            self.city = city


        def greet(self):
            print("Hello, " + self.name + "!")


# Create three objects based on the Customer class
```

```
c1 = Customer("Sarah", "Atlanta")
c2 = Customer("Robert", "Florence")
c3 = Customer("Thomas", "Denver")

# Add the customer objects to a list
customers = [c1, c2, c3]

# Iterate through list, greet, then display information
for c in customers:
        c.greet()
        print(c.name + " lives in " + c.city + ".")
```

When you run this code, here's what you'll see:

```
Hello, Sarah!
Sarah lives in Atlanta.
Hello, Robert!
Robert lives in Florence.
Hello, Thomas!
Thomas lives in Denver.
```

This example builds on our existing `Customer` class. First, we use the `__init__` method to set internal (to the class) variables `name` and `city`. They are referenced by `self` because they belong to each object based on that class.

We accept three parameters on the `__init__` method, but only two are for our use—the `self` argument allows us to reference the class variables inside the `__init__` method. Then we assign the values in the arguments passed called `name` and `city` to `self.name` and `self.city`, which are really just variables inside the class.

Recall that the `__init__` method is special in that Python calls it automatically when an object is created. Because of this unique status, we can pass values to it when we create the object (figure 25).

I added a method called `greet()`, which simply says "Hello", to the name instance variable found in each customer object.

As in the previous examples, we created three objects from the class, `c1`, `c2`, and `c3`, and added them to a list called `customers`. Because they're in a list, we can iterate over them and perform the same action on each—in this case, first calling `greet()` and then displaying the name and city.

The key takeaway here is that each object has its own copy of the `name` and `city` variables. But that doesn't change the class. Just like adding sprinkles to one of your cookies doesn't change your cookie cutter, the `Customer` class isn't changed by giving each object a unique `name` and `city`. It only serves as a template. The objects (cookies) have these unique values.

```
def __init__ (self, name, city):


c1 = Customer("Sarah", "Atlanta")
```

Comparing the `__init__` method arguments with the creation of the customer object.

Class Variables

While instance variables are unique to each object, ***class variables*** are established inside the class and are shared by each object created from that class. To continue with our cookie metaphor, adding sprinkles to the cookies doesn't change the cookie cutter, but modifying the cookie cutter will change every cookie.

We've already used class variables once at the beginning of this chapter in our "Hello World!" class.

```
# Define the World class
class World:
        # Define our greeting
        greeting = "Hello, World!"

# Run this whenever the object is created
def __init__ (self):
        # Print the greeting
        print(self.greeting)

# Use the class World to create a world object named w
w = World()
```

The `greeting` class variable is set for all the objects created from the `World` class. You can create as many objects from `World` as you like and they'll all have `w.greeting` set to "Hello, World!" Even though this class uses the `print` function to display `self.greeting` automatically upon creation (because it's in `__init__`), we can use `print(w.greeting)` outside the class (right below the `w = World()` line) to do the same thing. Inside the class, we have to use `self.greeting` because we need a reference to the instance of the class, and `self` provides that. But outside, `w` *is* the object (in our example) and simply accessing `w.greeting` produces the same result.

Another interesting attribute of class variables is that they are accessible from the class itself.

06-03.py

```
# Define the World class
class World:
        # Define our greeting
        greeting = "Hello, World!"


print(World.greeting)
```

If this seems a bit strange, that's good! It should, because when we talk about classes in Python, we really are more focused on what they produce—objects. Nevertheless, having some data structures accessible at the class level can be quite useful, especially when using these values outside of the class. We'll be doing more of that in future chapters.

Scope in Classes

In chapter 5 we discussed scope in regard to functions, but now, since we're introducing classes that contain methods, it's important to talk about this new layer of the Python onion.

Classes contain variables and methods, and those belong to the class. Code that isn't part of that class cannot interact with those variables or methods directly—another reference point is needed by which to access them.

Let's look at some code that will demonstrate the scope of variables.

06-04.py

```
# This variable exists in the main scope
name = "Sarah"

# Define a new class with a class variable called name
class Customer:
        name = "Robert"

# Create a new customer so that __ init __ is called
customer = Customer()
```

```
# Display the name in the main scope
print(customer.name)
```

Here, we define a string called `name` with the value "Sarah". Then we define a new class called `Customer` and create a class variable within it called `name` and assign it the value "Robert".

When we run the code, it displays "Robert". It does this because the `print` function displays the value of `customer.name`, not the name variable in the main scope.

The same situation occurs with instance variables.

SNIPPET

06-05.py

```
# This variable exists in the main scope
name = "Sarah"

# Define a new class with a class variable called name
class Customer:
        def __ init __ (self, name):
                self.name = name

# Create a new customer so that __ init __ is called
customer = Customer("Robert")

# Display the name in the main scope
print(customer.name)
```

In this example, the same situation occurs—the `name` variable in the main scope is "Sarah" but `customer.name` is "Robert".

Object Lifecycle

Objects are born, live their life within the Python interpreter, and eventually die. In figure 26, we can see the cycle of an object and the various methods that are automatically called at each stage of its existence based on our `World` class.

Let's look at each of the special lifecycle methods in depth.

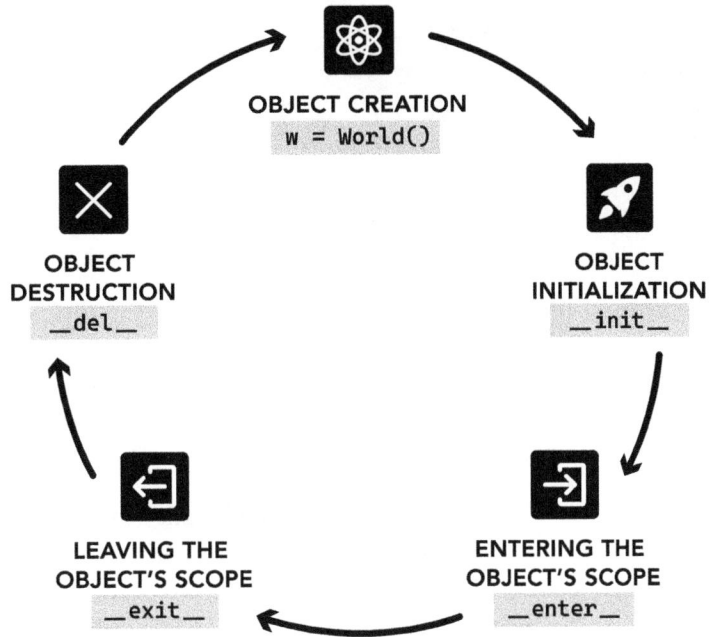

fig. 26

__init__

As we discussed earlier in this chapter, the __init__ method is automatically called whenever an object is created from a class. Generally, it is tasked with setting up any instance variables that the object will later need.

```
class World:
    # Define our greeting
    greeting = "Hello, World!"


    # Run this whenever the object is created
    def __init__(self):
        # Print the greeting
        print(self.greeting)
```

We don't have to create an __init__ method, but most classes will have them to set up variables the object needs to use. Arguments passed at the object's creation will be available in __init__, declared after the self argument in the method definition.

```python
# Define a new class
class Customer:
    # Define the init method, using name and city as arguments
    def __init__(self, name, city):
        self.name = name
        self.city = city


# Create three objects based on the Customer class
# The name and city are passed to __init__
c1 = Customer("Sarah", "Atlanta")
c2 = Customer("Robert", "Florence")
c3 = Customer("Thomas", "Denver")
```

__enter__ and __exit__

The `__enter__` method is called by the interpreter when we use the `with` statement. This handy feature allows us to run code within a block that makes use of a resource that we create (like an open file). This encourages us to use and manage resources wisely.

```python
# Define a new class
class Customer:
    def __init__(self, name, city):
        self.name = name
        self.city = city

    def __enter__(self):
        print("Entering scope.")
        # Run code upon entering scope of with statement
        return self

    def __exit__(self, exc_type, exc_value, traceback):
        print("Leaving scope.")
        # Run code upon leaving scope of width statement

    def greet(self):
        print("Hello, " + self.name + "!")

# Use with to create a scope
with Customer("Robert", "Florence") as robert:
    robert.greet()
```

The program's execution begins at the `with` statement at the end of the file. This creates a "temporary" object named `robert` from the `Customer` class. I say temporary because this object is created inline by the `with` statement and will be destroyed at the end of the indented code block contained in the `with` statement.

When the object is created, the `__init__` method fires. This takes the `name` and `city` arguments and sets them as instance variables. Since a `with` statement was used to create the object, the `__enter__` method is called right after that. Here, we display a quick message to tell ourselves where we are in the object lifecycle, then we can run any code we like at this point. However, once we're done, we must `return self` at the end of the `__enter__` method.

The `with` block provides the customer object (accessible as `robert`, which the `as robert` at the end of the `with` statement indicates) so that it can be used within the code block. Then the `greet` method is called on the `robert` object and the greeting is displayed.

After the code in the `with` block is done, the `__exit__` method is fired, which takes four arguments: `self`, `exc_type`, `exc_value`, and `traceback`. The `self` argument gives code within the method an anchor from which it can access other methods and variables in the class, and the `exc_type`, `exc_value`, and `traceback` arguments are populated with values if an exception occurs. Otherwise, they are optional. Inside `__exit__`, we display a message that lets us know where we are, and then we run any code we want when the `with` statement is about to end.

At the end of the processing of `__exit__`, control is returned to the last line of the with statement block, which then dispenses with the object (in this case, `robert`).

__del__

All good things must come to an end—including our objects. When we no longer need an object, we can use the `del` function to delete it. Deleting objects when we no longer need them reduces memory usage in a program. Deleting objects is permanent, but we can create more if we wish. To delte objects we can instruct Python to trigger a special method called `__del__`. Here's an example:

```
class World:
    def __ init __ (self):
        print("I'm alive!")
    def __ del __ (self):
        print("I'm gone!")


earth = World()
del(earth)
```

When we run this program, we'll see this:

```
I'm alive!
I'm gone!
```

When the object `earth` was created from the class `World`, the `__ init __` method was executed, thus printing "I'm alive!" When the object was deleted, the `__ del __` method was executed, printing "I'm gone!"

Be careful when using `__ del __`, because it has several drawbacks. First, excessively long or error-prone code in this method can interfere with *garbage collection*, the Python process that cleans up unneeded objects to keep resource usage low and prevents *memory leaks* (the gradual decline of free memory caused by data consuming more and more memory). Additionally, an object might not be deleted when you think it is (unless you explicitly delete it with `del`), so relying on this method can be risky.

Properties and Private Variables

We're already familiar with instance variables—that is, variables that belong to an object and are referenced by `self.variable _ name` inside the class and `object.variable _ name` outside the class. These fill most of our object variable needs. However, sometimes we want to perform actions when accessing that variable. That's where *properties* come in handy.

Let's look at two different approaches. Both accomplish the same thing but in different ways.

```
# Convert kilometers to miles
class Converter:
    def __ init __ (self, km):
        self.km = km
```

```
        def to_miles(self):
            return self.km / 1.609

# Convert 3 kilometers to miles
distance1 = Converter(3)
print(distance1.to_miles())
```

In this first example, we use the traditional approach—specifying the number of kilometers when we create the object `distance1` from the class `Converter`. This sets the `km` instance variable, and then `to_miles` returns this instance variable value divided by 1.609, which yields a rough approximation of miles. This works, but there's another way.

SNIPPET

06-10.py

```
class Distance:
        def __init__(self, km):
            self._km = km
        @property
        def km(self):
            return self._km
        @property
        def miles(self):
            return self._km / 1.609

distance2 = Distance(3)
print(str(distance2.km))
print(str(distance2.miles))
```

The first thing you may notice about this approach is that the class name is `Distance` rather than `Converter`. I named it that because the main purpose of the class is not to convert but rather to store a value of a distance. In other words, the objects created from this class represent an actual value, not just a container for a utility function. That may seem like a subtle and perhaps unimportant difference, but as we explore usage patterns of classes throughout the rest of the book, you'll appreciate the distinction.

Also, the instance variable `_km` has an underscore in front of it. When we add `_` in front of a variable, this, by convention, denotes a *private variable*—that is, a variable not directly accessible from outside the class. It is private, or internal, to the class itself. To access it, we'll use one of the property methods available, either `km` or `miles`.

Property methods have @property above them. This is called a ***decorator*** (because it "decorates" a function) and it tells Python to treat it more as a variable than as a function. In the first example, we used to _ miles() with parentheses because it was a function. However, km and miles are properties in this example, so from the outside, we access them just like we would instance variables. We don't have to do anything to convert kilometers to kilometers, so the km property simply returns self. _ km, our private variable. Converting to miles involves a bit of math, so our miles property returns self. _ km after dividing it by 1.609.

In addition to modifying a variable before we return it, we can also run code when we set a property. This is especially useful for validating data.

SNIPPET

06-11.py

```python
class Distance:
    def __ init __ (self, km):
        self. _ km = km

    @property
    def km(self):
        return self. _ km

    @km.setter
    def km(self, value):
        self. _ km = value

    @property
    def miles(self):
        return self. _ km / 1.609

    @miles.setter
    def miles(self, value):
        self. _ km = value * 1.609

distance2 = Distance(3)
print("3 kilometers is " + str(distance2.miles) + " miles.")
distance2.miles = 3
print(str(distance2.miles) + " miles is " + str(distance2.km) + " kilometers.")
```

In this example, we set an initial value to the `distance2` object in kilometers but can easily get both kilometers and miles from it. And, if we want to give it a distance in miles, we can simply set `distance2.miles = 3` and we internally set `self._km` to the correct value in kilometers, thanks to the `@miles.setter` property.

As we covered previously, putting the `@property` decorator above a function converts it into a property. Once it's a property, we can define a ***setter***, that is, a property that sets a value internal to the object. We do this by adding a decorator with the `@` sign, then the name of the property with `.setter` at the end of it. In this example, the setter for `km` simply sets `self._km` to the value provided, because internally we're storing the value as kilometers anyway, but when we use the `miles` setter, we multiply it by 1.609.

When I learned about properties in Python, I was a bit confused at first. I think this is partially because the idea of a function acting more like a variable was weird to me. Additionally, the examples that I saw used somewhat contrived problems to demonstrate how properties worked. My understanding of properties didn't solidify until I used them for unique, real-world issues in my programming work.

I tell you this for two reasons. First, you can program in Python and never create properties and you'll be just fine. They aren't essential for Python programming. Nevertheless, I think they give you tremendous flexibility in the way you design your classes, and this leads to better programs. Second, if you don't quite see the value in Python properties right now, or it's a bit fuzzy, don't worry. We'll use them more as the book progresses, and as various use cases pop up in examples and in our Coffee Shop game, I believe you'll find them as indispensable as I do.

Inches to Centimeters

Our `Distance` class does a great job of converting between miles and kilometers. Let's expand on that concept a bit and create a `Length` class. Instead of using miles and kilometers, we can convert inches and centimeters.

The principles are the same, but you'll have to adjust several parts of the code, including the math required for the new conversion. Try this on your own, but if you get stuck, you can refer to the appendix for a solution.

(Hint: 1 inch is equal to 2.54 centimeters.)

ClydeBank Coffee Shop: Our Second Refactor

We now have lots of classes to empower our coffee shop simulator game. With this new level of organization and functionality, we can complete the basic game loop. First, let's look at the new code.

```python
# ClydeBank Coffee Shop Simulator 4000
# Copyright 2022 (C) ClydeBank Media, All Rights Reserved.


# Import the random module
import random


def welcome():
    print("ClydeBank Coffee Shop Simulator 4000, Version 1.00")
    print("Copyright (C) 2022 ClydeBank Media, All Rights Reserved.\n")
    print("Let's collect some information before we start the game.\n")


def prompt(display="Please input a string", require=True):
    if require:
        s = False
        while not s:
            s = input(display + " ")
    else:
        s = input(display + " ")
    return s


def convert_to_float(s):
    # If conversion fails, assign 0 to it
    try:
        f = float(s)
    except ValueError:
        f = 0
    return f


def x_of_y(x, y):
    num_list = []
    # Return a list of x copies of y
    for i in range(x):
        num_list.append(y)
    return num_list
```

```
class CoffeeShopSimulator:

    # Minimum and maximum temperatures
    TEMP_MIN = 20
    TEMP_MAX = 90


    def __init__(self, player_name, shop_name):
        # Set player and coffee shop names
        self.player_name = player_name
        self.shop_name = shop_name

        # Current day number
        self.day = 1

        # Cash on hand at start
        self.cash = 100.00

        # Inventory at start
        self.coffee_inventory = 100

        # Sales list
        self.sales = []

        # Possible temperatures
        self.temps = self.make_temp_distribution()

    def run(self):
        print("\nOk, let's get started. Have fun!")

        # The main game loop
        running = True
        while running:
            # Display the day and add a "fancy" text effect
            self.day_header()

            # Get the weather
            temperature = self.weather

            # Display the cash and weather
            self.daily_stats(temperature)
```

```
            # Get price of a cup of coffee
            cup_price = float(prompt("What do you want to charge per cup of coffee?"))

            # Get advertising spend
            print("\nYou can buy advertising to help promote sales.")
            advertising = prompt("How much do you want to spend on advertising (0 ↦
            ↪ for none)?", False)

            # Convert advertising into a float
            advertising = convert_to_float(advertising)

            # Deduct advertising from cash on hand
            self.cash -= advertising

            # Simulate today's sales
            cups_sold = self.simulate(temperature, advertising, cup_price)
            gross_profit = cups_sold * cup_price

            # Display the results
            print("You sold " + str(cups_sold) + " cups of coffee today.")
            print("You made $" + str(gross_profit) + ".")

            # Add the profit to our coffers
            self.cash += gross_profit

            # Subtract inventory
            self.coffee_inventory -= cups_sold

            # Before we loop around, add a day
            self.increment_day()
    def simulate(self, temperature, advertising, cup_price):
        # Find out how many cups were sold
        cups_sold = self.daily_sales(temperature, advertising)

        # Save the sales data for today
        self.sales.append({
            "day": self.day,
            "coffee_inv": self.coffee_inventory,
            "advertising": advertising,
            "temp": temperature,
```

```
            "cup_price": cup_price,
            "cups_sold": cups_sold
    })

    # We technically don't need this, but why make the next step
    # read from the sales list when we have the data right here
    return cups_sold

def make_temp_distribution(self):
    # This is not a good bell curve, but it will do for now
    # until we get to more advanced mathematics
    temps = []

    # First, find the average between TEMP_MIN and TEMP_MAX
    avg = (self.TEMP_MIN + self.TEMP_MAX) / 2
    # Find the distance between TEMP_MAX and the average
    max_dist_from_avg = self.TEMP_MAX - avg

    # Loop through all possible temperatures
    for i in range(self.TEMP_MIN, self.TEMP_MAX):
        # How far away is the temperature from average?
        # abs() gives us the absolute value
        dist_from_avg = abs(avg - i)
        # How far away is the dist_from_avg from the maximum?
        # This will be lower for temps at the extremes
        dist_from_max_dist = max_dist_from_avg - dist_from_avg
        # If the value is zero, make it one
        if dist_from_max_dist == 0:
            dist_from_max_dist = 1
        # Append the output of x_of_y to temps
        for t in x_of_y(int(dist_from_max_dist), i):
            temps.append(t)
        return temps

def increment_day(self):
    self.day += 1

def daily_stats(self, temperature):
    print("You have $" + str(self.cash) + " cash on hand and the temperature is " + ↦
    ↳ str(temperature) + ".")
```

```
        print("You have enough coffee on hand to make " + str(self.coffee_inventory) ↦
            ↳ + " cups.\n")


    def day_header(self):
        print("\n-----| Day " + str(self.day) + " @ " + self.shop_name + " |-----")


    def daily_sales(self, temperature, advertising):
        return int((self.TEMP_MAX - temperature) * (advertising * 0.5))


    @property
    def weather(self):
        # Generate a random temperature between 20 and 90
        # We'll consider seasons later on, but this is good enough for now
        return random.choice(self.temps)


# Print welcome message
welcome()


# Get name and store name
t_name = prompt("What is your name?", True)
t_shop_name = prompt("What do you want to name your coffee shop?", True)


# Create the game object
game = CoffeeShopSimulator(t_name, t_shop_name)


# Run the game
game.run()
```

Now the game is functionally complete. I say *functionally* because it's not really done, but it is playable. The structure has changed quite a bit though, so let's step through the changes.

The Game Class

Most of the game's logic has been moved into the CoffeeShopSimulator class. This better organizes the structure and lets us streamline variable sharing within the game. Since most of the content is in the class, the main program simply gets the name, shop_name, and then creates an object called game derived from the CoffeeShopSimulator class. Then the run method is called on the game object, which starts the show.

The __init__ Method

The game sets up needed variables in the `__init__` method, including the `sales` list that will contain the player's daily progress. It also calls a method named `make_temp_distribution`, which sets up a list of possible temperature values.

The make_temp_distribution Method

I wanted to make the temperatures seem somewhat realistic rather than just a random smattering of possible values. While this method is in no way optimized or even ideal for the problem at hand, it does the job. It still doesn't account for seasons, but it gives a somewhat passible approximation of a typical swing of temperatures in a temperate climate in spring or fall.

Let's step through it line by line, as it is a bit complex. First, we create an empty list named `temps`. Then we find the average between `self.TEMP_MIN` and `self.TEMP_MAX` by adding both together and dividing them by 2. Then we get the maximum distance from average by subtracting the average from `self.TEMP_MAX`.

Armed with this information, we start a loop that uses `range` to iterate between `self.TEMP_MIN` and `self.TEMP_MAX`. Then we use the `abs` function to find the absolute value of the average minus our current position in the loop between `self.TEMP_MIN` and `self.TEMP_MAX`.

Next, we calculate how far this distance is from the maximum. The purpose of this is to derive the distance from max distance, which essentially tells us how close the current position in the loop `(i)` is from the extreme hot and cold points in the list. Using this value, we append the temperature to the final list (`temps`)`dist_from_max_dist` times using the function `x_of_y` times. By this I mean that the the temperature is repeated `dist_from_max_dist` times in a list that is then appended to the final result.

Our final list (`temps`), which is returned, provides a range of values that more commonly occur near the center, or peak, of the bell curve.

The Game Loop

The `run` method now starts the loop, displays the header, gets a temperature for the day, and prompts the player for price and advertising information. With this information, it runs the simulation via the `simulate` method, which runs the `daily_sales` method to simulate sales. For now, this is just a simple calculation that favors colder temperatures and more advertising, but we'll expand on it later. After that method returns with the sales, it appends a dictionary to the `sales` list and then returns control to the main loop. Once there, it displays the day's sales, adds the profit of the day, subtracts the inventory, and increments the day counter.

Then it's rinse and repeat for the next day.

Even though the game is technically working right now, there are quite a few problems. First, there is no inventory check to prevent running out of coffee, or a prompt to buy any if there was. We need to add a prompt that asks the user to buy more coffee each day, preferably at the end of the day. Also, there's no way to leave the game other than closing the terminal or pressing CTRL+C, so we'll need to add an escape hatch.

There are a lot of deficiencies, but as it stands it is technically playable. We'll continue to improve it as we go through the book. Why not have a bit of fun and play a few days of the simulator?

ON YOUR OWN

Here's a suggestion. Modify the constructor of the `CoffeeShopSimulator` class to accept optional `player_name` and `shop_name` values so you can construct a game object without prompts.

If you choose to do this, copy the folder with the game code to another location (perhaps `coffee-shop-no-prompts` or similar) and work on that new copy, because this modified code won't be compatible with the future additions we're going to make to the game. Nevertheless, this will be a good exercise to help you better understand classes and constructors.

Chapter Recap

»   Classes allow us to organize data and logic into reusable containers.

»   Classes are like cookie cutters, serving as a template for objects to be created.

»   Objects have a lifecycle and automatically call __ init __ upon their creation.

»   Properties are preferred over instance variables when we need to run code upon getting or setting a value from an object.

| 7 |
Inheritance and Design Patterns

Chapter Overview
» Classes can inherit methods and variables from parent classes
» Classes can have multiple parents and ancestors
» Using class design patterns can save time in development

Inheritance in object-oriented programming is a way for a class to be based on another class. A class inherited from its parent class will acquire all the parent's structure, including methods, class variables, and properties.

Before we dive into an example, let's consider furniture. I'm sure you never expected a discussion about furniture in a programming book, but there's a first time for everything. We'll need furniture in our coffee shop, and although it will be just a small part of our game, this paradigm will nevertheless explain the concept of inheritance.

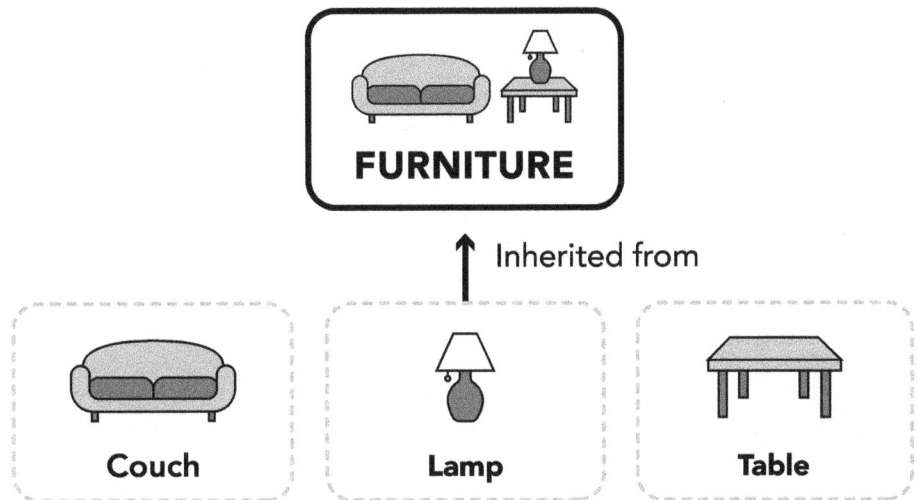

Many classes of furniture, all inherited from the Furniture class.

If we were to create a `Furniture` class, it might have properties like width, height, and perhaps even the material of which it's made. Now consider a `Chair`. I've capitalized the word so that you can see my intent—let's imagine it's a class. Chairs are furniture. They have width and height and are made of materials. But they also have a seat, and some have backs and some have arms. A chair has the base properties of `Furniture` but also properties of its own.

Parent and Child

Consider our furniture metaphor—a chair is a piece of furniture. Let's convert that concept into Python code. I'm going to use instance variables for the basic properties because (currently) we don't need to perform any kind of transformation on those properties when accessing or setting them. This may change in the future, and that situation would call for properties, but for now, instance variables will do.

```
# First, let's define the Furniture class
class Furniture:
    def __init__(self, width = 0, height = 0, material = "Wood"):
        self.width = width
        self.height = height
        self.material = material


# Next, let's define the Chair class
class Chair(Furniture):
    def __init__(self, width = 0, height = 0, material = "Wood", arms = True, back = True):
        super().__init__(width, height, material)
        self.arms = arms
        self.back = back
```

Two new elements are introduced here—the parentheses after `class Chair` and the `super()` function.

DETOUR

Why would width and height be 0? In practice (except maybe in the realm of science fiction), we certainly wouldn't find a piece of furniture with no width or height. The reason I defaulted these values to zero is an old habit from when I designed graphical user interface applications. In some situations, it was advantageous to spawn a window or control that had no width or height but could still receive events.

If we really were constructing software dealing with furniture, we probably wouldn't allow these values, but even in that case this kind of escape hatch from reality could be helpful. In fact, a few years ago I worked on a website where a hidden, fake product was added to the cart when certain industry customers (rather than the public) placed an order. The presence of this hidden product told the checkout code how to process the customer.

First, with the parentheses, we specify `Furniture` in `class Chair(Furniture)` because that's the base, or parent, class of the child class `Chair`. Both parent and child classes can be used independently of one another, but the child class `(Chair)` inherits everything from the parent. So the `Chair` class has instance variables named `arms` and `back`, as well as `width`, `height`, and `material`. `Furniture` is still usable as a separate class and has only `width`, `height`, and `material`.

Second, the `super()` function is a shortcut to the parent class (in this case, `Furniture`). Just as `self` allows instance methods to interact with instance variables, `super()` lets us make use of the parent's functionality.

You might wonder why this is necessary, though, because I stated that child classes inherit all their functionality from their parents. They do, but we defined an `__init__` method in `Chair`, and this overrode the `__init__` method in `Furniture`. Since we need both, as soon as we enter the `__init__` method of `Chair`, we call `super().__init__(width, height, material)`, which calls the `__init__` method of `Furniture`. This lets us blend the functionality of both `__init__` methods.

Using `super()` wouldn't be necessary if we hadn't defined a custom `__init__` method for `Chair`, but we did because we want to give it some initial instance variables of its own (i.e., `arms` and `back`). Since the line `super().__init__(width, height, material)` calls the `__init__` function in the parent `Furniture` class, it allows for three arguments: `width`, `height`, and `material`. They aren't required because they have default values in the `Furniture` `__init__` function, but I wanted them to be able to be set to non-default values, so I added them to `Chair`'s `__init__` function as well.

Expanding Child Classes

`Chairs` have other unique properties that most `Furniture` doesn't. Consider the idea of a folding chair. In this case, we'll add a method to the `Chair` class:

```
# First, let's define the Furniture class

class Furniture:

    def __init__(self, width = 0, height = 0, material = "Wood"):

        self.width = width

        self.height = height

        self.material = material


# Next, let's define the Chair class

class Chair(Furniture):

    def __init__(self, width = 0, height = 0, material = "Wood", arms = True, back = True):

        super().__init__(width, height, material)

        self.arms = arms

        self.back = back


    def fold(self):

        self.folded = True

        print("The chair is now folded and ready for transport.")

    def unfold(self):

        self.folded = False

        print("The chair is now unfolded and ready for use.")
```

In this example, I added two methods to the `Chair` class: `fold` and `unfold`. The `fold` method sets `self.folded` to `True`, and the `unfold` method sets `self.folded` to `False`. It is important to note that only the `Chair` class gets these extra methods and the additional instance variable. The original `Furniture` class, its parent, remains unchanged.

You may have noticed that I didn't add an argument to `__init__` for `folded`. I wanted it to always default to `False`, with no possibility of override at object creation. It isn't necessary to allow every instance variable to be set by arguments to the `__init__` method. Until `fold()` or `unfold()` is called, `self.folded` doesn't exist. Another approach to this would be to make `folded` a property and set it to `True` or `False`, then do some action on each state.

If I come back later and add an instance variable, property, or method to the `Furniture` class, the `Chair` class will receive those "upgrades" as well.

Multilevel Inheritance

Python allows for a class to have an ancestral line of inheritance. When a class has a chain of ancestors, this is called *multilevel inheritance*. The child class gains all the methods, instance variables, and properties of the ancestor at each level of inheritance.

The best way to explain this is to dive right into an example. We'll expand on our furniture metaphor with an additional class, Bench.

```python
class Furniture:
    def __init__(self, width = 0, height = 0, material = "Wood"):
        self.width = width
        self.height = height
        self.material = material


class Chair(Furniture):
    def __init__(self, material, width = 0, height = 0, arms = True, back = True):
        super().__init__(width, height, material)
        self.arms = arms
        self.back = back


class Bench(Chair):
    pass
```

In this example, we define the Furniture and the Chair classes as normal. Then we create a new class—a Bench. Since at this point there isn't anything substantial to add to the Bench class, I just add pass, which allows me to create a new, empty class. I can always add to it later.

But Bench isn't empty. It contains the instance variables width, height, and material from Furniture, and arms and back from Chair.

We can get a glimpse into our objects with the built-in vars() function.

```python
class Furniture:
    def __init__(self, width = 0, height = 0, material = "Wood"):
        self.width = width
        self.height = height
        self.material = material


class Chair(Furniture):
    def __init__(self, material, width = 0, height = 0, arms = True, back = True):
        super().__init__(width, height, material)
        self.arms = arms
        self.back = back


class Bench(Chair):
    pass
```

```
sofa = Bench("Metal")
print(vars(sofa))
```

When we run this code, the following is displayed:

```
{'width': 0, 'height': 0, 'material': 'Metal', 'arms': True, 'back': True}
```

Even though we didn't give `Bench` any additional content, it still inherited its values (and their initial defaults) from `Chair` and `Furniture`.

> **NOTE**
>
> The `vars()` function is very useful for testing and debugging. Providing it an object for its argument returns the dictionary for the object in question. This contains all the mutable (i.e., writable) attributes and their values.

Multiple Inheritance

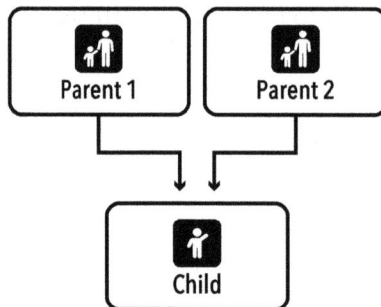

Additionally, a Python class can have multiple parents. Children of multiple parents share attributes of both parents. In object-oriented programming, this is called *multiple inheritance* (figure 28).

fig. 28

Multiple inheritance compared to multilevel inheritance.

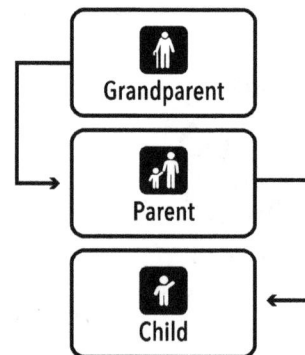

To demonstrate this, I've reworked our furniture example to include the parent classes `Furniture` and `Surface`, then created a new class called `Table`. A `Table` is, of course, both a piece of `Furniture` and a `Surface`, so it has both classes as parents.

```python
class Furniture:
    def __init__(self, width, height, material):
        self.width = width
        self.height = height
        self.material = material


class Surface:
  def __init__(self, flat):
      self.flat = flat


class Table(Furniture, Surface):
    def __init__(self, width = 0, height = 0, material = "Wood", flat = True):
        Furniture.__init__(self, width, height, material)
        Surface.__init__(self, flat)
        self.legs = 4


a = Table()
print(vars(a))
```

When we run this code, it displays as follows:

```
{'width': 0, 'height': 0, 'material': 'Wood', 'flat': True, 'legs': 4}
```

This indicates it received `width`, `height`, and `material` from `Furniture`, `flat` from `Surface`, and has `legs` added as its own unique instance variable. It's important to note that the `legs` instance variable is part of `Table` and is not part of `Furniture` or `Surface`.

Also, instead of `super().__init__`, I specified `Furniture.__init__(self, width, height, material)` and `Surface.__init__(self, flat)` in the `__init__` function for the `Table` class. Since `Table` has two parents, `super()` isn't specific enough; therefore, each `__init__` is used directly.

You may have noticed I dropped the default arguments on `Furniture`. I did this because I'm not directly using `Furniture`. Instead, I created a `Table` object, and that's what will ultimately require the arguments. I put all the defaults in the `__init__` of `Table`, so the table object doesn't need any arguments. I can provide them, of course, if necessary.

REMEMBER

I advised using keyword arguments when there are many arguments or the arguments are subject to change. This is a perfect example of an instance when keyword arguments would be handy and avoid a lot of referencing back and forth between the class definition and the object's creation. If I wanted to specify custom values for each, I could replace

```
a = Table()
```

with

```
a = Table(width = 5, height = 5, material = "Metal", flat = True)
```

Introduction to Design Patterns

The possibilities with inheritance and class design are almost infinite, but as you write more Python code, you'll find yourself using similar patterns to solve problems. In fact, using a *design pattern*—that is, a structured way of solving a problem—is a very useful technique when you have classes that share many things in common.

Design patterns help prevent "blank page syndrome," a term that usually refers to writing. Staring at a blank page can be intimidating, whether you're writing the next great novel or a simple Python program. Having a pattern to build from is incredibly helpful. If I'm writing a large application, I typically start by thinking about the data I intend to store and designing classes around that data.

If there are going to be many classes, I think about what those classes have in common and then create base classes. Like a `Chair`, a `Table` is also a piece of `Furniture`, and by having the `Furniture` base to work from, I can create a `Table` class and save myself the hassle of giving it `height`, `width`, and `material` instance variables. Doing this keeps us on the Don't Repeat Yourself design pattern that encourages us to code once and reuse when needed.

There are quite a few abstract design patterns in computer science, and although it's always tempting to delve into the theory behind what we do, I'd rather introduce you to the actual real-world scenarios you may encounter and how to solve them than to fill the glossary with a wide assortment of conceptual terms. So, while these are actual design patterns you'll encounter, we'll explore them with relevant examples rather than dry chalkboard-type lecturing that can put any beginning (and expert) Python programmer to sleep.

To explore these patterns further, let's consider our furniture paradigm more carefully. We have a wide variety of types of furniture, and as we add more and more to our collection—each with its own instance variables and properties—our argument list upon object creation will soon grow to become long and potentially confusing.

Python has named parameters, so we don't have to remember the position of many different arguments on object creation. Nevertheless, it's still a pain to enter so many parameters when creating a new object. And if we're creating a lot of different types of furniture, the process can become tedious and error-prone. Let's consider some ways to make it easier.

Default Arguments

Default arguments can make this simpler. They can make your code clearer and save typing.

SNIPPET

07-04.py

```python
class Furniture:
    def __init__(self, width, height, material):
        self.width = width
        self.height = height
        self.material = material


class Surface:
    def __init__(self, flat):
        self.flat = flat
class Table(Furniture, Surface):
    def __init__(self, width = 0, height = 0, material = "Wood", flat = True):
        Furniture.__init__(self, width, height, material)
        Surface.__init__(self, flat)
        self.legs = 4
```

The `Table` class uses all default arguments, so you can use `a = Table()` and you're off to the races with the `a` object containing reasonable default values. After all, how many tables aren't flat?

If you need to change the object's properties after creation, you can—and this is preferred if it's the exception, not the rule.

```python
# Two quiet, unassuming, regular tables. Nothing fancy here.
# We create them with no parameters and they receive defaults.
a = Table()
b = Table()

# And then there's a weird table named fred. Poor fred.
# He's not like the other tables a and b, he's not flat!
fred = Table(flat = False)
```

Collection of Objects

If you need to create a lot of objects and want to iterate through them with a loop, using lists and dictionaries is a very handy way to do that. Let's fill the coffee `bar` with `Stool` objects. For brevity, the specific details of the classes have been removed from this example.

SNIPPET

07-05.py

```python
class Furniture:
    pass


class Chair(Furniture):
    pass


class Stool(Chair):
    def __init__(self, number):
        self.number = number


# Create an empty list named bar
bar = []


# Add 8 Stools to the bar
for i in range(8):
    bar.append(Stool(i))
```

QUESTION

Q: What type of inheritance is this? Multilevel or multiple inheritance?

In this example, we create blank `Furniture` and `Chair` classes and a `Stool` class that takes a parameter named `number`. Then we create an empty list with `bar = []`. This will hold our collection of `Stool` objects.

Next we'll start a loop with a range of 0 to 7, then call the `append` method. You might find it odd that I say *method* rather than *function*. That's because a list (`bar`, in this case) is a special kind of object that has methods of its own, and `append` is a method that adds a value to the list. In this case, we're supplying a new `Stool` object as the argument to the `append` method while setting the `number` argument to `i`.

The result is a collection of eight `Stool` objects in the `bar` list. We can access them by their number.

```python
print(bar[2].number)
```

This results in 2 being displayed in the interpreter.

You can change any of the stools, too:

```
bar[4].number = 54
```

This will set the number instance variable of the fourth `Stool` object in the `bar` list to 54. Note that it doesn't change the index position in the `bar` list. You can't use `bar[54]` because it's still `bar[4]` (i.e., the fifth `stool` object in the list—remember, counting in indexes starts at zero). However, the `number` instance variable in the object is changed, and you can verify it with `print`.

```
print(bar[4].number)
```

This displays 54.

You can always add a ninth `Stool` object (or more).

```
bar.append(Stool)
```

This can be verified with

```
print(len(bar))
```

It will now show 9, indicating there are 9 stools in the list.

The `bar` list can just as easily be a dictionary. Since dictionaries contain keys rather than just index positions, you can give your `Stool` objects names or otherwise associate some meaningful data to them so they can be easily accessed in the dictionary.

```
class Furniture:
    pass


class Chair(Furniture):
    pass


class Stool(Chair):
    pass
```

```
# Create an empty dictionary named bar
bar = {}

# Create several Stool objects
fred = Stool()
marvin = Stool()

# Add them to the bar dictionary
bar["Fred"] = fred
bar["Marvin"] = marvin
```

In this example, we create our `Stool` object inherited from `Chair` (which is inherited from `Furniture`), then create an empty `bar` dictionary. Then we create `fred` and `marvin`, our two new favorite stools with spiffy names. Since dictionaries are key:value data structures, we can give a friendly key to each when we add them to the dictionary.

Then we can reference, oh, say `fred`, for example, with:

```
bar["Fred"]
```

There are many more design patterns to explore when working with classes and objects, and we'll use several throughout this book. For now, I wanted to introduce you to the concept, so you'll look for these patterns in the future and use them to help solve your programming problems more easily and with less work.

A Fantasy World

As an up-and-coming video game developer, you've set your sights on something a bit bigger—a role-playing game. That's an ambitious task for any programmer, because there are many elements that go into a game of this genre, not to mention the code it would take to display a graphical user interface and possibly three-dimensional elements on the screen.

Nevertheless, the humble beginnings of a large game could start with some simple class design. Let's create some classes that will contain elements you might find in a role-playing game, like these:

» Players
» Player classes (types of players, like fighters, healers, mages, etc.)
» Weapons

- » Armor
- » Magic spells
- » Monsters

Feel free to add more to this list if you like, but this should get us off to a good start. The object of this exercise is not to worry about methods, variables, etc., but to focus on the design of the classes and how they use inheritance. Still, if you want to make your healer heal, your rogue steal, or your fireballs incinerate a monster, go for it!

It's critical to note here that there are no wrong answers in these exercises. How you choose to lay out this game data is entirely up to you. Let your imagination run wild!

If you get stuck or would like to see an example I came up with, please refer to the appendix.

Chapter Recap

- » Inheritance allows classes to obtain methods and variables from parents. Classes can have one parent or multiple parents and inherit structure from each.

- » Multilevel inheritance forms a chain of ancestors passing a growing collection of traits to their children. Multiple inheritance allows classes to inherit structure from more than one parent.

- » Design patterns are systematic approaches to solving real-world programming issues. Both abstract and practical programming design can help jump-start your development projects.

| 8 |
Saving Time with Dataclasses

Chapter Overview

- » The dataclasses module can save you a lot of time
- » Instance variables can be created automatically with dataclasses
- » The `@dataclass` decorator can be customized with keyword arguments

If your project has a lot of classes—especially if those classes contain extensive functionality—you'll find yourself repeating the same patterns. The dataclasses module will save you time by eliminating much of the redundant lifecycle and setup code that's common in Python applications.

Dataclasses is a standard module that was added in Python 3.7 and is incredibly helpful. You might not find it in many existing projects because it is relatively new, but if you use more than a few classes, I highly recommend it.

Automatic Instance Variables

Dataclasses can automatically add instance variables for you. You may recall our `Customer` class example from chapter 6:

```
# Define a new class
class Customer:
    def __init__(self, name, city):
        self.name = name
        self.city = city
```

Let's rewrite it, this time with dataclasses. We'll cover importing in chapter 9, so don't worry about that yet.

```
# Include the dataclasses module
from dataclasses import dataclass
```

```
# Define a new class
@dataclass
class Customer:
    name: str
    city: str
```

NOTE

In dataclasses, the `str` references strings.

That's it! When Python runs this code, the `Customer` class will be identical to the previous one. The `@dataclass` decorator from the dataclasses module will automatically add an `__init__` method and add `name` and `city` as instance variables, including the code necessary to set the `self.name = name` and `self.city = city`.

In this code, the format for instance variables in the `Customer` class is the variable name, then a colon, then the type of variable. If you wanted to add a variable called `bonus_points`, it would look like this:

```
# Include the dataclasses module
from dataclasses import dataclass

# Define a new class
@dataclass
class Customer:
    name: str
    city: str
    bonus_points: int
```

We can also define default values. If we want a customer to start with 100 bonus points (unless otherwise specified during object creation), we can. These bonus points are loyalty reward points that a customer earns on each purchase, but we can start off every new customer with 100.

```
@dataclass
class Customer:
    name: str
    city: str
    bonus_points: int = 100
```

Now if we create a new customer, like this:

```
c1 = Customer()
```

... the customer will have 100 bonus points.

```
print(c1.bonus_points)
```

produces:

```
100
```

But let's give just one customer 200 points at the start.

```
c2 = Customer("John Smith", "Anytown", 200)
print(c2.bonus_points)
```

produces:

```
200
```

Let's add one more instance variable, `total_spent`:

```
@dataclass
class Customer:
    name: str
    city: str
    bonus_points: int = 100
    total_spent: float = 0.00
```

We set a default on `total_spent` to 0.00 because it's assumed that a new customer won't have spent anything with us yet. Though we haven't specifically shown it in an example, we can set a default value for strings `(str)` too.

```
@dataclass
class Customer:
    name: str
    city: str = "Florence"
    bonus_points: int = 100
    total_spent: float = 0.00
```

So by only specifying the name, the one variable for which we haven't set a default value, we get the others filled in for us automatically.

```
c1 = Customer("Robert")
print(c1)
```

produces:

```
Customer(name='Robert', city='Florence', bonus_points=100, total_spent=0.0)
```

This is already a timesaver, but imagine what a real-life `Customer` class might look like. If we had fields like `first_name`, `last_name`, `address`, `city`, `state`, `country`, and `postal_code`, the savings would really add up. Not only that, but by automatically generating the initialization code and `__init__` method, we're less likely to accidentally make a mistake.

Dataclass Features

Behind the scenes, `dataclass` does a lot more than make it easier to set up variables. We can toggle its functionality with keyword arguments to the `@dataclass` decorator. These arguments control the features that the decorator injects into the class that is defined on the next line.

As we explore the functionality of each feature, we will also get acquainted with some new special methods you haven't used yet.

```
@dataclass(init=True, repr=True, eq=True, order=False, frozen=False)
```

NOTE

You don't have to include all these arguments. Specify only the ones for which you want to define a value other than the default value. Moreover, I've left off a few arguments that are rarely used or are specific to extremely recent versions of Python, which aren't well supported by most installed versions.

Since there are quite a few arguments, let's explore each in detail, including their defaults. Each of these accepts `True` or `False`.

init

The `init` argument defaults to `True` and instructs the `dataclass` decorator to automatically generate the `__init__` method.

repr

The `repr` argument allows our class to represent itself as a string. A practical purpose for this is to compare objects. The `repr` argument defaults to `True`. If it is `True`, the `repr()` function will call this method on the class to obtain the string.

We can see an example of this behavior with our Customer class:

```python
@dataclass
class Customer:
    name: str
    city: str = "Florence"
    bonus_points: int = 100
    total_spent: float = 0.00


c1 = Customer("Robert")
print(repr(c1))
```

When we run this code, we'll get this:

```
Customer(name='Robert', city='Florence', bonus_points=100, total_spent=0.0)
```

eq

The `eq` argument defaults to `True`. If it is `True`, the `__eq__` method will allow for a comparison of two objects from the same class using the `==` operator.

For example:

```python
c1 = Customer("Robert")
c2 = Customer("Marsha")


print(c1 == c2)
```

This will output `False`. The functionality that `dataclass` provides for the `__eq__` method is good, but we can define this ourselves, as with any other method. If we define an `__eq__` method in our class, we can craft a specific way to test for equality. For example:

```python
def __eq__(self, other):
    if isinstance(other, Customer):
        return self.name == other.name
    return False
```

This does two things. First, it checks whether `other` is an instance (object) of `Customer` via the `isinstance` function, which returns `True` if the first argument is an instance of the second argument, a class. If not, it returns `False`. Otherwise, it checks to see if `name` on both the `self` object and the `other` object are equal. If so, it returns `True`.

This comparison is done outside the class via `c1 == c2` (or any other two objects, as long as they're the same kind of object).

order

The `order` argument defaults to `False`. If it's set to `True`, though, dataclass automatically creates `__lt__`, `__le__`, `__gt__`, and `__ge__` methods (less than, less than or equal to, greater than, and greater than or equal to, respectively).

Similar to the `__eq__` method, these methods allow for comparisons between two objects using <, <=, >, and >=.

frozen

By default, the `frozen` argument is set to `False`. If we set it to `True`, the objects from this class will be read-only (immutable), which would allow the class to be stored in a set or as a key in a dictionary.

Dataclasses Compatibility

Dataclasses are incredibly useful, and since they've been a part of Python's standard library since version 3.7, it's hard to justify not using them. I've used them in my projects since their introduction in 2018. If your programs are run on a Python version earlier than 3.7, or were written before mid-2018, you may want to consider omitting them until your Python version can be upgraded.

Since 3.7 has been out for about five years as of this publication, you probably won't run into many issues, but this should be considered if you plan on running your programs on slightly older machines.

Chapter Recap

» In projects using multiple classes, we'll save a lot of time by using the dataclasses module, added in Python version 3.7.

» Instance variables can be created automatically with dataclasses. We can specify the type of variable (`str`, `int`, `float`) as well as provide a default value.

» The `@dataclass` decorator can be controlled via a wide assortment of keyword arguments, but we only need to provide them when we want to deviate from defaults.

| 9 |

Reusing Code with Modules and Packages

Chapter Overview
» A module is a Python program file
» Modules can be used in other Python programs
» Packages are collections of *modules*

Classes are powerful tools that give us the flexibility to create nearly any project we can imagine. But with this power comes great responsibility—namely, the responsibility to keep our code maintainable. As our game grows larger, we'll need to keep it organized or else it will become more difficult for us to work on. If we want to bring in another programmer or are lucky enough to have a game publisher take our coffee shop simulator game to the next level, we'll have a whole team working on the project. Whether a project is just for ourselves or written by a large organization, maintaining a tidy, well-structured workspace is essential.

Python *modules* are simply Python code files that provide one or more classes, functions, or variables together. This module then creates a reusable package that can be used in other programs. A Python module doesn't even have to be written in Python! Other programming languages (namely, C/C++) can construct modules, and the interpreter can load them and make them accessible as though they were native Python.

Namespaces

Before we get into building our own modules, let's look at how modules are organized in a Python program. To do that, we need to see exactly how `import` works and how it adjusts the namespace in our program.

Let's look at the `locale` standard module, which handles internationalization (i.e., a set of character, time, currency, and number formatting conventions for a country). We'll use the `locale` module to get a dictionary of all the available locales installed on the system.

```
import locale
for l in locale.locale_alias:
    print(l)
```

When we run this code, we'll see a list of our computer's supported locales. The list will vary from computer to computer, and it will likely be quite long.

In this example, the module magic begins with the first line of code: `import`. The `import` function brings into the current code all the classes, functions, and variables that are defined in the module named `locale`, and then we can reference them with the name of that module.

For example, if we run this …

```
import locale
```

… we can access `locale.locale_alias`. But we can't just use `locale_alias` by itself because it is in the `locale` *namespace*. A namespace is a collection of code that exists in a separate space. Recall that there are various scopes within a Python program. For example, instance variables need to be accessed with `self` because they exist one level up from the function calling them and thus are part of the class's namespace, or scope. You can think of namespaces like concentric rings of access, and to access something in another ring you must have a pointer to that namespace (figure 29).

NAMESPACE EXAMPLE

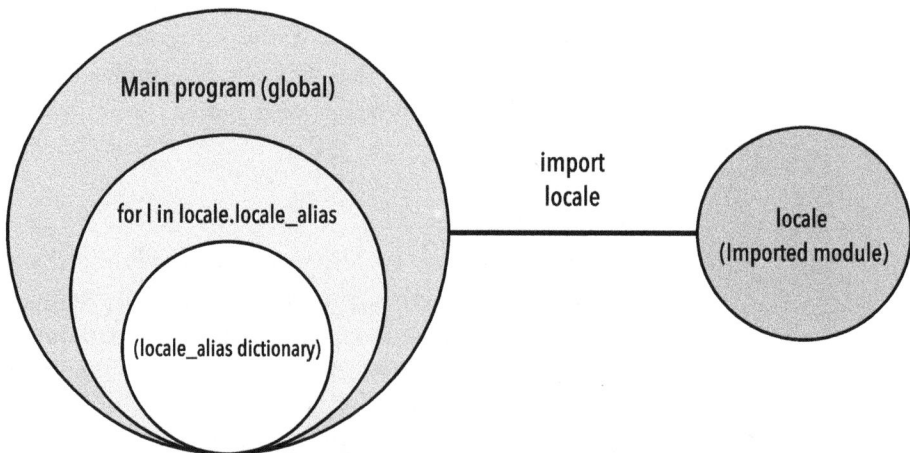

GRAPHIC

fig. 29

The namespace relationships of the main program, its classes and methods, and the imported module named `locale`.

In figure 29, the concentric rings each define a namespace. The circle off to the right side is the `locale` module, included in the program via the `import` function. It exists outside the main program, which is why we need to reference its name, `locale`, when using functionality within it. The main program is its own namespace, often referred to as the "global" namespace. The `for` loop defines its own namespace, referenced by `l`, which becomes each item of the dictionary `locale.locale_alias`.

> **IMPORTANT**
>
> When we are accessing functionality in other namespaces (i.e., not within the current namespace), we specify the name of the namespace, then a dot, before the resource so Python knows how to find it.

Importing Modules

To use a standard module, simply include:

```
import name
```

In this example, `name` refers to the name of the module we want to import. Generally, `import` statements are at the top of a program. There are some possible exceptions, which we'll address in chapter 18.

We can also import a module as another name if we so choose. For example, if I wanted to name the `locale` module `robert`, I could:

```
import locale as robert
```

And then I would use `robert.locale_alias` instead of `locale.locale_alias`.

> **MY TAKE**
>
> Unless there's a naming conflict, or the module's name you want to use is long, I wouldn't recommend this. It can confuse you and others if they work on your code. I would avoid renaming modules unless it makes your code more readable. You might ask why I mentioned it only to recommend against using it. Because, as you see other Python code and use third-party modules, you'll no doubt encounter this usage pattern. Now you'll be able to spot it and use it if desired—but I would recommend doing so sparingly, if at all.

We can also import particular functionality from a module. For example, let's say I need to process an email, but I don't need to send or receive a message.

```
from email import parser
```

In this case, I'm importing only the `parser` code from the `email` module. I can then use the `parser` namespace to access its logic and process my mail. If I had used the traditional route:

```
import email
```

... then I would have to use `email.parser` to access those methods.

To dig deeper into the contents of modules, let's launch the Python interpreter rather than using Visual Studio Code for the moment, because some of the commands below require an interactive session, which is easier to do directly in the interpreter.

Remember the `vars` function that lists the variables inside a class? It works on modules too.

```
vars(email)
```

We'll see a long list of variables contained within the module. If we want a list of functions/methods from a module (or class), the `dir` function has us covered:

```
dir(email)
```

And finally, if we want to see a helpful documentation on a module, we'll use the `help` function:

```
help(email)
```

The `help` function is, well, incredibly helpful. It provides a reference for using a module without requiring internet access, a search engine, or even a book! When the help browser launches, we use the arrow keys or page down/up to navigate its contents. We can search for specific text with the / key and then type what we want to search for and press ENTER. To quit the help viewer, we press the Q key.

Creating Your Own Module

Python modules are easy to write. In fact, you already know everything you need to know to make a Python module, because, at its core, a module in Python is just a Python code file with one or more classes, variables, and/

or functions. Nevertheless, you'll need a bit of organizational knowledge to assemble a module.

Let's construct a simple module, then use it in a program. First, create a new file called `distance.py` and add this code. It might look familiar—it's our `Distance` class!

```
class Distance:
    def __init__(self, km):
        self._km = km

    @property
    def km(self):
        return self._km
    @km.setter
    def km(self, value):
        self._km = value
    @property
    def miles(self):
        return self._km / 1.609
    @miles.setter
    def miles(self, value):
        self._km = value * 1.609
```

Save the file, then create a new file called `moduletest.py`.

```
import distance

dist = distance.Distance(3)
print("3 kilometers is " + str(dist.miles) + " miles.")
dist.miles = 3
print(str(dist.miles) + " miles is " + str(dist.km) + " kilometers.")
```

Save this file and run it. If all goes well, you'll see our familiar output:

```
3 kilometers is 1.8645121193287757 miles.
3.0 miles is 4.827 kilometers.
```

If you get an error, check to make sure both files are in the same directory and that you don't have any typos.

Let's step through what's happening in the `moduletest.py` code. First, we import the `distance` module. If you're wondering how `distance.py` is a module, that's only natural. As we discussed before the example, a module is essentially just a Python code file.

Then we create a `Distance` object named `dist`, but we must use `distance.Distance` to reference the `Distance` class because it is part of the `distance` namespace due to our module import.

The rest of the code uses the `miles` and `km` properties of the `Distance` class to display (and set) the distance in both measurement systems as it did in chapter 6. Congratulations! You've written your first module.

Standard Modules

Standard modules are those that are built in to Python and provide a wide assortment of functionality in the base system. These modules are quite extensive; in fact, there are too many to list here, but as we progress through the book we'll explore and use quite a few of them. For a full list, please see https://docs.python.org/3/py-modindex.html.

Packages

As we've learned in this chapter, a module is a single `.py` file. For larger modules, it isn't practical to include everything we need in one file. If a module contains many classes, splitting it up into multiple files makes it easier to maintain.

A *package* is simply a collection of regular Python program files (like our `distance.py` file) that are arranged in a structured pattern. This pattern can be as simple as several files in a folder or a collection of subfolders containing additional parts of a larger module. This organization is necessary so that Python knows how to assemble the namespace. Just like modules, packages can be imported into a program via the `import` function.

Let's browse the contents of an example package. Our `distance.py` will be part of it, but I added an `area.py` and a `timecalc.py` file. I named it `timecalc.py` instead of `time.py` because `time` is a standard module built in to Python. In `area.py`, I added the following:

```
class Area:
    pass
```

This creates a blank `Area` class for later expansion. Then I created a `timecalc.py` file and added:

```
class Timecalc:
    pass
```

Our new package, combined in a folder I created called `calculations`, contains (I should say, will someday contain) classes necessary for dealing with area, time, and distance to help us solve those infamous "A train has been traveling at sixty miles per hour in a southwestern direction for three hours. What flavor of pie is the conductor eating?" math problems.

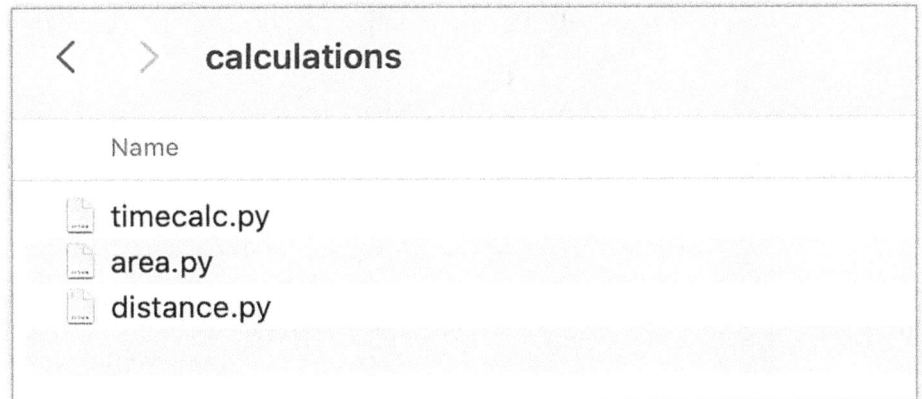

The `time`, `area`, and `distance` modules (i.e., Python code files) in a folder named `calculations`, as shown in the macOS Finder file browser.

If you have a file called `program.py` in the directory with your package files, you can use these:

```
import area
import distance
import timecalc
```

This works fine, but it isn't very convenient. As they exist right now, these are three simple stand-alone modules. However, since they're related in functionality, it makes sense to bundle them together in a package. To do so, we only need to add an __ init __ .py file to this folder.

An `__ init __.py` file must be in a folder for Python to treat that folder as a package. In it, we'll import the modules (i.e., Python code files) so that when the package is imported into the main program one folder above the package contents, it will load all the modules. When an object is created, its `__ init __` method is run, and in the same way, when a package is imported, the `__ init __.py` is executed.

```
from .distance import *
from .area import *
from .timecalc import *
```

There are two components of this `__ init __.py` file that are new—the dot before the module name and the star/asterisk after the `import` statement. The dot before `distance`, `area`, and `timecalc` tells Python to look in the current folder (relative to the `__ init __.py` file) for the modules. The star/asterisk tells Python to import all the contents of the module.

We could say:

```
from .distance import Distance
```

... which would import only the `Distance` class. But, as modules often contain multiple classes, using `*` would ensure that we got all the module's contents.

Once we have the `__ init __.py` file created, we can create our `program.py` (or any other file name) program one level up from the `calculations` folder (i.e., above it) and use ...

```
import calculations
```

... to import all three modules. The resulting namespace is `calculations`, so to use our `Distance` class, we would specify ...

```
d = calculations.Distance(5)
```

... to create a `Distance` object with a default value of five kilometers.

Armed with this knowledge, you can now create packages of your classes (and functions) and reuse them in other programs.

ClydeBank Coffee Shop: Modularizing the Game

Right now, our game exists in one module. This isn't ideal, because it's clumsy to navigate. Let's fix that. We'll move the CoffeeShopSimulator class into its own file, then move the utility functions (including welcome, prompt, convert_to_float, and x_of_y) to a module named utilities. Then we can include both in the main.py file.

SNIPPET

CCS-07.py

main.py

```python
# ClydeBank Coffee Shop Simulator 4000
# Copyright 2022 (C) ClydeBank Media, All Rights Reserved.

# Import all functions from the utility module
from utilities import *

# Import the game class from the coffee_shop_simulator module
from coffee_shop_simulator import CoffeeShopSimulator

# Print welcome message
welcome()

# Get name and store name
t_name = prompt("What is your name?", True)
t_shop_name = prompt("What do you want to name your coffee shop?", True)

# Create the game object
game = CoffeeShopSimulator(t_name, t_shop_name)

# Run the game
game.run()
```

SNIPPET

CCS-08.py

utilities.py

```python
def welcome():
    print("ClydeBank Coffee Shop Simulator 4000, Version 1.00")
    print("Copyright (C) 2022 ClydeBank Media, All Rights Reserved.\n")
    print("Let's collect some information before we start the game.\n")

def prompt(display="Please input a string", require=True):
    if require:
        s = False
        while not s:
            s = input(display + " ")
```

```
        else:
            s = input(display + " ")
        return s


def convert_to_float(s):
    # If conversion fails, assign it to 0
    try:
        f = float(s)
    except ValueError:
        f = 0
    return f


def x_of_y(x, y):
    num_list = []
    # Return a list of x copies of y
    for i in range(x):
        num_list.append(y)
    return num_list
```

coffee_shop_simulator.py

```
# Import needed modules
import random
import re
from utilities import *


class CoffeeShopSimulator:
    # Minimum and maximum temperatures
    TEMP_MIN = 20
    TEMP_MAX = 90


    def __init__(self, player_name, shop_name):

        # Set player and coffee shop names
        self.player_name = player_name
        self.shop_name = shop_name

        # Current day number
        self.day = 1
```

```python
        # Cash on hand at start
        self.cash = 100.00


        # Inventory at start
        self.coffee_inventory = 100


        # Sales list
        self.sales = []


        # Possible temperatures
        self.temps = self.make_temp_distribution()

    def run(self):
        print("\nOk, let's get started. Have fun!")


        # The main game loop
        running = True
        while running:
            # Display the day and add a "fancy" text effect
            self.day_header()


            # Get the weather
            temperature = self.weather


            # Display the cash and weather
            self.daily_stats(temperature)


            # Get price of a cup of coffee
            cup_price = float(prompt("What do you want to charge per cup of coffee?"))


            # Get advertising spend
            print("\nYou can buy advertising to help promote sales.")
            advertising = prompt("How much do you want to spend on advertising (0 ↦
            ↪ for none)?", False)


            # Convert advertising into a float
            advertising = convert_to_float(advertising)


            # Deduct advertising from cash on hand
            self.cash -= advertising
```

```python
            # Simulate today's sales
            cups_sold = self.simulate(temperature, advertising, cup_price)
            gross_profit = cups_sold * cup_price

            # Display the results
            print("You sold " + str(cups_sold) + " cups of coffee today.")
            print("You made $" + str(gross_profit) + ".")

            # Add the profit to our coffers
            self.cash += gross_profit

            # Subtract inventory
            self.coffee_inventory -= cups_sold

            # Before we loop around, add a day
            self.increment_day()

    def simulate(self, temperature, advertising, cup_price):
        # Find out how many cups were sold
        cups_sold = self.daily_sales(temperature, advertising)

        # Save the sales data for today
        self.sales.append({
            "day": self.day,
            "coffee_inv": self.coffee_inventory,
            "advertising": advertising,
            "temp": temperature,
            "cup_price": cup_price,
            "cups_sold": cups_sold
        })

        # We technically don't need this, but why make the next step
        # read from the sales list when we have the data right here
        return cups_sold

    def make_temp_distribution(self):
        # This is not a good bell curve, but it will do for now
        # until we get to more advanced mathematics
        temps = []
```

```
        # First, find the average between TEMP_MIN and TEMP_MAX
        avg = (self.TEMP_MIN + self.TEMP_MAX) / 2
        # Find the distance between TEMP_MAX and the average
        max_dist_from_avg = self.TEMP_MAX - avg


        # Loop through all possible temperatures
        for i in range(self.TEMP_MIN, self.TEMP_MAX):
            # How far away is the temperature from average?
            # abs() gives us the absolute value
            dist_from_avg = abs(avg - i)
            # How far away is the dist_from_avg from the maximum?
            # This will be lower for temps at the extremes
            dist_from_max_dist = max_dist_from_avg - dist_from_avg
            # If the value is zero, make it one
            if dist_from_max_dist == 0:
                dist_from_max_dist = 1
            # Append the output of x_of_y to temps
            for t in x_of_y(int(dist_from_max_dist), i):
                temps.append(t)
        return temps


def increment_day(self):
    self.day += 1


def daily_stats(self, temperature):
    print("You have $" + str(self.cash) + " cash on hand and the temperature is ↦
    ↪ " + str(temperature) + ".")
    print("You have enough coffee on hand to make " + str(self.coffee_inventory) ↦
    ↪ + " cups.\n")


def day_header(self):
    print("\n-----| Day " + str(self.day) + " @ " + self.shop_name + " |-----")


def daily_sales(self, temperature, advertising):
    return int((self.TEMP_MAX - temperature) * (advertising * 0.5))


@property
def weather(self):
    # Generate a random temperature between 20 and 90
```

```
# We'll consider seasons later on, but this is good enough for now
return random.choice(self.temps)
```

The game now consists of three files (`main.py`, `utilities.py`, and `coffee_shop_simulator.py`), and everything is much easier to find. Also, the `main.py` file is extremely simple to read and understand.

As we explore advanced functionality in Python, we'll learn how to add the finishing touches our game needs to be a fun game to play—and replay!

Chapter Recap

» Python's standard modules provide a wealth of functionality.

» Every Python code file is a module. Packages are collections of Python modules.

» Both modules and packages can be imported into other Python programs via the `import` statement.

PART III

PYTHON IN ACTION

| 10 |
Advanced Strings

Chapter Overview
» Python contains extensive text manipulation functionality
» Using regular expressions is a powerful way to spot patterns in text
» Compressing data saves resources

Throughout this book we've worked with strings in a rather basic way, but in this chapter we'll explore some of the extremely powerful ways that Python can manipulate strings.

Before we get deep into it, let's expand the definition of a string in Python. Sure, we've already discussed that strings are just text in a variable. But strings are also objects and therefore have built-in functionality (i.e., methods) that we can use to do all sorts of helpful things.

One note, though, before we begin. In previous chapters, I've explained the details of each line of example code, even if we've covered it before. Now that we've explored the basics of Python, including its object-oriented features, I'm going to spend a bit less time doing that and instead rely more on code comments. Don't worry—anytime a new concept is introduced, we'll cover it in detail.

Standard String Operations

Finding and Replacing Text
You'll likely be interacting with text a lot in Python, and a common task you'll need to be able to do is to search and modify strings. Python makes this easy.

```
# Create a string
a = "Hello, World!"
```

SNIPPET

10-01.py

```
# Search for "World" in the string
if a.find("World") != -1:

    # Replace "World" with "Reader"
    b = a.replace("World", "Reader")

    # Display the results
    print(a)
    print("... was replaced with ...")
    print(b)
```

In this example, we use the find method on the string named a and provide an argument with "World". This will return a True value (specifically, it returns 7, because that's the character position in the string where "World" starts), so the code inside the if conditional block is executed. That said, it may also return a -1 value if World isn't found, so we must make sure the result of find isn't equal to -1.

Inside the block, we create a new string b that stores the results of a.replace("World", "Reader"). The replace method looks through the string and replaces the first argument with the second argument. So "Hello, World!" becomes "Hello, Reader!" Then we print the strings named a and b with a brief message in between them. Note that the string a remains "Hello, World!" because replace doesn't change the value of the a string, it just returns the replaced value.

Here's the result:

```
Hello, World!
... was replaced with ...
Hello, Reader!
```

We could have simplified the code further:

```
# Create a string
a = "Hello, World!"

# Search for "World" in the string
if a.find("World") != -1:

    # Replace "World" with "Reader"
```

```
print(a)
print("... was replaced with ...")
print(a.replace("World", "Reader"))
```

This version does the same thing but doesn't create a string named b; instead, it runs the replace method on the string a inline in the print statement. If we might need that string later, and didn't just want to display it, we would store it in a separate variable (like we did when we assigned the result to b), or overwrite the original variable, like this:

```
a = a.replace("World", "Reader")
print(a)
```

But be careful with this approach, because the string a is forever changed, and if you needed a copy of the original for some reason, it would be lost.

Cases
We can do some other neat things with strings in Python. Here are some methods for dealing with capitalization.

SNIPPET

10-03.py

```
# Create our string
title = "Python QuickStart Guide"


# Display it all uppercase
print(title.upper())


# Display it all lowercase
print(title.lower())
```

When we run this, it displays:

```
PYTHON QUICKSTART GUIDE
python quickstart guide
```

Pattern Counting
If we need to know the number of times a character (or string of characters) occurs in a string, the count() method has us covered.

SNIPPET

10-04.py

```
# Create our string
tongue_twister = "She sells seashells by the seashore."
```

```
# Count the number of 's' in tongue_twister and display it
print("There are " + str(tongue_twister.count("s")) + " letter s in:")
print(tongue_twister)
```

With `count()`, we get an integer with the number of times the character(s) in the argument is present in the string. In this case, it's 7, but since it's an integer, we must convert it to a string to use it with `print`. When we run this, we get:

```
There are 7 letter s in:
She sells seashells by the seashore.
```

Splitting and Joining

Sometimes it's helpful to split a string into characters and put them in a list. Conversely, we may also want to combine the contents of a list into a string. The `split` and `join` methods let us do just that (figure 31).

The quick brown fox jumps over the lazy dog.

```
['The', 'quick', 'brown', 'fox', 'jumps', 'over', 'the', 'lazy', 'dog.']
```

Splitting strings into lists in Python.

Here's an example that splits a sentence into words.

```
# A simple string
fox = "The quick brown fox jumps over the lazy dog."

# Split the string
fox_list = fox.split()

# Display the resulting list
print(fox_list)
```

This example will display as follows:

```
['The', 'quick', 'brown', 'fox', 'jumps', 'over', 'the', 'lazy', 'dog.']
```

By default, without arguments, `split` will separate a string with spaces (or any whitespace—multiple spaces work, too). However, if we provide a character or string to `split` as an argument, we can split a string with any *delimiter* (that is, any character used to separate segments of data—in this case, to break apart the string).

10-06.py

```python
# An (obviously fake) ID number
id = "123-45-6789"

# Split id by a dash character
id_segments = id.split("-")

# Display it
print(id_segments)
```

This code displays:

```
['123', '45', '6789']
```

You can also use multiple characters as your delimiter:

10-07.py

```python
# New glossary terms
glossary = "delimiter, module, package, class, object"

# Split by comma then a space
glossary_list = glossary.split(", ")

# Display it
print(glossary_list)
```

This produces:

```
['delimiter', 'module', 'package', 'class', 'object']
```

Now that we've broken a string into multiple pieces with `split`, let's put it back together again.

10-08.py

```python
# Our glossary terms
glossary = ['delimiter', 'module', 'package', 'class', 'object']
```

```
# The new joined string
glossary _ string = ", ".join(glossary)


# Display it
print(glossary _ string)
```

Don't be alarmed if the `join` line made you do a double take. It's odd, I'll admit. The method `join` is used on a string object, but that string object is the character or string that will be used to join the pieces (i.e., parts of the list) together. In this case, it's a comma and a space, but it could be anything. Then the argument to `join` is the list (in this case, `glossary`).

Input Validation

Input validation is the process of confirming that a variable fits a certain pattern. Validating the data we receive from users (or from files or network sources) is important in preventing errors and ensuring that our code will be able to operate properly on the data provided to it.

```
# Ask user for a value
value = input("Please enter a value: ")


# Check if every character is a number
# "3102" - True
# "4111123412341234" - True
# "04/22/2022" - False
# "1600 Pennsylvania Avenue" - False
if value.isnumeric():
    print("It's a number.")


# Check if every character is a letter
# Spaces, punctuation, and numbers don't count
# "Yes" - True
# "Yes " - False
# "Yes 3" - False
# "Yes!" - False
if value.isalpha():
    print("It is filled with alphabet characters only.")


# Check if the string is alphanumeric (i.e., letters and numbers)
# "1600 Pennsylvania Avenue" - False
```

```
# "Washington, D.C." - False
# "Washington DC" - False
# "Washington" - True
if value.isalnum():
    print("It's alphanumeric.")
```

NOTE

A common oversight when working with `isalnum()` is forgetting that it will not count spaces as alphanumeric characters. Only letters and numbers—no punctuation, spaces, or otherwise—will be `True` with `isalnum()`.

These functions are very useful for validating data, but they do have shortcomings in that they don't consider exceptions to the rules (i.e., spaces, punctuation, etc.). Next, we'll examine regular expressions, which will let us work around these issues and add a whole new set of abilities to validate input.

Regular Expressions

Regular expressions (often called regex for short) are a weird, sometimes arcane set of symbols that tell Python how to search through strings and match specific portions.

I'll be honest up front about regular expressions—you'll love them or you'll hate them. Either way, you'll use them quite a bit in your Python programming career, because they're exquisitely powerful.

Despite their incredible capability, it took me years, perhaps even a decade, to truly use regular expressions well. In programming years (not to be confused with, but similar in scope to, dog years) that might as well be an eternity. I muddled along with searching and replacing text in more traditional ways and borrowing regular expressions from open-source software and public sources to accomplish what I needed to.

But once I truly understood them, I commanded a powerful text processing engine at my fingertips. Now you, the owner of this book, can skip ahead of my decade of string searching ambiguity and unlock the true power of the regular expression.

Before we get started, allow me to talk up regular expressions just a bit more. Nearly all programming languages and many programs that work with text (including Visual Studio Code and even Microsoft Word) have built-in support for regular expressions. That means that what you learn here will apply not only to Python but to other programming languages and hundreds—possibly thousands—of other programs.

Basically, a regular expression is a string of characters and special codes that are designed to match certain patterns in strings. With them, we can search for more than just characters in a string—we can find complex patterns that we can't otherwise locate with find or replace.

Additionally, complex types of input validation are possible with regular expressions, ones that go beyond simple methods like isnumeric or isalpha.

Let's start with the simplest possible example of a regular expression in Python.

SNIPPET

10-10.py

```python
# Import the regular expression engine
import re

# Define our content
text = "Hello, World!"

# Is "Hello" in our string?
if re.search("Hello", text):
    print("Hello is in the string.")
else:
    print("Hello isn't in the string.")
```

When we run this code, we'll see this:

```
Hello is in the string.
```

At first glance, we're not doing anything substantially new. The search function from the re module (i.e., re.search) takes two parameters, the regular expression and the string that will be searched. Since our regular expression was merely a word ("Hello" in this case), the expression wasn't anything more than an exact match. The search function simply looked for "Hello" in the string and found it, and thus it evaluated to be True. Since it was True, the "Hello is in the string" message was printed.

Admittedly, that's not impressive, but you just learned how to create your first regular expression. Now let's build on that to do more advanced things.

SNIPPET

10-11.py

```python
# Import the regular expression engine
import re

# Define our content
text = "Hello, World!"
```

```
# Is "Hello" in our string?
if re.search("hello", text, re.IGNORECASE):
    print("hello is in the string.")
else:
    print("hello isn't in the string.")
```

When we run this, we'll see:

```
hello is in the string.
```

In this case, we supplied `hello` as our regular expression, and it will serve the exact same function as the `Hello` regex, except it won't match by default because the regular expression has a capital `H` at the beginning. By default, these expressions are *case-sensitive*, meaning they do not make allowances for case deviation (if we specify lowercase, we will only match a lowercase string).

That's where the third (and optional) parameter to `search` comes into play. The `re.IGNORECASE` is really just a *flag*, another word for "option" in programming terminology, that tells the search function to ignore the case and treat "`hello`" and "`Hello`" as the same string.

MY TAKE

You can shorten `re.IGNORECASE` to `re.I`, and this is far simpler to type. However, `IGNORECASE` makes it clear to other programmers (especially ones who may not know about `re.I`) what you intend to do with your regular expression search. If you use `re.I`, I suggest leaving a comment above it to note that it is a case-*insensitive* search. This helps you and anyone else that may come along later to read or edit your code.

`search` can do more than just return a `True` or `False` if there's a match. We can fetch the contents of that match. Matching text in regular expressions could fill a chapter all by itself, but let's walk through an example you're likely to encounter in real life.

SNIPPET

10-12.py

```
# Import the regular expression engine
import re

# Define our content
text = "The quick gray fox jumped over the lazy dog!"
```

```
# Find
match = re.search("(gray|grey)", text, re.IGNORECASE)

# Print the match
print(match.group(0))
```

In this example, we use `re.search` in the exact same way, but instead of evaluating for `True`/`False` we fetch the result of the search and place it in `match`. Our regex is `(gray|grey)`, and the parentheses tell Python to find and return any text (or evaluation of other regex code) inside the parentheses. In this case, we have the US and UK spellings of the same word (*gray* in the US and *grey* across the pond), and the pipe symbol between them specifies that either the first or second variation is acceptable. Finally, the last line prints the match.

The object returned by `re.search` (`match` in this case) also contains other information about the matching result. The `span` method gives us the exact position in the string where the match occurred.

```
match.span()
```

contains:

```
(10, 14)
```

The first value specifies the start of the match, and the second specifies the index of the character after the end of the match. We can use this data to alter the string.

```
# Import the regular expression engine
import re

# Define our content
text = "The quick gray fox jumped over the lazy dog!"

# Find
match = re.search("(gray|grey)", text, re.IGNORECASE)

# Get start and end of match
match _ start = match.span()[0]
match _ end = match.span()[1]
```

```
# Replacement text
replace_text = "grey"

# Replace gray with grey using the position from span
new_text = text[:match_start] + replace_text + text[match_end:]

# Display results
print("Old text: " + text)
print("New text: " + new_text)
```

The new code starts when we get the `match_start` and `match_end` from the `span` method. The first result in the `span` method is the start, and the second the end, so we store these values for the next step. The `replace_text` is the UK spelling that we're going to substitute for the US spelling.

Next we construct a new string called `new_text` that begins with the `text` string, starting at the beginning and including everything up to the position `match_start`. The colon *before* the index position tells Python to return the portion of the string up to (but not including) the position. We then add (concatenate) the `replace_text` string and add the rest of the original `text` string. The colon *after* the position index tells Python to return the portion of the string starting at the position, including that portion and everything up to the end.

In other words, our `new_text` string consists of the first part of the `text` string up to the `match_start` position, then the `replace_text` string, then the remainder of the original `text` string starting at the `match_end` position.

So when we run the code, here is what we get:

```
Old text: The quick gray fox jumped over the lazy dog!
New text: The quick grey fox jumped over the lazy dog!
```

Let's do some more searching through strings, this time with a more advanced regex. It might seem a bit obscure at first, but bear with me.

You'll notice sequences `\b` and `\w`. Before we go into their purpose, it's important to understand that this is a special sequence of characters called an *escape sequence*. It's given this name because, in the context of regular expressions, they escape the normal processing of the regular expression and tell Python that the character immediately after the backslash is to be considered not part of the expression but a character to match.

The regular expression symbols \b and \w are ***metacharacters***—symbols that have special meaning. They denote a type of character or string of characters in a string.

Escape sequences exist beyond the realm of regular expressions, so I stated "in the context of regular expressions" to make it clear that escape sequences have other uses (e.g., recall the \n sequence that signals a newline). In general, escape sequences are groups of characters that mean something other than what they literally state. For example, in regular expressions, \b is not telling the program to match a backslash then a b.

Now let's look at an example that uses a more advanced regex involving metacharacters. We'll go through it in detail after the example.

SNIPPET

10-14.py

```python
# Import the regular expression engine
import re

# Define our content
text = "This is the the house. It has red red paint."

# Regular expression to find duplicate words
# Use prefix r before to treat as raw (unescaped) string
regex = r"\b(\w+)\s+\1\b"

# Find any duplicate words
matches = re.findall(regex, text, re.IGNORECASE)

# Print the duplicate words
for match in matches:
    print(match)
```

When you run this code, it finds the duplicate words.

```
the
red
```

You'll notice a few things different with this code, so let's step through them. First, we predefine our regular expression into a string called `regex`, but there's something new here. The r in front of the string tells Python to treat the string as a raw string. When it does this, it doesn't perform any escaping; that is, the \b, \w, etc., are treated as literal values. So, if \n were in this string, it wouldn't generate a newline—instead it would be exactly \n with no newline. This is necessary to prevent Python from turning the \b escape code into a backspace, which would cause an error in our regular expression.

We'll step through the regular expression in a moment, but first, note that we used re.findall. This returns a dictionary of the matches it finds. That's why we're able to iterate over them in the last loop, displaying each that was found in the string. You can even use len(matches) to determine the number of matches found, since matches is a dictionary.

Now, the elephant in the room—the weird-looking regex. Let's go through it symbol by symbol and it will make sense. To keep things easily digestible, I've constructed a handy table (figure 32).

GRAPHIC

fig. 32

SYMBOL	OBJECTIVE
\b	Matches empty string at the beginning or end of a word (i.e., a word boundary).
\w+	\w matches any single word character (i.e., a-z, A-Z, 0-9). The + causes the \w to match unlimited times.
(\w+)	The parentheses around the \w+ tell Python to capture (save for later) what is matched inside them.
\s+	\s matches any single whitespace character (including but not limited to spaces). Unlike \b, this doesn't have to be at the beginning or end of a word. The + causes the \s to match unlimited times.
\1	Matches the first capturing group again, which is (\w+). The 1 denotes the first group.
\b	Matches empty string at the beginning or end of a word.

Regular expression metacharacters and symbols in the regex
"\b(\w+)\s+\1\b" as shown in the code the example.

Don't worry if this doesn't make sense to you. Regular expressions like this didn't make sense to me for years. However, the more I used them in my programs and copy/pasted expressions I found online, the more I learned how they work. One of the most useful ways to learn about regular expressions is to take an existing regex and modify it to suit your needs.

Regex Anchors

What if I want to see if a string starts with the letter H? To do that, I'll use the ^ *regex anchor*. A regex anchor is a character that signifies a certain position in a string, and the caret (^) signifies the beginning of a string.

SNIPPET

10-15.py

```
# Import the regular expression engine
import re

# Define our content
text = "Hello, World!"

# Does the string begin with the letter H?
if re.search("^H", text):
    print("The string begins with H.")
else:
    print("The string does not begin with H.")
```

When we run this, we'll see:

```
The string begins with H.
```

The regular expression ^H tells Python to search for a capital letter H at the beginning of the strong (we didn't use the case-insensitive flag, so it must match a capital letter). Since the regular expression matched, it evaluated to be True, and the proper message was displayed.

Let's do the same thing in reverse—that is, use the $ symbol to denote the end of a string.

SNIPPET

10-16.py

```
# Import the regular expression engine
import re

# Define our content
text = "Hello, World!"

# Does the string end in an exclamation point?
if re.search("\!$", text):
    print("The string ends with an exclamation point.")
else:
    print("The string doesn't end with an exclamation point.")
```

Here's what we see when we run the code:

```
The string ends with an exclamation point.
```

When this regular expression runs, it matches, because at the end of the string (denoted by the $ in the regex) an exclamation point exists (denoted by a backslash and an exclamation point: \!) .

There are two new things in this example. First, we specify the dollar symbol ($) to tell Python to start from the end of the string with the match, not the beginning. Second, we place a backslash (\) before the exclamation mark (!) because the exclamation mark itself is a regex symbol, and putting a backslash before it tells Python that we don't mean to use the regex symbol but rather the actual character (often called a *literal character* in programming parlance).

If we wanted to see if the string ended in a period or any other non-letter or non-number, we would have to escape that character as well with an escape sequence. With a regular expression of \.$ we could see if the string ended in a period. If we wanted to detect whether a string ended in the letter o, the regex would be o$, with no escaping necessary via the backslash because o is an alphanumeric character.

When we work with multiline strings, we often want to match the beginning or end of each line, rather than the beginning or end of the whole string. To do so, we can specify the re.MULTILINE flag, which changes the behavior of ^ and $ to match the start and end of each line, respectively.

But that raises an interesting question: how do we make multiline strings? The triple-quote delimiter is our new friend.

```
text = """This is a multiline string.
It has multiple lines to it.
So, fittingly, it's called a multiline string.
When you type a string and hit ENTER,
a special character is inserted in the string.
That special character is a backslash followed by n."""
```

In chapter 1, we discussed the `\n` sequence that inserted a newline. By entering a multiline string in our editor, this `\n` sequence is already added for us because it's on a new line.

If we want a regex that matches the exact beginning of the string, even if it has multiple lines, we use `\A`. Conversely, `\Z` matches the end of the string. So `re.search("\AThis", text)` would work because the first line starts with "`This`" and the `\A` anchor directs the regular expression to start at the very beginning.

Match

The `re.match` function takes the same parameters as the `re.search` function except it tries to match the regex pattern at the beginning of the string and not the entire string. The `re.match` function is faster, so if you're looking for something at the beginning, it's better to use it instead of `re.search`.

10-17.py

```python
# Import the regular expression engine
import re
# Our string
test = "Hello, World!"
# Match
if re.match("e", test):
    print("re.match says it has an e in it.")
# Search
if re.search("e", test):
    print("re.search says it has an e in it.")
```

When we run the code, we see this:

```
re.search says it has an e in it.
```

We do not see the `match` conditional `print` statement. Since `match` looks only at the start of the string, the capital `H` that begins the string invalidates the match. The `re.search` function, on the other hand, finds every occurrence of `e` in the string, so the statement evaluates to be `True` because it found at least one match.

Splitting Strings with Regexes

You can use `re.split` to break apart strings using a regular expression. Recall that the regular `split` function splits strings based on a delimiter of one or more characters. The `re.split` function is similar except the splitting delimiter can be a regular expression, giving you considerably more flexibility.

In the next example, we'll split a string with spaces and then with non-word characters using the \s and \W metacharacters. Recall that \s means any whitespace character—that's simple enough.

As for \W, this matches any non-word character (space, punctuation, etc.). You might be wondering why we didn't use \w (which matches any word character). It might be great for finding individual words, but this is the delimiter we are providing to `split`, so if we split by words we'd end up with no meaningful results because we'd match only the space between the words. So we use \W as the delimiter to match the spaces between the words, and thus `split` returns each word. Adding the + at the end matches one or multiple non-word characters.

Just like the regular `split` function, `re.split` returns a list of the split strings.

10-18.py

```
# Import the regular expression engine
import re

# Our string
test = "The quick brown fox is fast!"

# Split by spaces using the \s metacharacter
# Since we want to account for multiple spaces, we add +
space_split = re.split("\s+", test)
print(space_split)

# Split by word using the non-word metacharacter
# Since we want to account for multiple
# non-word characters, we add +
word_split = re.split("\W+", test)
print(word_split)
```

This code produces the following:

```
['The', 'quick', 'brown', 'fox', 'is', 'fast!']
['The', 'quick', 'brown', 'fox', 'is', 'fast', '']
```

An interesting note here is that the split by spaces gives us the exclamation mark at the end of the word "fast", whereas splitting by non-word characters omits this. Since `\W+` splits by one or more non-word characters, it doesn't return the exclamation mark at the end of the word "fast" but instead uses it to split the string, leaving an empty entry at the end.

Substitution

The `re.sub` function allows us to perform a find-and-replace operation using regular expressions.

SNIPPET

10-19.py

```
# Import the regular expression engine
import re

# Our string
test = "The quick brown fox is fast!"

# Substitute spaces with +
plus_test = re.sub("\s+", "+", test)
print(plus_test)
```

When we run the code, we'll see this:

```
The+quick+brown+fox+is+fast!
```

The first argument for `re.sub` is the regex pattern to find. The second argument is the character(s) to replace in the string when the regex pattern is matched. Finally, we provide the string that will be used to replace matches in the third argument. The function returns the modified string (in this example, `plus_test`).

DIGITAL ASSETS

For more regular expression symbols, please see the "Regular Expression Cheat Sheet" included with your Digital Assets at go.quickstartguides.com/python.

String Formatting

We've been using `print` quite a lot, and it works great for strings. But when we need to add numbers to the mix, we have to convert them via `str()` and use the + symbol to combine elements of the data to be displayed. While this technically works, it's not very elegant and can make the lines of code quite complex to follow if we need to sprinkle a lot of variable data in our string.

The formatting system introduced in Python 3 is quite expansive, so let's start with its basic functionality and work up from there. In this first example, we'll use curly brackets (i.e., `{ }`) in the middle of a string to define where we want to insert another string.

SNIPPET

10-20.py

```python
# Define the name
name = "Robert"

# Print a friendly message
print("Hello, {}!".format(name))
```

This produces:

```
Hello, Robert!
```

In this example, the `format` method to the inline string `"Hello, {}!"` substitutes the value in the `name` string at the location of the curly braces. This isn't a huge improvement over the previous `+` string concatenation we've been using, but this approach becomes a lot more powerful with multiple variables.

```
# Define our greeting
greeting = "Hello, {name}! It's currently {temp} and the time is {time}."

# Print the message
print(greeting.format(name = "Robert", temp = "54F", time = "3:42 PM"))
```

Here, we're passing keyword arguments to the `format` method, providing values for `name`, `temp`, and `time`. For now, we're just using example values; we'll talk about getting the actual time in chapter 11.

We can even format digits, including `floats`, with the `format` method.

```
total = 6.95
message = "Your total is ${:.2f}."

print(message.format(total))
```

This code displays:

```
Your total is $6.95.
```

Inside the curly braces, we use the pattern `:.2f`, which is a bit arcane but can be quite simply explained. Python has a set of formatting codes, or shorthand, that allows us to define what the `format` method returns inline between the braces. The colon tells `format` that a formatting code is being used, and the `f` at the end denotes a floating-point value. The `.2` portion of the formatting code sets the `float` display to two decimal places. In this case, 6.95 is already formatted in that pattern, but let's change things a bit.

```
total = 6.95333
message = "Your total is ${:.2f}."

print(message.format(total))
```

This code will still display:

```
Your total is $6.95.
```

The `:.2f` pattern also instructs `format` to round the float to two decimal places. We can change the `2` to another number to adjust the number of decimal places to be displayed.

There are quite a few other patterns we can use. Figure 34 is a chart displaying the most frequently used codes for the `format` method.

fig. 33

FREQUENTLY USED FORMATTING CODES

CODE	DESCRIPTION	EXAMPLE	DISPLAY
:n	integer format	`"There are {:n} continents."`	There are 7 continents.
:f	Floating point number	`"Your total is ${:.2f}."`	Your total is $6.95.
:,	Use comma-separators	`"In 2020, the USA had {:,} people"`	In 2020, the USA had 329,500,000 people.
:%	Percentage format	`"Take an additional {.0%} off today!"` *(the 0 defines decimal places in percentage display)*	Take an additional 20% off today!
:e	Exponent (scientific) notion	`"The speed of light is {:e} m/s."`	The speed of light is 3.000000e+08 m/s.
:E	Exponent (scientific) notion (Capital E)	`"The speed of light is {:E} m/s."`	The speed of light is 3.000000E+08 m/s.

DIGITAL ASSETS

For more string formatting codes, please refer to your Digital Assets at go.quickstartguides.com/python.

F-Strings

You're going to see traditional Python string formatting quite a bit in existing code, but f-strings (short for formatted string literals) could be used beginning with Python 3.6.

F-strings provide tremendous flexibility when we're constructing strings with inline variables.

SNIPPET

10-23.py

```python
first_day = "Monday"
second_day = "Wednesday"
print(f"We are closed this week from {first_day} till {second_day}.")
```

With f-strings, we can avoid the awkward plus signs and a call to `format()`.

We can also perform evaluations inside the curly brackets, like this:

```
print(f"Testing evaluations in f-strings: {3 * 9}")
```

When we run this code, we get the following:

Testing evaluations in f-strings: 27

Those evaluations aren't limited to mathematics. You can call functions inside the brackets.

```
word = "cool!"
print(f"Testing functions in f-strings: {word.upper()}")
```

This produces:

```
Testing functions in f-strings: COOL!
```

Consider using f-strings in the ClydeBank Coffee Shop Simulator game.

Python 3.6 was released on December 23, 2016. As of this printing, that's more than six years ago. It's growing increasingly unlikely that you'll run into an installed version of Python that old. However, there are versions of Linux, especially those running on servers, that will still have older versions installed, so that could be something to consider when using f-strings. If you do run your Python code on a server with Python 3.5 or earlier, there's an excellent case to be made for upgrading. Nevertheless, you will still run into plenty of code written before this time that doesn't have f-strings.

Data Compression

Compression is a technique that reduces redundant data in strings, causing the string to take up less space in memory or on the disk. The strings we've been working with are quite small, but sometimes you'll be working with massive sets of data.

You've likely heard of zip files—archives of files (and sometimes folders) condensed into a single package. Zip files use compression to help minimize space and transfer time.

Python has built-in methods for creating compressed files. You can easily compress a string. To demonstrate this, we'll need a rather large string. Let's create a multiline string with the triple-quote delimiter.

```
data = """To compress data, we'll need a long string.
Not a short string. No, that would be too small.
To get any meaningful benefit from compression,
you must use a decent length of data or else the
overhead of compression isn't worth the gains.
This will be enough data, containing enough redundant
patterns, to be compressible."""
```

Now that we have the string, we must import the zlib module to include compression logic in our program.

```
import zlib
```

To be compressed, the string data must be encoded to *UTF-8* format. Recall that UTF-8 is a type of character encoding that vastly expands on the traditional *ASCII* character set, which includes mostly numbers, English letters, and a few symbols. UTF-8 has a wide assortment of non-Latin characters, emojis, and other helpful symbols. Like most tasks, Python makes this easy via encode.

```
encoded_data = data.encode()
```

To compress the data, we simply call the compress function inside the zlib module that we imported. Let's put it all together, along with code to show how many characters we saved.

```
# Load the zlib module
import zlib

# Define our data
data = """To compress data, we'll need a long string.
Not a short string. No, that would be too small.
To get any meaningful benefit from compression,
```

```
you must use a decent length of data or else the
overhead of compression isn't worth the gains.
This will be enough data, containing enough redundant
patterns, to be compressible."""

# Compress the data
compressed_data = zlib.compress(data.encode())

# Display stats
data_len = len(data)
compressed_data_len = len(compressed_data)
print("Length of uncompressed data: " + str(data_len))
print("Length of compressed data: " + str(compressed_data_len))
```

When we run this code, we see that the uncompressed data consists of 323 characters, and the compressed data 203 characters. Compression gave us roughly 37% more space. That doesn't sound like much, but if you needed to compress gigabytes of data, it could provide an enormous amount of storage and bandwidth.

Even though in this example we provided the string directly in the code, you can compress any data you want with Python, including data you load from and write to disk.

ClydeBank Coffee Shop: Inventory Woes

Two outstanding features need to be addressed: our inventory isn't properly managed, and we have no way for the player to quit. Let's fix both. I'm going to show only the updated files. The utilities module (`utilities.py`) hasn't changed.

MY TAKE

You might find it odd that I used a prefix of `t_` in front of some variable names, like `t_name` and `t_shop_name`. I use this prefix for variables that are intended to be temporary. This is a convention I adopted quite early in my programming career and have kept it ever since. When I see it in my own code, I immediately know what I meant by it. I am not necessarily encouraging this particular convention, only using it as an example. Over time, you'll develop your own habits and conventions. Pick what works best for you.

main.py

```
# ClydeBank Coffee Shop Simulator 4000
# Copyright 2022 (C) ClydeBank Media, All Rights Reserved.


# Import all functions from the utility module
from utilities import *


# Import the game class from the coffee_shop_simulator module
from coffee_shop_simulator import CoffeeShopSimulator


# Print welcome message
welcome()


# Get name and store name
t_name = prompt("What is your name?", True)
t_shop_name = prompt("What do you want to name your coffee shop?", True)


# Create the game object
game = CoffeeShopSimulator(t_name, t_shop_name)


# Run the game
game.run()


# Say goodbye!
print("\nThanks for playing. Have a great rest of your day!\n")
```

coffee_shop_simulator.py

```
# Import needed modules
import random
import re
from utilities import *


class CoffeeShopSimulator:

    # Minimum and maximum temperatures
    TEMP_MIN = 20
    TEMP_MAX = 90


    def __init__(self, player_name, shop_name):
```

```python
        # Set player and coffee shop names
        self.player_name = player_name
        self.shop_name = shop_name

        # Current day number
        self.day = 1

        # Cash on hand at start
        self.cash = 100.00

        # Inventory at start
        self.coffee_inventory = 100

        # Sales list
        self.sales = []

        # Possible temperatures
        self.temps = self.make_temp_distribution()

    def run(self):
        print("\nOk, let's get started. Have fun!")

        # The main game loop
        running = True
        while running:
            # Display the day and add a "fancy" text effect
            self.day_header()

            # Get the weather
            temperature = self.weather

            # Display the cash and weather
            self.daily_stats(temperature)

            # Get price of a cup of coffee (but provide an escape hatch)
            response = prompt("What do you want to charge per cup of coffee? (type ↦
            ↪ exit to quit)")
            if re.search("^exit", response, re.IGNORECASE):
                running = False
                continue
```

```
    else:
        cup_price = int(response)


    # Do they want to buy more coffee inventory?
    response = prompt("Want to buy more coffee? (hit ENTER for none or ↦
    ↳ enter number)", False)


    if response:
        if not self.buy_coffee(response):
            print("Could not buy additional coffee.")
    # Get advertising spend
    print("\nYou can buy advertising to help promote sales.")
    advertising = prompt("How much do you want to spend on advertising ↦
    ↳ (0 for none)?", False)


    # Convert advertising into a float
    advertising = convert_to_float(advertising)


    # Deduct advertising from cash on hand
    self.cash -= advertising


    # Simulate today's sales
    cups_sold = self.simulate(temperature, advertising, cup_price)
    gross_profit = cups_sold * cup_price


    # Display the results
    print("You sold " + str(cups_sold) + " cups of coffee today.")
    print("You made $" + str(gross_profit) + ".")


    # Add the profit to our coffers
    self.cash += gross_profit


    # Subtract inventory
    self.coffee_inventory -= cups_sold


    if self.cash < 0:
        print("\n:( GAME OVER! You ran out of cash.")
        running = False
        continue
```

```python
                # Before we loop around, add a day
                self.increment_day()


    def simulate(self, temperature, advertising, cup_price):
        # Find out how many cups were sold
        cups_sold = self.daily_sales(temperature, advertising)


        # Save the sales data for today
        self.sales.append({
            "day": self.day,
            "coffee_inv": self.coffee_inventory,
            "advertising": advertising,
            "temp": temperature,
            "cup_price": cup_price,
            "cups_sold": cups_sold
        })


        # We technically don't need this, but why make the next step
        # read from the sales list when we have the data right here
        return cups_sold


    def buy_coffee(self, amount):
        try:
            i_amount = int(amount)
        except ValueError:
            return False


        if i_amount <= self.cash:
            self.coffee_inventory += i_amount
            self.cash -= i_amount
            return True
        else:
            return False
    def make_temp_distribution(self):
        # This is not a good bell curve, but it will do for now
        # until we get to more advanced mathematics
        temps = []


        # First, find the average between TEMP_MIN and TEMP_MAX
        avg = (self.TEMP_MIN + self.TEMP_MAX) / 2
```

```python
        # Find the distance between TEMP_MAX and the average
        max_dist_from_avg = self.TEMP_MAX - avg


        # Loop through all possible temperatures
        for i in range(self.TEMP_MIN, self.TEMP_MAX):
            # How far away is the temperature from average?
            # abs() gives us the absolute value
            dist_from_avg = abs(avg - i)
            # How far away is the dist_from_avg from the maximum?
            # This will be lower for temps at the extremes
            dist_from_max_dist = max_dist_from_avg - dist_from_avg
            # If the value is zero, make it one
            if dist_from_max_dist == 0:
                dist_from_max_dist = 1
            # Append the output of x_of_y to temps
            for t in x_of_y(int(dist_from_max_dist), i):
                temps.append(t)
        return temps


def increment_day(self):
    self.day += 1


def daily_stats(self, temperature):
    print("You have $" + str(self.cash) + " cash on hand and the temperature is " ↦
        ↪ + str(temperature) + ".")
  print("You have enough coffee on hand to make " + str(self.coffee_inventory) + ↦
        ↪ " cups.\n")


def day_header(self):
    print("\n-----| Day " + str(self.day) + " @ " + self.shop_name + " |-----")


def daily_sales(self, temperature, advertising):
    sales = int((self.TEMP_MAX - temperature) * (advertising * 0.5))
    if sales > self.coffee_inventory:
        sales = self.coffee_inventory
        print("You would have sold more coffee but you ran out. Be sure to buy ↦
            ↪ additional inventory.")


@property
def weather(self):
```

```
# Generate a random temperature between 20 and 90
# We'll consider seasons later on, but this is good enough for now
return random.choice(self.temps)
```

We've added several improvements. First, there's a check each time the player is asked to provide a price for the coffee: the word `exit`. This uses a regular expression and `re.IGNORECASE` to allow for the possibility of their using capital letters in the word. If it matches, it sets `running` to `False` and then uses `continue` to skip to the next iteration of the loop, which will exit because `running` is no longer `True`. The newly added `print` message *after* the `game.run()` line tells them the game has ended and thanks them for playing.

Next we add a method called `buy_coffee()` that does the heavy lifting of purchasing coffee by subtracting money from our `cash` and adding it to the `coffee_inventory`. It includes checks to make sure the player has enough money to buy the coffee and an exception handler to ensure that the conversion to `int` is successful.

The amount of coffee sold is now subtracted from `coffee_inventory`, and checks were added to prevent buying coffee with money we don't have or selling coffee with inventory that doesn't exist. And finally, there's a check to make sure the player isn't negative in cash. If so, the game is over.

The game is in a lot better shape now, but if you play it for a while, you'll notice that it's quite easy to ensure a successful sales day. I won't specifically mention the bug here, but if you examine the code closely and play for a few days, you might see a pattern.

In any event, we'll clear that up and provide a more realistic gameplay experience in the coming chapters.

Chapter Recap

» Python's standard string offers extensive functionality for finding, replacing, and processing text.

» Regular expressions are a unique and powerful tool for manipulating text. They go beyond basic find and replace operations to spotting and iterating over complex patterns.

» Data compression can save substantial amounts of disk and memory resources by reducing redundancies in data.

| 11 |
Math in Python

Chapter Overview

» Python is frequently used for math, science, and statistics
» Python primarily works in integer and floating-point math
» Python provides excellent statistical and time/date functionality

Python is capable of some incredibly complex math. But if math isn't your thing, don't worry. We're not going to dive into differential calculus. Remember, I said I wouldn't use the A-word again in this book, and I intend to keep my promise. We'll take an in-depth look at the math functionality you're likely to use in general-purpose and business programming, and I'll show some quick examples of the higher-level stuff that the brilliant minds at NASA and leading laboratories use, in case you ever need to calculate the phases of the moon.

Integer Math

Most math performed by computers is based on integers. This functionality is generally called integer math. We've covered basic math operations in our discussion up to this point, but in this section we'll expand our knowledge to include multiplication, exponents, and more.

Addition, Subtraction, Multiplication, and Division

Python can easily take care of the third R in the "reading, writing, and 'rithmetic" trifecta. Arithmetic is performed using the symbols shown in figure 34.

If we divide a number by another number, we'll get a floating-point number (called a `float`) as the quotient, even if there is no remainder. Otherwise, adding, subtracting, multiplying, and calculating exponents with integers will produce integers as the result.

fig. 34

OPERATION	SYMBOL	EXAMPLE
Addition	**+**	3 + 5 + 8
Subtraction	**–**	5 - 2 = 3
Multiplication	*****	5 * 5 = 25
Division	**/**	6 / 3 = 2
Exponent	******	3 ** 3 = 27

The basic symbols involved in Python math.

Order of Operations

In Python, just as in eighth-grade math class, you still must Please Excuse My Dear Aunt Sally. Depending on where in the world you went to school, you may be more familiar with the BODMAS order of operations (figure 35).

fig. 35

ORDER OF OPERATIONS					
P (Parentheses)	**E** (Exponent)	**M** (Multiply)	**D** (Divide)	**A** (Add)	**S** (Subtract)
B (Brackets)	**O** (Order)	**D** (Divide)	**M** (Multiply)	**A** (Add)	**S** (Subtract)
( )	$\sqrt{x}$ or x^2	÷ or x		+ or –	

The order of operations in Python.

Let's look at an example that covers each of these operations.

```
# PEMDAS
result = (5 * 4) / 6 - (1 + 2) + 3 ** 2
print(result)
```

results in:

```
9.333333333333334
```

The Math Module

Python has a standard module named `math` that adds a lot of math functionality to the language. Let's explore some examples.

SNIPPET

11-01.py

```python
# Import the math module
import math

# Ask user for a number
number = input("Please enter a number: ")

# Convert to int
number = int(number)

# Calculate result
result = math.sqrt(number)

# Display result
print("The square root of {:n} is {:.6f}".format(number, result))
```

In this example, I've used several techniques that are worth discussing beyond the new `sqrt` function, which calculates square roots of numbers. Once we get the input from the user, we convert it to an integer right away (as `input` returns a string). We could have done this inline on the "calculate result" line of code, but I chose to do it separately because we use the number twice—once to calculate the result and the second time to display the original number in the results.

If we're going to use a calculation or conversion multiple times, we should perform whatever action we need to do with that variable, or else we'll have to duplicate our work each time we need it. This is not only an inefficient use of our time but also makes the program slower. Granted, in this example, we wouldn't have noticed the performance loss if we had converted `number` twice, but if we're in a loop with millions of iterations it can make a huge difference.

Additionally, rather than create a separate value to store the integer conversion of `number`, I set `number` to equal the new `int` result. This is fine if we don't need the original value, and in this case we don't because when we display it in the last line, the `format` function takes care of converting the integer back into a string for use in `print`.

Now to the star of the show, the `sqrt` function. We can provide any integer or float to the function, and it returns the square root of that value (if it's not negative). Then the last line displays the original number and the square root in floating-point form with 6 decimal places via the `{:.6f}` format code.

There are many other functions in the `math` module. A few of the more common ones are shown in figure 36.

GRAPHIC

fig. 36

COMMON MATH STANDARD MODULE FUNCTIONS		
FUNCTION	DESCRIPTION	EXAMPLE
floor(n)	Find largest integer less than or equal to n	`print(str(math.floor(5.9)))` Result: 5
ceil(n)	Find smallest integer greater or equal to n	`print(str(math.ceil(4.9)))` Result: 5
fabs(n)	Return the absolute value of n as float	`print(str(math.fabs(-5)))` Result: 5.0
fmod(x, y)	Return remainder from x / y	`print(str(math.fmod(3, 2)))` Result: 1.0
cos(n)	Find cosine of n	`print(str(math.cos(1)))` Result: 0.5403023058681398
sin(n)	Find sine of n	`print(str(math.sin(1)))` Result: 0.8414709848078965
tan(n)	Find tangent of n	`print(str(math.tan(1)))` Result: 1.5574077246549023
pi	Return the value of pi	`print(math.pi))` Result: 3.141592653589793

For more math functionality, please see https://docs.python.org/3/library/math.html.

Floating-Point Math

Floating-point math involves operations that either use or produce non-integer numbers. Before we get too far into this topic, let's quickly review the basics of floating-point operation.

```
# Convert integer to floating-point
number = 5
floating _ number = float(number)

# Display both
print(number)
print(floating _ number)
```

When we run this code, we get this:

```
5
5.0
```

We can round `floats` to their nearest whole number with the `round` function.

```
# Some floats to round
a = 1.2
b = 1.49
c = 1.51

# Displaying results
print(round(a))
print(round(b))
print(round(c))
```

This code produces:

```
1
1
2
```

NOTE   If you supply an integer to the `round` function, it will simply return the same integer, so the `round` function is safe to use on both integers and `floats`.

Floating-Point Precision

Using floating-point numbers can be a bit tricky in all programming languages, Python included. You might think this should be simple for a computer, but by default Python stores floating-point numbers in memory using a method that favors speed over accuracy. To witness this quirk firsthand, fire up the Python interpreter (or input this in your `scratch.py` file) and enter the following:

```
n = 0.2 + 0.2 + 0.2
```

You would expect the answer to be `0.6`, right? Well, it is.

11-04.py

```
# Display n with 2 decimal precision
print("The total is {:.2f}".format(n))
```

Until you take a closer look.

```
# Display n with 30 decimal precision
print("The total is {:.30f}".format(n))
```

What in the world is this nonsense?

```
0.600000000000000088817841970013
```

No, the laws of space and time haven't collapsed around you. Internally, Python stores floating-point values as fractions. When it needs to display them, it converts them back into decimals, and this conversion isn't always as precise as you might think. Fortunately, there's a standard module that helps deal with that issue.

11-05.py

```
# Import the Decimal class from the decimal module
from decimal import Decimal

# Define some numbers
a = Decimal("0.2")
b = Decimal("0.2")
c = Decimal("0.2")

# Add them together
result = a + b + c

# Display the result as a string
print(str(result))
```

This code yields:

```
0.6
```

The `float` logic built into Python is usually fine for simple tasks, but as you can see, when precision matters, the `decimal` module helps considerably.

The `decimal` module contains more functionality to help us process complex decimal math. For more information, please see https://docs.python.org/3/library/decimal.html.

Percentages

Python, like most programming languages, doesn't have a dedicated feature set for percentages, but we can easily convert `floats` into a percentage by multiplying them by 100.

SNIPPET

11-06.py

```
# Float value
value = 0.34

# Percent value
p_value = value * 100

# Display both
print(value, p_value)
```

When we run this code, we'll see this:

```
0.34 34.0
```

By the way, this demonstrates an interesting aspect of the `print` function. We can send it multiple arguments, in fact as many as we want.

```
print(1, 2, 3, 4, 5, 6, 7, 8, 9)
```

This code produces:

```
1 2 3 4 5 6 7 8 9
```

`print` accepts an arbitrary number of arguments. Internally, it iterates through the multiple variables we send it and displays them all.

If you use percentages more than once or twice in your program, defining a function to handle them will likely be a big timesaver.

```
def percent(n):
    return(str(n * 100) + "%")
```

Now, anytime you want to use it:

```
print(percent(0.42))
```

and it will produce:

```
42.0%
```

Remember, if you catch yourself doing something more than once or twice, it's probably time for a function. Don't repeat yourself!

Statistical Math

Statistics is a very popular field in Python, as the language is favored by the scientific community. Most of this functionality is in separate modules, but the standard library includes a statistics module that offers most of the statistical functionality you'll likely need for general and business use. Let's go over some of the essential statistics functionality.

```
# Import statistics module
import statistics

# Define a list of numbers
numbers = [1, 4, 17, 62, 12, 84, 5, 8, 21]

# Calculate mean
mean = statistics.mean(numbers)

# Calculate median
median = statistics.median(numbers)

# Calculate mode
mode = statistics.mode(numbers)
```

```
# Calculate standard deviation
stdev = statistics.stdev(numbers)
# Print the results

print("Mean: {:f}".format(mean))
print("Median: {:f}".format(median))
print("Mode: {:f}".format(mode))
print("Standard Deviation: {:f}".format(stdev))
```

For a complete list of in-depth statistics functionality, please see https://docs.python.org/3/library/statistics.html.

Date and Time

The `datetime` standard module contains functionality to process dates and times in Python. If you write a scheduling, reporting, or business application, this may be the most frequent standard module you'll use.

I recall writing a program for a service that required scheduling time slots, and at first I felt this would be an easy task. As I started to dig into the nuts and bolts of finding available time slots, scheduling provider breaks and availability, finding the optimum time for both client and provider, and addressing shifting schedules throughout the day, I realized that the task was excruciatingly complex. Fortunately, the standard library did a lot of the heavy lifting, but the project still required careful planning.

Let's examine some of the `datetime` module's features. First, let's get the current time.

SNIPPET

11-09.py

```
# Import datetime
import datetime

# Get the current time and date
now = datetime.datetime.now()

# Display it
print(now)
```

When we run this code, we'll see the current date and time. While this displays the entire date and time, we can obtain only certain parts if we like.

```
# Import datetime
import datetime
```

```
# Get the current time and date
now = datetime.datetime.now()

# Display the year
print(now.year)

# Display the month
print(now.month)
```

NOTE

The `datetime.datetime.now()` line isn't a typo. We must repeat "datetime" because of the way the `datetime` module is organized.

In addition to `year` and `month`, we can also use the properties `day`, `hour`, `minute`, `second`, and `microsecond`.

We can format the date and time however we like with the `strftime` function.

SNIPPET

11-10.py

```
# Import datetime
import datetime

# Get the current time and date
now = datetime.datetime.now()

# Display date and time in a custom format
print(now.strftime("%A, %B %d, %Y at %I:%M %p"))
```

Running this on my machine displays the exact time that I'm writing it:

```
Monday, April 04, 2022 at 09:31 PM
```

The secret is out—you discovered I'm a night owl!

But what are those strange codes supplied as the arguments for `strftime`? Well, one of them, the word "at," isn't a code at all. And the colon character serves as the hour and minute separator. But the rest are codes that tell the function what to display (figure 37).

To calculate differences in time, we can use the `timedelta` logic from `datetime`. I used this module extensively when writing the scheduling app mentioned previously. The `timedelta` function lets us do time arithmetic or, in other words, find the *delta*, the change in value between one time and another.

CODE	DESCRIPTION	RESULTS
%a	Abbreviated weekday	Sun, Mon, Tue, etc.
%A	Weekday full name	Sunday, Monday, etc.
%w	Weekday as number (i.e., day of the week)	Sunday is 0, Saturday is 6
%d	Day of the month	01 through 31
%b	Abbreviated month	Jan, Feb, Mar, etc.
%B	Month full name	January, February, etc.
%m	Month number	01 through 12
%y	2-digit year	00 through 99
%Y	4-digit year	0001 through 9999
%H	Hour (24-hour clock)	00 through 23
%I	Hour (12-hour clock)	00 through 12
%p	AM or PM	AM, PM
%M	Minute	00 through 59
%S	Second	00 through 59
%f	Microsecond	000000 through 999999
%z	UTC offset	(empty), +0000, -0100, etc.
%Z	Time zone	(empty), UTC, GMT, etc.
%j	Day of the year	001 through 366 (366 is possible in leap year)
%U	Week number of the year	00 through 53
%W	Week (Mon as first day) number of the year	00 through 53
%c	Locale's date and time representation	Mon Apr 4 21:31:00 2022
%x	Locale's date representation	04/04/2022
%X	Locale's time representation	21:31:00
%%	A literal '%' character	%

GRAPHIC

fig. 37

Possible strftime format codes. These values are adjusted to meet the standards of the locale selected on the computer. For example, if the selected country typically lists year first, %c and %x will reflect this.

This is no simple matter. Sure, it's easy to take 50 seconds and subtract 12 seconds or go back 2 hours from 9 o'clock to 7 o'clock. But subtracting minutes that straddle midnight, therefore going back a day, or adding weeks when you must consider a leap year, gets insanely complex.

Don't worry, though—`timedelta` will do all the work for us.

```python
# Import datetime
import datetime

# Get the current time and date
now = datetime.datetime.now()

# Create a delta of 18 hours and 49 minutes
delta = datetime.timedelta(hours = 18, minutes = 49)

# Subtract delta and store in previous_time
previous_time = now - delta

# Display time and time minus the delta
print(now)
print(previous_time)
```

The `delta` variable contains an object representing a time difference, which can then be added or subtracted from a time (in this case, `now`, the current time) and the time difference it represents (in this case, 18 hours and 49 minutes).

The `datetime` standard module is packed with temporal goodness that will make your programming life a lot simpler. And the broader lesson from this and previous chapters is that the Python standard library is an expansive collection of functionalities that will aid you immensely with your programs. We'll cover more of it as we progress in future chapters.

Counting the Days

How many days is it until your birthday? Until Christmas? New Year's? Perhaps, like me, you can't wait until the first day of fall. Rather than asking Google, let's ask Python to help.

Use the code in the previous section to determine how long it is until a day you're looking forward to this year. To do this, you'll need to know one additional thing—how to create an arbitrary `datetime` object that isn't now.

```python
future = datetime.datetime(2023, 12, 25, 0, 0)
```

Now the future object contains a reference to Christmas in the year 2023. The trailing zeros at the end are the hour and minute and can be omitted.

Armed with this knowledge, you can now create a few lines of code to find out how long it is until a day you're looking forward to in the future.

Try this exercise on your own, but if you get stuck, you can find a solution in the appendix.

NOTE

HINT: You can subtract `datetime` objects to find the difference in time between them. Additionally, if you decide to use the `print` function to display a string alongside your time difference (or perhaps even include the future date for reference), then you need to cast the `datetime` object as a string with `str(now)` and `str(future)`.

ClydeBank Coffee Shop: A More Accurate Simulation

Our simulation is predictable. Advertising has the same effect no matter what day it is, temperature always has the same effect, and an expensive cup of coffee sells just as well as one that's practically free. Moreover, the temperature generator method, `make_temp_distribution`, can be simplified.

With this round of changes, only the `coffee_shop_simulator` module was modified.

SNIPPET

CCS-12.py

coffee_shop_simulator.py

```python
# Import needed modules
import random
import re
import numpy
from utilities import *


class CoffeeShopSimulator:

    # Minimum and maximum temperatures
    TEMP_MIN = 20
    TEMP_MAX = 90


    # Length of temperature list
    # (higher produces more realistic curve)
    SERIES_DENSITY = 300


    def __init__(self, player_name, shop_name):
```

```python
        # Set player and coffee shop names
        self.player_name = player_name
        self.shop_name = shop_name

        # Current day number
        self.day = 1

        # Cash on hand at start
        self.cash = 100.00

        # Inventory at start
        self.coffee_inventory = 100

        # Sales list
        self.sales = []

        # Possible temperatures
        self.temps = self.make_temp_distribution()

    def run(self):
        print("\nOk, let's get started. Have fun!")

        # The main game loop
        running = True
        while running:
            # Display the day and add a "fancy" text effect
            self.day_header()

            # Get the weather
            temperature = self.weather

            # Display the cash and weather
            self.daily_stats(temperature)

            # Get price of a cup of coffee (but provide an escape hatch)
            response = prompt("What do you want to charge per cup of coffee? ↦
            ↳ (type exit to quit)")
            if re.search("^exit", response, re.IGNORECASE):
                running = False
                continue
```

```
        else:
            cup_price = int(response)


        # Do they want to buy more coffee inventory?
        print("\nIt costs $1 for the necessary inventory to make a cup of coffee.")
        response = prompt("Want to buy more so you can make more coffee? ↦
        ↪ (ENTER for none or enter number)", False)


        if response:
            if not self.buy_coffee(response):
                print("Could not buy additional coffee.")


        # Get price of a cup of coffee
        print("\nYou can buy advertising to help promote sales.")
        advertising = prompt("How much do you want to spend on advertising ↦
        ↪ (0 for none)?", False)


        # Convert advertising into a float
        advertising = convert_to_float(advertising)


        # Deduct advertising from cash on hand
        self.cash -= advertising


        # Simulate today's sales
        cups_sold = self.simulate(temperature, advertising, cup_price)
        gross_profit = cups_sold * cup_price


        # Display the results
        print("\nYou sold " + str(cups_sold) + " cups of coffee today.")
        print("You made $" + str(gross_profit) + ".")


        # Add the profit to our coffers
        self.cash += gross_profit


        # Subtract inventory
        self.coffee_inventory -= cups_sold


        if self.cash < 0:
            print("\n:( GAME OVER! You ran out of cash.")
            running = False
            continue
```

```python
            # Before we loop around, add a day
            self.increment_day()


    def simulate(self, temperature, advertising, cup_price):
        # Find out how many cups were sold
        cups_sold = self.daily_sales(temperature, advertising, cup_price)


        # Save the sales data for today
        self.sales.append({
            "day": self.day,
            "coffee_inv": self.coffee_inventory,
            "advertising": advertising,
            "temp": temperature,
            "cup_price": cup_price,
            "cups_sold": cups_sold
        })


        # We technically don't need this, but why make the next step
        # read from the sales list when we have the data right here
        return cups_sold


    def buy_coffee(self, amount):
        try:
            i_amount = int(amount)
        except ValueError:
            return False


        if i_amount <= self.cash:
            self.coffee_inventory += i_amount
            self.cash -= i_amount
            return True
        else:
            return False


    def make_temp_distribution(self):
        # Create series of numbers between TEMP_MIN and TEMP_MAX
        series = numpy.linspace(self.TEMP_MIN, self.TEMP_MAX, self.SERIES_DENSITY)


        # Obtain mean and standard deviation from the series
        mean = numpy.mean(series)
```

```
            std_dev = numpy.std(series)


        # Calculate probability density and return the list it creates
        return (numpy.pi * std_dev) * numpy.exp(-0.5 * ((series - mean) / std_dev) ** 2)


    def increment_day(self):
        self.day += 1


    def daily_stats(self, temperature):
        print("You have $" + str(self.cash) + " cash on hand and the temperature is ↦
        ↳ " + str(temperature) + ".")
        print("You have enough coffee on hand to make " + str(self.coffee_inventory) ↦
        ↳ + " cups.\n")


    def day_header(self):
        print("\n-----| Day " + str(self.day) + " @ " + self.shop_name + " |-----")


    def daily_sales(self, temperature, advertising, cup_price):
        # Randomize advertising effectiveness
        adv_coefficient = random.randint(20, 80) / 100


        # Higher priced coffee doesn't sell as well
        price_coefficient = int((cup_price * (random.randint(50, 250) / 100)))


        # Run the sales figures!
        sales = int((self.TEMP_MAX - temperature) * (advertising * adv_coefficient))


        # If price is too high, we don't sell anything
        if price_coefficient > sales:
            sales = 0
        else:
            sales -= price_coefficient


        if sales > self.coffee_inventory:
            sales = self.coffee_inventory
            print("You would have sold more coffee but you ran out. Be sure to buy ↦
            ↳ additional inventory.")
        return sales


@property
def weather(self):
```

```
# Generate a random temperature between 20 and 90
# We'll consider seasons later on, but this is good enough for now
return int(random.choice(self.temps))
```

Let's walk through the modifications individually. First, I improved the temperature generator by using the `numpy` module. This module isn't included in Python by default, so you'll need to install it to use this code. To do so, simply open a console or terminal window and run the following:

```
pip3 install numpy
```

If that fails on Windows, it's probably because Python isn't in the system path. In that case, try running the command in the terminal window of Visual Studio Code.

`numpy` has no external dependencies, so it should install fine on any system with Python. In this code, I used the `linspace`, `mean`, `std`, and `exp` functions. `linspace` provides a list of evenly spaced numbers, `mean` provides the mean, `std` provides the standard deviation, and `exp` gives us an exponent. Using this, I generated a curve that is far more realistic and uses fewer lines of code.

For more reasonable sales figures, I created a price coefficient that punishes higher-priced coffees with fewer sales. But the coefficient isn't necessarily applied evenly—there is a random element to it to keep the player guessing. I did the same with advertising, giving a random element to the effect it has on sales.

There are some small changes to text that provide the user with a better experience and a bit of help along the way. I've also added a fair number of comments to better explain functionality. I encourage you to play a few rounds and see if you can spot the differences. As always, feel free to experiment with different multipliers on the coefficients. I found the values that seem to match what I thought was best in terms of sales, advertising, and price performance, but you could easily derive better results with some more experimentation.

Chapter Recap

» Python follows the standard order of operations.

» Python provides built-in floating-point math functionality, but for maximum precision and capability, use the `decimal` module.

» Python has a wide range of statistical functions via the `statistics` module.

» The `datetime` module allows for date/time math. The `strftime` function allows the formatting of dates and times in an incredibly customized way.

| 12 |
Input and Output

Chapter Overview

> » Computers accept input, process data, and generate output
> » Python can write and read to the disk in multiple modes and encoding schemes
> » Serialization lets us save an object to disk for later recreation

Computers do a tremendous amount of complex work, but each task can be essentially broken down into three parts: collecting input, processing those data, and outputting results. We've already covered some simple input and output commands and the processing of various kinds of data, but in this chapter we'll learn how to read from, and write to, files on disk.

The phrase "*input* and *output*" is frequently abbreviated as I/O. Input is defined as data that are provided to the computer, either by the user via a keyboard, mouse, or similar device, or read from a disk or network. Output is the result of computation and can be displayed on the screen, sent over a network, or saved to disk.

INPUT   **OUTPUT**

GRAPHIC

fig. 38

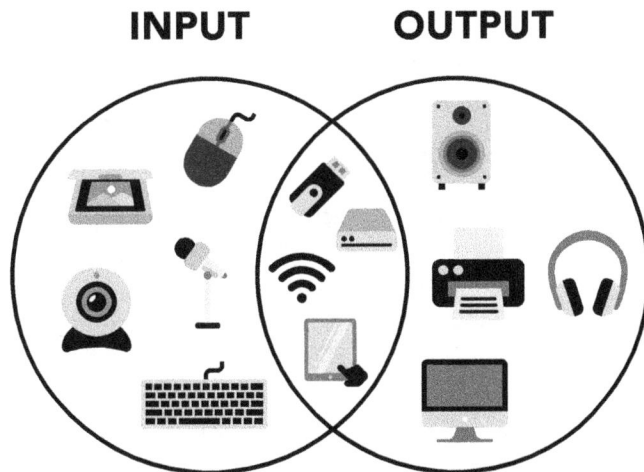

A wide variety of input and output devices. Some serve both roles.

While most devices serve a well-defined purpose on the input-output spectrum, some, like disks, accept both input (reading files) and output (writing files). See figure 38 for some examples. In this chapter, we'll focus on disk I/O.

Disk I/O

There are many times when we want to load data from files and save the results to disk. Most every activity performed on a modern computer involves using the disk—including booting the operating system, starting a program, and loading a document. Despite this wide range of disk activity, most users are concerned with loading and saving *their* data, be it a spreadsheet, a presentation, or the next great novel.

In this section, we're going to focus on reading and writing *text files*. Text files are simply files filled with string data—that is, human-readable characters. In this example, we'll write a text file and then read it.

```python
# String to write
data = "The lazy red fox slept instead of jumping over a dog."

# Write the data
with open("fox.txt", mode = "w", encoding = "utf-8") as f:
    f.write(data)

# Read the file
with open("fox.txt", mode = "r", encoding = "utf-8") as f:
    read_data = f.read()

# Display the results
print("Original  : " + data)
print("From disk : " + read_data)
```

When we run this program, here's what we'll see:

```
Original  : The lazy red fox slept instead of jumping over a dog.
From disk : The lazy red fox slept instead of jumping over a dog.
```

First, we create one line of sample data, then use the `with` statement paired with `open` to open a file (in this case, `fox.txt`), for writing (i.e., `mode = "w"`) with an encoding of UTF-8.

Before we proceed, let's unpack that a bit. When we open the file, we haven't written anything to it yet; we're simply asking the operating system to create the file and return a `handle`, or reference to a file (which is represented as the `f` object). The mode, in this case `"w"`, means that we will be writing to the file.

The `encoding` is the type of system used to represent the text. For many years, computers used ASCII to store text. The ASCII encoding format had 127 characters that consisted of the numbers, English letters, punctuation marks, and various symbols commonly found on a computer keyboard. This standard is still used in some computer operations, but computers now store data with UTF-8 encoding, a format that allows for just over a million characters. Operating systems and programs have gradually shifted to this standard to accommodate non-Latin letters, additional symbols, and emojis.

Inside the `with` block, the object `f`, which represents the file, is accessible. We call the method `write` on the file, and for the argument we pass the `data` string. This writes the file to the `fox.txt` file. When the `with` block ends, the file is closed. By closing a file, we are signifying to the operating system that we aren't going to access the file in that mode (write, or `"w"`, in the first operation) for the time being. This allows other programs to use the file.

In the next `open` statement, we use the same arguments except for the mode, which in this case we specify as `"r"` for read. When we open a file for reading, it is read-only to us. It's possible to tie up the file system by keeping a file open, preventing it from being used in other programs. Because of this, it's a good practice to open a file for writing only when we're going to write to it and to close it when we're done.

NOTE I'm sure you've encountered the frustrating situation of trying to delete or move a file and receiving an error message saying the file is open or is otherwise in use. This indicates that some program on your computer has the file open and hasn't closed it yet, and to prevent data corruption or error, the operating system blocks the request.

When we read the file, we place the contents from the read operation in the `read_data` variable. Leaving the second block closes the file, and then we display both variables so we can see what was written to, and read from, the disk.

This file was created in the same directory in which you stored your program, so you can navigate to this file in your file manager and open it with any text editor—either Visual Studio Code or another editor like Notepad on Windows, TextEdit on macOS, or gedit on Linux. Once the program has finished, feel free to delete the file—or keep it as a souvenir of your first program written to the disk!

Reading Part of a File

We can also read *part* of a file, rather than its entire contents, into a string. This is especially useful if we're dealing with a large file, for several reasons. First, if the file is (or could possibly be) large, this could consume an enormous amount of memory—possibly more than is available on the system. Second, the read time could be considerable, especially on a slower system. Let's modify our example to read just 16 characters.

SNIPPET

12-02.py

```python
# String to write
data = "The lazy red fox slept instead of jumping over a dog."

# Write the data
with open("fox.txt", mode = "w", encoding = "utf-8") as f:
    f.write(data)

# Read the file
with open("fox.txt", mode = "r", encoding = "utf-8") as f:
    read_data = f.read(16)

# Display the results
print("Original  : " + data)
print("From disk : " + read_data)
```

When we run this program, we'll see this:

```
Original  : The lazy red fox slept instead of jumping over a dog.
From disk : The lazy red fox
```

In this case, we passed the number 16 to `read` and received only the first 16 characters. With a string this small, you won't notice the speed difference, even on an extremely slow computer, but if we were dealing with an enormous file, this could be a tremendous timesaver.

When working with large files, it can often be advantageous to read them in small chunks, processing one chunk of data and then proceeding to the next. Reading files like this is usually done with the binary mode (i.e., `"rb"`).

```python
with open("fox.txt", mode = "rb") as f:
    while (c := f.read(32)):
        # Do something with data in c
```

This loop iterates over the file, reading up to 32 bytes at a time. What makes it unique is the `:=` operator (sometimes called the "walrus operator" because it's reminiscent of a walrus lying on its side), which tells Python to assign the return value from `f.read` to the variable `c` and return `True` if successful, thus satisfying the `while` loop condition. Once it reaches the end of the file (or is otherwise unable to read again), the comparison becomes `False`, and the loop is exited.

Working with Multiple Lines

Working with binary mode is not for the faint of heart. Did you notice that in the example in the previous section I didn't specify the encoding? That's because binary mode doesn't support encoding. Generally, binary mode is best used for binary files (files that contain machine code rather than text). If you're using text files, which is our focus in this chapter, and you want to read a large text file in chunks, the `readlines` method is extremely useful.

```python
with open("fox.txt", mode = "r") as f:
    while (l := f.readline()):
        # Do something with the line in l
```

This works just like the previous loop except it reads an entire line at once and puts it in the variable named `l`, returning `True` if it was able to read the line. If it wasn't, it evaluates to `False` and exits the loop. Reading text one line at a time is more efficient for larger files and causes Python to consume fewer resources while running, as it only needs to keep one line at a time in memory.

The `readlines()` (note the plural spelling) is another variation of `read` that reads all the lines of the file into a list.

SNIPPET

<!-- snippet icon -->

12-03.py

```python
# String to write
data = """The lazy red fox slept instead of jumping over a dog.
    The lazy dog ignored the fox and slept as well."""

# Write the data
with open("fox2.txt", mode = "w", encoding = "utf-8") as f:
    f.write(data)

# Read the file
```

```
with open("fox2.txt", mode = "r", encoding = "utf-8") as f:
    read_data = f.readlines()

# Display the results
print("Original  : " + data)
print("From disk : " + str(read_data))
```

When we run this example, we get this:

```
Original  : The lazy red fox slept instead of jumping over a dog.
The lazy dog ignored the fox and slept as well.
From disk : ['The lazy red fox slept instead of jumping over a
dog.\n', 'The lazy dog ignored the fox and slept as well.']
```

The read_data in this example is no longer a string; it's a list, and we must use str with the last print statement to convert it into a string (inline, not permanently).

Standard I/O

You've already outputted text to the screen, which is generally called *standard out*, or stdout for short, and received input from the keyboard, which is generally called *standard in*, or stdin for short. When you do this, you're essentially inputting and outputting from and to special files, and the operating system is translating those reads and writes into requesting input from the keyboard and displaying text on the screen.

However, we can explicitly read and write to standard input and output, which, by default, reads from the keyboard and writes to the screen. The user (or other programs) can then redirect those standard input and output devices to their own input and output, much like a telephone operator from the early 1900s would connect the output of a caller to the input of the number they wanted to reach.

Let's take a quick look at reading from standard in and then outputting to standard out. Afterward, we'll walk through a quick example on how to make use of this functionality. Start a new file in Visual Studio Code and call it inout.py.

SNIPPET

```
# Import sys module
import sys
```

12-04.py

```
# Read stdin into data_in
data_in = sys.stdin.read()

# Write to stdout
bytes_written = sys.stdout.write(data_in)

# Display stats
print("Wrote {} bytes to stdout.".format(bytes_written))
```

When you run this code, you'll need to provide some input via the keyboard. Just type "Hello" or anything else you wish, hit ENTER for a blank line, then hit CTRL+D on macOS and Linux or CTRL+Z followed by ENTER on Windows. The CTRL+D or CTRL+Z keyboard combination tells the `read` function that the data input is finished.

Once you finish with the input, it will display what you typed and how many bytes it wrote to standard output.

```
Testing, 123!
Testing, 123!
Wrote 14 bytes to stdout.
```

Now let's make use of standard out via the terminal. Click on the *Terminal* tab (where the results are displayed) and type the following:

```
python3 inout.py > inout.txt
```

NOTE

The python3 command might not work on Windows. If it doesn't, run the command `python inout.py > inout.txt`

You'll again need to enter some input. Type some text, hit ENTER, then CTRL+D (or CTRL+Z followed by ENTER on Windows). When the program finishes, its standard output will be redirected (via the > symbol on the command line) into a file called `inout.txt`. You can open the text file in Visual Studio Code or another text editor to verify that the contents match what you entered.

You can also use the < symbol on the command line to read data from a file into the standard input device. In fact, both < and > can be used on the same command if you wish.

The benefits of standard in and out are perhaps greatest not for your program but for your users. Being able to redirect the output from the screen to a file can be especially useful for power users and system administrators.

Serialization with Pickle

Serialization is the process of describing every detail of an object in a text format that is stored in a string (and then often written to disk). This process makes it easy to save complex patterns of data without having to format it yourself before writing it.

In addition to saving an object, we can load a serialized object and bring it to life. This is a very common design pattern found in any program that needs to save structured data.

12-05.py

```python
# Import the pickle module
import pickle

# Our data
customer_names = ["Jim Smith", "Amber Dobson", "Al James"]

# Write to disk
with open("customers.dat", mode = "wb") as f:
    pickle.dump(customer_names, f)

# Load the data
with open("customers.dat", mode = "rb") as f:
    loaded_data = pickle.load(f)

print("Original data : " + str(customer_names))
print("Loaded data   : " + str(loaded_data))
```

When we run this program, we'll see this:

```
Original data : ['Jim Smith', 'Amber Dobson', 'Al James']
Loaded data   : ['Jim Smith', 'Amber Dobson', 'Al James']
```

There are several things to note about this example. First, we open the file for writing with the `"wb"` flag, meaning we're writing binary data. This is why I named the file `customers.dat` rather than `customers.txt`. I could have used `customers.txt`, but `.dat` is a generic file extension for binary data. The same binary mode, except with reading specified (`"rb"` for reading binary), is used to load the data. Once the data is loaded with `pickle.load`, the `loaded_data` variable now becomes a list with the exact same contents.

Data serialized with `pickle` can be insecure. A hacker can create a serialized data stream that matches an object you wish to recreate and fill it with malicious data. While a simple video game is probably not a substantial target for this kind of attack, any internet-based application or website that loads data supplied to it by users must do so extremely carefully to avoid security problems.

ClydeBank Coffee Shop: Saving Your Game

It would be nice if our users could save their game mid-progress and restore it whenever they wanted to. Before we get into the code to do just that, you should know that I removed the `utilities.py` file. I wanted to move the game into the `CoffeeShopSimulator` class for easier pickling. Also, this makes the code simpler to read.

In any event, let's first look at the code, then dive into the walk-through.

main.py

CCS-13.py

```python
# ClydeBank Coffee Shop Simulator 4000
# Copyright 2022 (C) ClydeBank Media, All Rights Reserved.

import pickle
import re
from pathlib import Path

# Import the game class from the coffee_shop_simulator module
from coffee_shop_simulator import CoffeeShopSimulator

print("ClydeBank Coffee Shop Simulator 4000, Version 1.00")
print("Copyright (C) 2022 ClydeBank Media, All Rights Reserved.\n")

# If save file exists, see if the player wants to load it
run_game = True
if Path(CoffeeShopSimulator.SAVE_FILE).is_file():
    # Save game exists, do they want to load it?
    response = CoffeeShopSimulator.prompt("There's a saved game. Do you want to load ↦
    ↪ it? (Y/N)", True)
    if re.search("y", response, re.IGNORECASE):
        # Load the game and run!
        with open(CoffeeShopSimulator.SAVE_FILE, mode="rb") as f:
            game = pickle.load(f)
            game.run()
```

```
                # We don't need to run the game again
                run_game = False
        else:
            print("HINT: If you don't want to see this prompt again, remove the " + ↦
            ↪ CoffeeShopSimulator.SAVE_FILE + " file.\n")


if run_game:
    # Create the game object and run it!
    game = CoffeeShopSimulator()
    game.run()


# Say goodbye!
print("\nThanks for playing. Have a great rest of your day!\n")
```

coffee_shop_simulator.py

```
import pickle
import random
import re
import numpy

class CoffeeShopSimulator:

    # Minimum and maximum temperatures
    TEMP_MIN = 20
    TEMP_MAX = 90


    # Length of temperature list
    # (higher produces more realistic curve)
    SERIES_DENSITY = 300


    # Save game file
    SAVE_FILE = "savegame.dat"


    def __init__(self):

        # Get name and store name
        print("Let's collect some information before we start the game.\n")
        self.player_name = self.prompt("What is your name?", True)
        self.shop_name = self.prompt("What do you want to name your coffee shop?", True)
```

```python
        # Current day number
        self.day = 1

        # Cash on hand at start
        self.cash = 100.00

        # Inventory at start
        self.coffee_inventory = 100

        # Sales list
        self.sales = []

        # Possible temperatures
        self.temps = self.make_temp_distribution()

def run(self):
    print("\nOk, let's get started. Have fun!")

    # The main game loop
    running = True
    while running:
        # Display the day and add a "fancy" text effect
        self.day_header()

        # Get the weather
        temperature = self.weather

        # Display the cash and weather
        self.daily_stats(temperature)

        # Get price of a cup of coffee (but provide an escape hatch)
        response = self.prompt("What do you want to charge per cup of coffee? ↦
        ↪ (type exit to quit)")
        if re.search("^exit", response, re.IGNORECASE):
            running = False
            continue
        else:
            cup_price = int(response)
```

```python
# Do they want to buy more coffee inventory?
print("\nIt costs $1 for the necessary inventory to make a cup of coffee.")
response = self.prompt("Want to buy more so you can make more coffee? ↦
↪ (ENTER for none or enter number)", False)

if response:
    if not self.buy_coffee(response):
        print("Could not buy additional coffee.")

# Get price of a cup of coffee
print("\nYou can buy advertising to help promote sales.")
advertising = self.prompt("How much do you want to spend on advertising ↦
↪ (0 for none)?", False)

# Convert advertising into a float
advertising = self.convert_to_float(advertising)

# Deduct advertising from cash on hand
self.cash -= advertising

# Simulate today's sales
cups_sold = self.simulate(temperature, advertising, cup_price)
gross_profit = cups_sold * cup_price

# Display the results
print("\nYou sold " + str(cups_sold) + " cups of coffee today.")
print("You made $" + str(gross_profit) + ".")

# Add the profit to our coffers
self.cash += gross_profit

# Subtract inventory
self.coffee_inventory -= cups_sold

if self.cash < 0:
    print("\n:( GAME OVER! You ran out of cash.")
    running = False
    continue

# Before we loop around, add a day
self.increment_day()
```

```python
            # Save the game
            with open(self.SAVE_FILE, mode="wb") as f:
                pickle.dump(self, f)

    def simulate(self, temperature, advertising, cup_price):
        # Find out how many cups were sold
        cups_sold = self.daily_sales(temperature, advertising, cup_price)


        # Save the sales data for today
        self.sales.append({
            "day": self.day,
            "coffee_inv": self.coffee_inventory,
            "advertising": advertising,
            "temp": temperature,
            "cup_price": cup_price,
            "cups_sold": cups_sold
        })


        # We technically don't need this, but why make the next step
        # read from the sales list when we have the data right here
        return cups_sold


    def buy_coffee(self, amount):
        try:
            i_amount = int(amount)
        except ValueError:
            return False


        if i_amount <= self.cash:
            self.coffee_inventory += i_amount
            self.cash -= i_amount
            return True
        else:
            return False


    def make_temp_distribution(self):
        # Create series of numbers between TEMP_MIN and TEMP_MAX
        series = numpy.linspace(self.TEMP_MIN, self.TEMP_MAX, self.SERIES_DENSITY)


        # Obtain mean and standard deviation from the series
        mean = numpy.mean(series)
```

```python
        std_dev = numpy.std(series)


        # Calculate probability density and return the list it creates
        return (numpy.pi * std_dev) * numpy.exp(-0.5 * ((series - mean) / std_dev) ** 2)


def increment_day(self):
    self.day += 1


def daily_stats(self, temperature):
    print("You have $" + str(self.cash) + " cash on hand and the temperature is ↦
    ↪ " + str(temperature) + ".")
    print("You have enough coffee on hand to make " + str(self.coffee_inventory) ↦
    ↪ + " cups.\n")


def day_header(self):
    print("\n-----| Day " + str(self.day) + " @ " + self.shop_name + " |-----")


def daily_sales(self, temperature, advertising, cup_price):
    # Randomize advertising effectiveness
    adv_coefficient = random.randint(20, 80) / 100


    # Higher priced coffee doesn't sell as well
    price_coefficient = int((cup_price * (random.randint(50, 250) / 100)))


    # Run the sales figures!
    sales = int((self.TEMP_MAX - temperature) * (advertising * adv_coefficient))


    # If price is too high, we don't sell anything
    if price_coefficient > sales:
        sales = 0
    else:
        sales -= price_coefficient


    if sales > self.coffee_inventory:
        sales = self.coffee_inventory
        print("You would have sold more coffee but you ran out. Be sure to buy ↦
        ↪ additional inventory.")


    return sales
```

```python
@property
def weather(self):
    # Generate a random temperature between 20 and 90
    # We'll consider seasons later on, but this is good enough for now
    return int(random.choice(self.temps))


@staticmethod
def prompt(display="Please input a string", require=True):
    if require:
        s = False
        while not s:
            s = input(display + " ")
    else:
        s = input(display + " ")
    return s


@staticmethod
def convert_to_float(s):
    # If conversion fails, assign it to 0
    try:
        f = float(s)
    except ValueError:
        f = 0
    return f


@staticmethod
def x_of_y(x, y):
    num_list = []
    # Return a list of x numbers of y
    for i in range(x):
        num_list.append(y)
    return num_list
```

This is quite a refactor! At first, it might seem that I've undone some of the previous refactors. That's correct, but there are several reasons. I want to make it clear that sometimes there is no perfect or right way to do something in programming. There's my way, your way, and perhaps a few dozen other methods that work just as well. Other programmers may not like your approach. *You* very well may not like your approach after putting away the code for a few days or weeks. But in this case, a fresh set of eyes helps.

While writing this book I realized that the `utility` module certainly served a purpose, but now that the game has been encapsulated into a single class, it's largely unneeded. To move some of these general-purpose functions into the class, I needed to use the `@staticmethod` decorator. This tells Python not to send a copy of `self` (the reference to the class) as the first argument and allows these methods to be used without first creating a copy of the class in object form. This lets us call our `prompt` function now as `CoffeeShopSimulator.prompt()` without using the object. That said, you can still use the object if you want, and even reference those functions within the class.

This wouldn't be ideal if we were interacting with multiple classes via this method. For example, if we had more than just a game object and we needed a function to make use of both (or multiple) objects, a utility function outside the scope of those classes would certainly be preferred. But that isn't the case here, and to make things simple and encapsulated, I moved the functions into the `CoffeeShopSimulator` class and decorated them with `@staticmethod`.

As for saving the game, this is done via `pickle` right before the loop cycles to the next day. Since everything is contained in the game object, we simply dump it to the `savegame.dat` file. When the game loads in `main.py`, it checks for the existence of this file via if `Path(CoffeeShopSimulator.SAVE_FILE).is_file()` and then uses the pickled content from that file to recreate the game object and execute `run()` to jump back into action. Since the loop starts at the beginning (and skips `__init__`), the variables that govern the game's progress won't be overwritten but instead will be loaded as though they were there all along.

Before each day ends, the game is saved via `pickle`, allowing the player to quit anytime and pick up wherever they left off in their previous gaming session.

Chapter Recap

»   Computers accept input from devices that interface with either
    humans (via keyboard and/or mouse), disks (e.g., hard drives, USB
    sticks), or the network. Data can be output to monitors, disks,
    sound devices, networks, and more.

»   Reading and writing data can be done directly from/to the disk or
    via standard I/O.

»   Python's `pickle` module allows us to serialize an object and save it
    for later re-creation.

| 13 |
The Internet

Chapter Overview
» Python has a wide assortment of modules for internet functionality
» The `urllib` module makes it easy to interact with web pages
» You can send email with Python's SMTP support

Python isn't confined to your computer. Armed with the power of the standard library, you have an assortment of tools to retrieve web pages, send and receive email, and even communicate with computers directly over the network.

Fetching a Web Page

Before we get into downloading a web page, we should first cover the terms we'll use in this section. When you enter a *URL* (Uniform Resource Locator) or web address, the browser first makes a connection to the site and then performs a *GET request*. A GET request tells the web server that the browser would like the contents of a page. The request is then filled by the server.

Let's grab the front page of the Python website at www.python.org using Python's standard `requests` module.

SNIPPET

13-01.py

```python
# Import the urllib module
import urllib.request

# URL to GET
url = "https://www.python.org"

# Get the page content
req = urllib.request.Request(url)
with urllib.request.urlopen(req) as response:
    page_content = response.read()
```

In this example, we first import `urllib.request`. The URL is in a separate variable so that it can easily be changed, but we can also specify it inline on the actual request in the next line. In the request, the `req` object is defined by the return value of `urllib.request.Request`, which creates a type of virtual file that can be `read()` to return the page content—which we store in `page_content`.

Since `page_content` is now a string filled with the HTML from the site, we can search that string (using either `find` or regular expressions) to fetch data we can use. Let's use the Wikipedia API (application programming interface—a mechanism for retrieving data with a program) to retrieve a page on Mount Tambora.

SNIPPET

13-02.py

```python
# Import urlopen from the urllib module
from urllib.request import urlopen

# Import regular expression functionality
import re

# Import unescape from HTML
from html import unescape

# URL to GET
url ="https://en.wikipedia.org/w/api.php?action=parse&prop=wikitext&fo ↦
↦ rmat=json&page=Mount_Tambora"

# Request the page
response = urlopen(url)

# Get the page content
page_content = str(response.read())

# Unescape the page
page_content = unescape(page_content)

# Use this regex to find the elevation of Mt. Tambora
regex = r"elevation\_m\s=\s(\d*)"

# Perform the search
result = re.search(regex, page_content)
```

```
# Fetch the second element of the match (which is the elevation)
elevation = result[1]

# Print the elevation
print("The elevation of Mt. Tambora is " + str(elevation) + ".")
```

If you run into any issues while running this code, especially any error regarding SSL certificates, you can implement the following fix. In our testing, some installations of Python used a different certificate authority store, which caused problems with retrieving the data from Wikipedia's API.

```
# Add this to the top of the code
import ssl

ctx = ssl.create_default_context()
ctx.check_hostname = False
ctx.verify_mode = ssl.CERT_NONE

# Then change: response = urlopen(url)
# to the following code:

urlopen(url, context=ctx)
```

This fix forces the `urlopen` function to avoid validating the SSL certificate. While this is perfectly acceptable to do with a non-sensitive site like Wikipedia, this fix would be unadvisable when sending secure data like credit card numbers or personally identifiable information. In that situation, fully uninstalling and then reinstalling Python should fix the issue.

We're doing a few new things in this code sample, so let's step through them. First, we're importing the `unescape` function from the `html` library. This prevents any special characters from interfering in our search. Then, after we fetch the content, we `unescape` the `page_content` string.

Next, we prepare a regular expression that matches a number (up to unlimited digits via the `*`) after `elevation_m` (and a space, equals sign, and a space). After that, we use `re.search` to search through the `page_content` variable and return our matches. This is the first element of the match result:

```
elevation_m = 2850
```

But we want the second (at index 1), which is this:

```
2850
```

It's all downhill from that point. We print the result, and the user is now informed as to the height of Mount Tambora.

NOTE

This functionality assumes that the Wikimedia (the software powering Wikipedia) API hasn't changed. This is the most current version as of this printing. It's remarkably stable, but if you find it has changed, you can consult www.mediawiki.org/wiki/API:Main_page for updated details. Generally, any change will merely involve modifying one of the parts of the API URL.

Saving a Web Page

We can retrieve a web page and then save the contents of that string to a file with the `html` file extension, which saves the page for offline viewing.

SNIPPET

13-03.py

```python
# Import the urllib module
import urllib.request

# URL to GET
url = "https://www.python.org"

# Get the page content
req = urllib.request.Request(url)
with urllib.request.urlopen(req) as response:
    page_content = response.read()

# Save to python.html, writing in binary mode
# to preserve encoding defined by web server
with open("python.html", mode = "wb") as f:
    f.write(page_content)
```

Notice that we open the file for writing in binary mode. This is done to preserve the encoding method from the HTML that we download from the web server. Not every web page uses UTF-8, especially those written in non-Latin languages.

Sending an Email

Sending an email in Python is easy, but email in general has become complex and error-prone. Most of this new complexity is well-intentioned (e.g., fighting spam, adding functionality to email that was never intended to be part of the standard, etc.), but the result is that it's difficult to guarantee that the code I'm about to show you will even work in your situation.

Nevertheless, the concepts in this example are important to learn, and if you're working on a server, this code will very likely work. Unfortunately, due to the nature of your internet service provider's or email provider's security settings, it may be difficult to find the mix of parameters that works for you.

IMPORTANT

The purpose of this code is not to give you an exact guide on working with your email, but rather a general overview of the flow you can use to send mail with most web providers.

You will need to consult your email provider's SMTP settings to get the values for your SMTP port and the SMTP server (Simple Mail Transfer Protocol, or outbound mail server). And, depending on your security settings, you may need to generate an SMTP password (Google calls this an "Application Password"). This code assumes you're using SSL (Secure Sockets Layer; when paired with SMTP this is sometimes called SMTPS), which is almost exclusively the default configuration now for mail servers.

SNIPPET

13-04.py

```python
# Import smtplib and ssl modules
import smtplib, ssl

# Define message parameters
from_email = "your@email.com"
to_email = "their@email.com"
subject = "Test email from Python"
message = "This is a test email from Python."

# Add subject to top of message
message = "Subject: " + subject + "\n\n" + message

# Define mail server parameters
smtp_server = "your.mail.server"
smtp_port = 465

# Get your email password
smtp_pass = input("Please enter your SMTP password: ")
```

```
# Create an SSL context
context = ssl.create_default_context()

# Send the mail
try:
    with smtplib.SMTP_SSL(smtp_server, smtp_port, context = context) as smtp_srv:
    smtp_srv.login(from_email, smtp_pass)
    smtp_srv.sendmail(from_email, to_email, message)
except Exception as e:
    # Display details about any error that occurred
    print(e)
```

There's a lot going on in this code, so let's break it down into manageable pieces. First, we import the `smtplib` and `ssl` modules. Next we assign some necessary parameters about the message. The message variable is then modified to have the subject inserted at the top, which the SMTP server expects.

After defining the server hostname and port, the code prompts the user for the SMTP server password. Technically, we could assign the password to the `smtp_pass` variable right in the code, but it's bad practice to include passwords in your code. If our source code were ever to become public, our email password would also be visible, creating a huge security problem.

Next, we set up SSL support and start a `with` block that establishes an object called `smtp_srv` that interfaces directly with the SMTP server. The `login` method of `smtp_srv` sets the credentials for the mail server, and the actual mail sending is done via the `sendmail` method. If any exceptions occur, they are displayed.

As I said before, sending email is a tricky subject and you may have to adjust this to work with your mail provider. It's impossible to cover all the variations and issues—in fact, the subject of email could possibly fill an entire book. But these are the general principles of interacting with a mail server.

Chapter Recap

» Python's `urllib` module allows us to download pages and interact with web servers.

» Once we have downloaded the contents of a page, we can extract data from our requests.

» Emails can be sent with Python using SMTP. The ISP or hosting provider needs to be consulted for SMTP hostname and credentials.

| 14 |
Debugging Python Code

Chapter Overview
» Debugging is the art of finding and fixing problems in code
» Logging is very useful for finding bugs
» Visual Studio Code can be a huge help in debugging

Even though we hold incredible power in our hands as they execute the code we've crafted through blood, sweat, and tears, we as programmers feel powerless at times over the smallest of bugs that creep into our code.

It's extremely helpful to have all the information you can possibly assemble about a problem when trying to solve it. Sometimes it's a simple typo. In fact, typos have been some of the hardest problems for me to find. Visual Studio Code and other development environments will point out if you've made a mistake with indentation or misspelling a function name, but those aren't exactly the typos I'm talking about. I'm talking about the perfectly valid code—complete with a swapped variable, a plus instead of a minus, a greater than instead of a less than, or some off-by-one index error—that has made me question my ability to program and, deep into the night right before a deadline, life in general.

As I've said several times before, things will go wrong. No matter how careful you are or how many exception handlers you use, your program will fail or, worse, produce incorrect results. That's where the art (notice I didn't say science) of debugging comes into play.

Logging
If I could choose only one debugging tool, it would be logging. Logging is the process of writing diagnostic data (oftentimes the value of variables at different stages of execution) to the screen or to disk. I can't think of any more effective and accessible technique for getting an internal view of what's going in inside a program.

Many programmers associate logging with log files written to disk. While this is certainly a common and useful method of logging data, we can also display it to the screen (under certain circumstances) or send it over the network to another system. We're going to discuss the first two methods in detail, as you'll use them the most in your Python programming work.

Displaying Data on the Screen

One of the easiest and most often used techniques in debugging is to print out the values of variables before, during, and after whatever misbehaving function calls them.

SNIPPET

14-01.py

```
x = input("What is x? ")

print("x = " + x)

y = input("What is y? ")

print("y = " + y)

if (x > y):
    print("x > y")
else:
    print("x < y")
```

If I was having problems with the comparison, the print statements after each input would show me what was collected each time, and then I could use this to help troubleshoot the comparison. This is, of course, a trivial example, but it highlights the usefulness of displaying variables as we go.

In other cases, we can use statements like this:

```
print("Reached first function call.")
```

or ...

```
print("Inside for loop.")
```

... to see if execution reaches certain points in our code. I've done this countless times when something I expected to function didn't run.

Knowing that we at least got to that part of the code, or made it into the loop, can help us figure out what's going wrong.

This technique of displaying messages to the screen is extremely useful while we're developing the program, but it has several disadvantages. First, it can get a bit messy. When I write these temporary values to screen, I tend to comment them out (to put comments in front of the lines of code) when I'm done with them but leave the print line there in case I need it again. Too many commented-out print functions in code can start to pile up and hurt readability.

But we don't necessarily have to get rid of all our temporary print statements to make things more readable. We can create a function that displays the data we want to show only if a variable named debug is set to True.

SNIPPET

14-02.py

```
# Define this in the main program
debug = True


def debug_msg(msg):
    if (debug):
        print(msg)
```

We can now call debug_msg whenever we want to show something on the screen, but only if the debug variable in the main scope is set to True. When we're ready to release our program to the public or no longer need the debugging feature, we can set debug = False in the top of our code to prevent the debug_msg function from printing anything to screen.

This is a primitive form of logging. We are "logging" the data in that we are displaying it for debugging use. That said, if we don't happen to see the debugging message (i.e., it scrolls by too fast), it doesn't do us much good. In that case, we may want to consider logging to a file.

Logging to Disk

Logging to disk is a bit more work than writing to the screen, but it's more durable and provides a better record of more complex events. Rather than hoping to catch certain messages on the display before they scroll away, we create and append to the log file that will have everything we need to find the problem in our code.

Fortunately, Python has a built-in module to help with that.

14-03.py

```
# Import the logging module
import logging

# Configure the module
logging.basicConfig(
    filename = "test.log",
    encoding = "utf-8",
    level = logging.DEBUG)
```

With this, I've imported the `logging` module and configured it with the following features:

» The log file is defined as `test.log`
» The encoding is UTF-8 (styled `utf-8` in Python)
» The log level is DEBUG, defined in the logging module, so we access it with `logging.DEBUG`

The logging level is the level at which we want to receive messages. Anything below the level of priority we specify doesn't get logged, and the level we supply in the `level` argument and above does get logged (figure 39).

GRAPHIC

fig. 39

LEVEL	PRIORITY	DESCRIPTION
`logging.DEBUG`	10	Provides the most detail. Useful for diving deep into problems.
`logging.INFO`	20	Used for basic information about execution.
`logging.WARNING`	30	Used for important warnings about potential hazards.
`logging.ERROR`	40	Used for events that could stop the program.
`logging.CRITICAL`	50	Reserved for the most serious problems.

Using this scheme, DEBUG will give us every log entry, and CRITICAL would skip everything except CRITICAL.

The `logging.DEBUG` value is uppercase to imply that it is a ***constant***—that is, a value that is immutable (read-only) and used as a reference for other code. Technically, though, it's not immutable. In this case, it's just another variable. We can (though we really shouldn't) change `logging.DEBUG` to be any value we wish, not just 10.

To specify a log level, use these functions:

```python
# Log a DEBUG message
logging.debug("This is a debug message.")


# Log an INFO message
logging.info("This is an info message.")


# Log a WARNING message
logging.warning("This is a warning message.")


# Log an ERROR message
logging.error("This is an error.")


# Log a CRITICAL message
logging.critical("Something major went wrong!")
```

Let's try a sample program, this time specifying `WARNING` as the level.

SNIPPET

14-04.py

```python
# Import the logging module
import logging

# Configure the module
logging.basicConfig(
    filename = "test.log",
    encoding = "utf-8",
    level = logging.WARNING)

# Log several messages
logging.debug("This is a debug message.")
logging.info("This is an info message.")
logging.warning("This is a warning message.")
logging.error("This is an error.")
logging.critical("Something major went wrong!")
```

When you run this code, you'll find a file called `test.log` in the same directory as your program. If you examine the file in Visual Studio Code or with any text editor, you'll see only this:

```
WARNING:root:This is a warning message.
ERROR:root:This is an error.
CRITICAL:root:Something major went wrong!
```

The log entries are added to the `test.log` file, and if a file already exists, they are appended so that the log file isn't overwritten. By default, the entries follow a colon-delimited format, where the first entry denotes the severity level (in this case, `WARNING`, `ERROR`, and `CRITICAL` are the only ones shown due to our log level being set to `logging.WARNING`).

The second entry is the name of the logger, and the third entry is the message.

Regarding the logger name, we can choose to use multiple loggers and give each a separate name. This is useful if we need to create multiple logs at once.

```
web_logger = logging.getLogger("jobs")
```

This would create two separate loggers named `web_logger` and `backend_logger` that we could use separately. We would use `web_logger.basicConfig(...)` to configure the first one and `backend_logger.basicConfig(...)` to configure the second, and subsequently call methods like `web_logger.warning("Web warning goes here!")` and `backend_logger.warning("Backend warning goes here!")`.

We can change the message format to show the time. We just need to provide the format argument to `basicConfig`.

SNIPPET

14-05.py

```
logging.basicConfig(
    filename = "test.log",
    encoding = "utf-8",
    format = "%(asctime)s - %(message)s",
    level = logging.WARNING)
```

With this configuration, we'll only see the time, followed by a dash and the message we supply.

```
2022-04-21 00:45:43,639 - Something REALLY bad happened!
```

We can also change the date and time format by supplying a `datefmt` argument to `basicConfig`. It accepts the `strftime` formatting codes found in chapter 11.

ON YOUR OWN

Now that you know how to use Python's logging to help debug, consider adding logging in the ClydeBank Coffee Shop Simulator game. This will be especially helpful if you decide to expand the game's features.

DIGITAL ASSETS

You can include a lot of helpful things such as the line number and function name. For a full list of logging formats, please refer to your Digital Assets at go.quickstartguides.com/python.

Debugging in Visual Studio Code

Visual Studio Code has some great tools for helping you debug your code. I'll cover some of them here, but I didn't include this section until the end of the debugging chapter because you may not always have Visual Studio Code (or any particular piece of software) in your environment.

For example, I often connect to remote machines via SSH (Secure Shell) and edit Python code files with Vim, a console-based text editor. While Vim is an excellent editor, it doesn't have the debugging features of Visual Studio Code or other Python development environments. In those situations, I must use other debugging methods, like logging, to figure out what's going on with the code.

So feel free to make use of these tools. But knowing how to survive without them—much like a digital form of survival bushcraft—is an excellent skill to have.

Let's start with debugging a sample program. It's quite simple, and it suffers from only one fatal flaw—it has an infinite loop. We set `running` to `True` at the beginning and it's never set to `False`, so the `while` loop continues forever.

SNIPPET

14-06.py

```python
# Import the time module so we can use sleep
import time

running = True
a = 0
```

```
while running:
    print("Hello, World!")
    print("a is " + str(a))
    a += 1

    # Pause execution for 1 second
    time.sleep(1)
```

When we run this program, we'll see something like this:

```
Hello, World!
a is 0
Hello, World!
a is 1
```

While it's running, Visual Studio Code is in debugging mode. You'll notice in the *Run* menu it says *Start Debugging*, not just *Start*. Technically, we've been launching the debugger all this time. But our programs up to this point have not had an ongoing process—they've executed and then finished.

NOTE

To stop the program, click the *Run* menu and click *Stop Debugging*. If you're running it in the terminal, you can press CTRL+C.

Now that we're in debugging mode and the `Hello, World!` messages are ticking away, let's look at what it has to offer. First, let's pause execution. We can do that by clicking the *pause* button on the floating debug toolbar near the top right of the screen (figure 40).

IMAGE

fig. 40

The debug toolbar bar that appears whenever a program is run in Visual Studio Code. The *pause* button is the first icon on the left (the two vertical lines).

When we click the *pause* button, it will temporarily halt execution and highlight the line it was currently running. The debug toolbar changes when we're in pause mode (figure 41).

fig. 41

The first icon resumes execution. The second steps over the current line. The third steps into the next function call or loop and pauses at the first line. The fourth steps out of the current function by finishing it, then pausing at the line of code that called it. The next icon restarts execution, and the square icon (stop) ends all execution.

Let's click the *step over* icon, which is the second in the debug bar. When we do so, the variables pane in the top left corner shows our variables (figure 42).

> In some cases, after clicking the *step over* icon, you may need to click *Run* and *Debug*.

fig. 42

∨ **VARIABLES**

  ∨ **Locals**

    > special variables

    a: 240

    running: **True**

    > time: <module 'time' (built-in)>

  > **Globals**

The variables pane of our sample debugging program.

This gives us a view of the current state of our variables, including a and running. If we double-click on one of them, a, for example, and change the value, it will edit the variable directly in our program's memory. When we resume execution by pressing the *play* button (the first button in the debug bar), we see that the variable named a has increased dramatically! If we double-click on the running variable and enter False, then resume execution, it will continue the current iteration of the while loop and then exit because running will no longer be True.

This example is simple, but it gives us a lot of insight into our program. Not only can we see the value of variables at certain points, but we can adjust them, playing what-if games to see where conditionals and loops are failing.

The next debugging feature I'd like to show you is the ***breakpoint***. A breakpoint is an instruction to the debugger to break (pause) execution on that line. If we want to pause execution at a certain point in our program automatically (rather than having to press pause and simply hope we hit the right line), we hover with our mouse just to the left of the line numbers and click the red circle that appears. A small symbol will appear indicating that a breakpoint has been set at that line (figure 43).

fig. 43

```
  5
  6  ∨ while True:
  7          print("Hello, World!")
▷ 8      |   print("a is " + str(a))
  9          a += 1
 10          time.sleep(1)
 11
```

A breakpoint has been set on line 8.

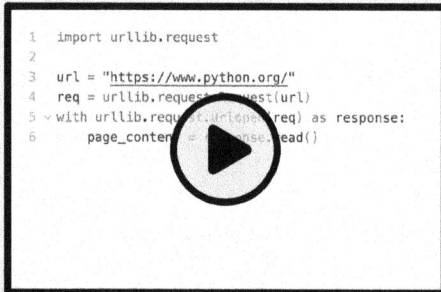

If we resume execution, Visual Studio Code will automatically pause when our program reaches that line, letting us examine and modify variables. If we click the *play* button, execution will resume but will stop again when it reaches this point. To clear the breakpoint when we're done with it, we right-click on the symbol next to the line number and select *Remove Breakpoint*.

Chapter Recap

» Debugging is more of an art than a science. Programs will have errors, and we can't expect them to always be immediately obvious. Developing debugging skills is essential.

» Logging is perhaps the single most important tool for finding bugs. If we're having problems spotting a bug, we should log everything that happens in our program (or at least the important parts) and examine the results.

» Visual Studio Code can be a huge help in debugging, with its variable view and breakpoint features. However, we should be prepared to fall back on other methods, such as logging, as we may not always have Visual Studio Code.

PART IV

ADVANCED PYTHON

| 15 |

Developing Websites

Chapter Overview
  » Python excels at website development
  » Popular lightweight frameworks include `web.py` and Flask
  » Django offers a fully featured website development stack

Python isn't limited to running programs on your computer. You can also use it to power websites and mobile application backends. Running a website with Python is not only completely feasible but highly desirable. Many sites you probably visit at least weekly are powered by Python; big players, including Google, Spotify, Netflix, YouTube, Dropbox, and many more, use Python in at least some capacity.

Even when Python isn't used to serve the actual website content, it's often found in the backend of servers, generating reports, sending emails, and running background tasks. While web development isn't the focus of this book, I'd nevertheless like to show you some common web frameworks and development workflows in Python.

I'll use a bit of HTML in the examples and explain that along the way, but I will warn you up front that any serious web development will utilize, if not require, at least basic knowledge of HTML, CSS, and perhaps some JavaScript. If you aren't familiar with HTML or JavaScript, or have no desire to develop websites with Python, I still encourage you to read through this chapter and follow along with the examples, because I'll be introducing new Python concepts as we go.

web.py

Let's dust off our old friend "Hello, World!" In this case, we'll use the `web.py` framework to host a simple website that displays nothing but our warm, familiar greeting. To do this, we'll first need to install web.py.

On macOS or Linux, open the terminal and run:

```
pip3 install web.py
```

If you're on Windows, run the console and run the same command. If that fails on Windows, it's probably because Python isn't in the system path. In that case, try running the command in the terminal window of Visual Studio Code.

You should see some download and installation messages scroll by as it proceeds. We'll get into `pip` a bit later, but for now, know that it manages our Python code dependencies, allowing us to request the install of a particular module (i.e., `web.py`).

Once `web.py` is installed, we can write our example (a lightly modified take on the featured example at webpy.org):

SNIPPET

15-01.py

```python
# Import web.py
import web

# Define the routes web.py will respond to
routes = (
"/(.*)", "home"
)

# Create app object, providing routes and globals as arguments
app = web.application(routes, globals())

# Define the home class which will respond to our default route
class home:
    # Method to respond to GET requests
    def GET(self, name):
        # Tell the browser we are sending HTML
        web.header("Content-Type", "text/html")
        # Set name to "World" if name not set
        if not name:
            name = "World"
        # Return string to display in browser
        return "<h1>Hello, " + name + "!</h1>"

# Make sure we're in the main program scope, then run!
if __name__ == "__main__":
    app.run()
```

When we run this code, we'll be presented with a URL that looks something like this:

```
http://0.0.0.0:8080
```

If this doesn't work, try http://127.0.0.1:8080/

Before we dive into precisely what this code is doing, let's talk a bit about this URL. The `0.0.0.0` is an ***IP address***. An IP address, or internet protocol address, is an identifier used to differentiate devices on a network. You can think of an IP address much like a street address, in that it helps others find a location.

Most sites have a routable address—that is, an address that can be routed, or delivered, to different networks to serve the request. However, the `0.0.0.0` address, in our situation, refers to any IP address on our local computer. When `web.py` listens to this address for requests from browsers, it's essentially saying "listen to any address on this computer and respond to it." This will work regardless of what internet connection we have, or even if we're not connected at all, because it will treat it as a local address.

The 8080 portion of the address, which is separated from the IP by a colon, is the ***port***. A port is even more specific than an IP address, providing a unique point at which to communicate with a particular application—in this case, our Python program. If IP addresses are like street addresses, then ports are much like room or suite numbers, or perhaps even individuals residing at that address.

To summarize, the URL `http://0.0.0.0:8080` lets a client (in this case, our web browser) know that it needs to make a connection to IP address `0.0.0.0` (that is, any local address) on port `8080`. Copy and paste this URL into your browser (while your Python code is still running) and view the glorious result. You should see `"Hello, World!"`

How does this work? Let's get into the particulars of the code. First, we import the `web` module, which is `web.py`. Then we define a tuple that can contain multiple URL patterns and the class that handles them. In our case, we simply define that every URL (i.e., via the regex `/(.*)`, which matches `/` and all URLs) should be handled by the `home` class. If we wanted to handle a list of specific URLs, we'd add multiple pairs to the tuple, the first being the URL pattern regex, and the second the Python class name that handles it. We can specify URL patterns that aren't regular expressions. For example, `"/hello"` would respond to a URL like `http://0.0.0.0/hello`.

Then we create the app object via the `web.application` method. This method takes two arguments: the tuple with the URL patterns and matching class names, and a list of *global variables*. A global variable is a variable that is within the scope of the main program. In our case, we just called inline the `globals()` function, which returns a dictionary of all variables, objects, classes, etc., in the global (i.e., main program) scope.

Next, we define the class `home`, which has one method: `GET`. In the past we've used method names that are lowercase, but in this situation, `GET`, the HTTP operation to "get" a web page from the server, is always styled in capital letters because that's the actual string sent to the web server. The method `GET` has `self` and `name` as arguments, but if `name` is not set to a value, the string `name` is set to "`World`".

We then use `web.header` to set the `Content-Type` header, that is, a key:value pair sent to the browser before the content of the page is sent, telling the web browser how to interpret the content it will receive. If we had specified `text/plain` instead of `text/html`, or even left out the `web.header` call, it would have rendered plain text and not HTML.

This `if not name` comparison is simply an inversion of `if name`, meaning that if the `name` variable isn't set and thus doesn't evaluate to `True`, the comparison will succeed, and its code block will be processed. This is helpful for when we want to see if a value isn't `True`, and in this case we do. In any event, we return "`Hello, `" and then the `name` variable, then an exclamation point.

In the return text, I've included the HTML tags `<h1>` and `</h1>` (opening the heading 1 tag and closing the heading 1 tag) to make sure the `Hello, World!` content is displayed in big bold heading type. We'll get to how to set the `name` variable in a moment.

Then, outside the `hello` class and back in the main program, we check to see if we're in the main scope (i.e., in the main program and not inside a module). When Python starts, it sets the `__ name __` global variable to `__ main __`. When execution occurs inside of module code, the `__ name __` variable inside of that module is the name of the module. So, by running this comparison, we can make sure that we're in the main program rather than being imported by another file.

When we run `app.run()`, the `web.py` server code launches, listens to the IP `0.0.0.0` and port `8080`, and displays the URL for us so we know how to access it. When we go to that URL in the browser, the `GET` method is executed in the `home` class, which returns the text to display.

The `name` variable doesn't have to be empty. How do we set it? In your browser, try going to the following URL (replacing "You" with your first name, no spaces).

```
http://0.0.0.0:8080/You
```

When I go there, I see this:

```
Hello, Robert!
```

This works because of our regular expression in the `routes` tuple. Recall from chapter 10 that parentheses in regular expressions match a value and return that value. In our route `/(.*)` we are saying "match anything after the forward slash" (i.e., the site root URL), so when we go to `/Robert` (in my case), the `Robert` portion is matched and set as the argument after `self` in the `GET` method. In `GET`, our comparison fails because `name` has a value, thus it's not changed to "`World`" and we see our name in the browser.

NOTE

To stop `web.py`, click the *Run* menu and click *Stop Debugging*. If you're running it in the terminal, you can press CTRL+C.

The `web.py` framework is simple and lightweight, but we've only scratched the surface of its capabilities. To learn more about web.py, please visit https://webpy.org.

Flask

Flask is another popular Python web framework. It has more active development than `web.py`, offers improved performance, and has extensive documentation. Even though Flask supports more modern features, it isn't necessarily the best choice for all web applications written in Python. Both web.py and Flask offer a lightweight system to power your website, so I don't believe there's necessarily a *wrong* choice.

Let's look at an example Hello World site in Flask. But first, we'll need to install it. On macOS or Linux, open the terminal (or open the console in Windows) and run the following:

```
pip3 install flask
```

REMEMBER

If you're having trouble using pip3 on Windows, try running the command in the terminal window of Visual Studio Code.

Once it's installed, create a new example file and name it `hello-flask.py`.

```python
# Import Flask
from flask import Flask

# Create the app object
app = Flask( __ name __ )

# Define the hello function, with route decorator
@app.route("/")
def hello():
    return "<h1>Hello, World!</h1>"
```

Now, go to the *Run* menu in Visual Studio Code and click *Add Configuration*. When prompted, pick *Python*, then *Flask*, then enter hello-flask.py as the file name. If you gave your sample code a different file name, you'll need to enter that instead. Hit ENTER, and when you do, a new file called launch.json will appear.

```json
{
    // Use IntelliSense to learn about possible attributes.
    // Hover to view descriptions of existing attributes.
    // For more information, visit: https://go.microsoft.com/fwlink/?linkid=830387
    "version": "0.2.0",
    "configurations": [
        {
            "name": "Python: Flask",
            "type": "python",
            "request": "launch",
            "module": "flask",
            "env": {
                "FLASK_APP": "hello-flask.py",
                "FLASK_ENV": "development"
            },
            "args": [
                "run",
                "--no-debugger"
            ],
            "jinja": true,
            "justMyCode": true
        }
    ]
}
```

Visual Studio Code generated this file for you and placed it in `.vscode/launch.json`. This file tells Flask how to run your application and sets important *environment variables* like `FLASK_APP` and `FLASK_ENV`. An environment variable is a variable set outside of the program (and outside of Python itself) that can be accessed inside your Python program. We'll talk more about environment variables in chapter 19, but for now, the main point is that they're useful for setting variables outside your program.

Go ahead and run the program. When you do, you'll see this:

```
* Serving Flask app 'hello-flask.py' (lazy loading)
* Environment: development
* Debug mode: on
* Running on http://127.0.0.1:5000 (Press CTRL+C to quit)
* Restarting with stat
```

In this case, the URL we need to open in our browser is `http://127.0.0.1:5000`. The `127.0.0.1` IP references the local machine, and the value after the colon references port `5000`. When you visit the page, you should see `Hello, World!` in big bold letters.

Before we delve more into how VS Code launches our Python program via the `launch.json` file, let's examine the code example. First, we import the `flask` module. Then we create a new object named `app` via Flask and pass the `__name__` global to it. This gives Flask the name of the module that created the object (`__main__` in this case).

Once the `app` object is up and running, functions are defined that determine what data to return. Rather than set up a predefined list of routes, in Flask we merely use a decorator, such as `@app.route("/")`, before the function that defines the behavior we want to perform when responding to that URL. Inside the `hello` function we merely return our favorite greeting. And that's what we see in our browser.

As for the `launch.json` file, the configuration file automatically created for us by Visual Studio Code is in *JSON*, or JavaScript Object Notation, a format that can be used to reconstruct objects in the JavaScript programming language—much like Pickle format can be used to reconstruct Python objects. We'll discuss JSON a little later in this chapter.

The `launch.json` file, in addition to setting some environment variables, also tells Flask about our application and sets some parameters it needs to properly run it. Granted, there isn't much configuration to do for our `Hello, World!` application, and the defaults in the file are fine for our purposes, but this gives us a lot of flexibility in how we launch Flask.

To stop Flask, click the *Run* menu and click *Stop Debugging*. If you're running it in the terminal, you can press CTRL+C.

This is just a taste of what Flask has to offer. It has an extensive set of features and can handle websites both large and small. To learn more about Flask, visit https://palletsprojects.com/p/flask.

Connecting to a Database

Python can be used to interface with nearly any *database* server. But before we get into that, we should discuss what databases do and how we interact with them. Databases store data. I know that's an incredibly simplistic and almost tautological definition, but that's essentially what they do. The magic of databases is in *how* they store the data.

Previously, we wrote text files to disk. This is a perfectly fine way to store data, but it's not easily *scalable*, meaning that it doesn't grow well with increased usage and complexity. Of course, we can store data on a disk with great efficiency and performance, but it's hard. Writing data in a linear fashion is easy, but modifying it in place—including saving enough space for anticipated data—can be incredibly tricky. Database programmers have spent decades optimizing these routines, taking a lot of the hard work off your back. Unless you have a good reason to avoid it, using a database to store anything but the most trivial data is strongly recommended.

There are two common types of databases—relational and document. In a relational database, data is stored in tables, much like a spreadsheet, with columns defining the fields of data and each row containing a new item to be stored. Relational databases are usually queried, or read from, using SQL (Structured Query Language). SQL allows us to pose questions to the database with a wide assortment of conditions, sort options, pagination, etc., and to receive spreadsheet-like answers with columns delineating separate rows of data.

A document storage database, a kind of "NoSQL" database, stores data in collections of documents (often in a JSON-like format) rather than using the table/column/row paradigm (figure 44). Unlike with relational databases, we don't have to define the columns up front; they can be added on the fly. Document storage databases aren't as fast at retrieving large numbers of records, but they can be faster at creating or updating large numbers of records.

RELATIONAL DATABASES

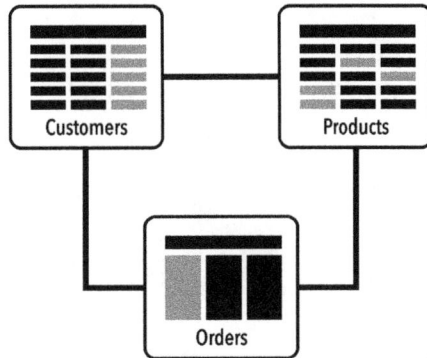

DOCUMENT DATABASES (NoSQL)

fig. 44

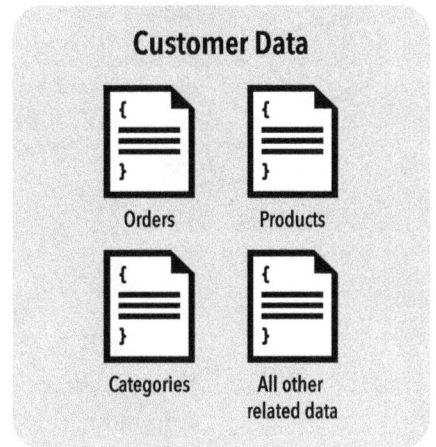

Whichever you choose to use, Python has you covered. Python can connect to pretty much every kind of database server, including MySQL, PostgreSQL, Microsoft SQL, Oracle, MongoDB, and more. Small applications can even use lightweight solutions like SQLite. Since SQLite is simple to set up and ideal for local development.

In the following example, we're going to demonstrate connecting to MySQL. However, setting up a database server is beyond the scope of this book, so we'll assume here that the database has already been set up for you.

You will need the `mysql-connector-python` package, and you can install it with this:

```
pip3 install mysql-connector-python
```

Your installation may fail if you don't have MySQL installed, so if you receive an error, you can go to https://dev.mysql.com and install it.

IMPORTANT

Installing a database server on your computer can take up memory and CPU time that you might not have to spare—especially if you have an older computer. You can install MySQL and choose to run it only when you're programming, then stop it. Or you can run MySQL on a cloud-based server and connect to it remotely. For more information on starting and stopping MySQL, please see https://dev.mysql.com/doc/mysql-startstop-excerpt/8.0/en.

Once you have the package installed, you can run the following code:

```
# Import mysql-connector-python
import mysql.connector


db = mysql.connector.connect(
    host = "localhost",
    user = "dbuser",
    password = "dbpass",
    database = "dbname"
)
```

You'll need to replace `localhost`, `dbuser`, `dbpass`, and `dbname` with the correct values, and they will vary. If you've just installed it on your computer, the hostname will almost certainly be `localhost` and the user is probably `root`. If you haven't set a password on the database server, you can probably leave that blank, but I highly recommend running the `mysql-secure-installation` tool (on the console/terminal) to set a root password and otherwise optimize the security of your installation. On Windows, the install wizard prompts you to do this, but on macOS and Linux, you may need to take this additional step.

The `dbname` parameter is the name of the database to use. Database servers like MySQL can host multiple databases, so specifying the name helps the server scope the queries to the tables and rows inside that database.

Once this code executes, you'll have a `db` object that is your gateway to the database server. Now let's query some data with SQL.

```
# Import mysql-connector-python
import mysql.connector


# Connect to the database
db = mysql.connector.connect(
    host = "localhost",
    user = "dbuser",
    password = "dbpass",
    database = "dbname"
)


# Grab a cursor object from the database connector
cursor = db.cursor()
```

```
# Run an SQL query to get all columns from the orders table
cursor.execute("SELECT * FROM orders")

# Return all results from the query
orders = cursor.fetchall()

# Step through orders and display order details
for order in orders:
    print(order)
```

In this example, we connect, then obtain a cursor context that allows us to execute queries on the database. Then we run SELECT * FROM orders, which means "select all columns from the orders table." The cursor.fetchall() method will obtain the results from the query and put them in an object named orders, which we can iterate over in the for loop.

NOTE *This code won't work on an empty database, because the table orders would have to exist first. If the orders table exists but is empty, the for loop will have nothing to iterate through, and execution will continue to the next line.*

This example is specific to MySQL, but other relational databases, such as PostgreSQL, are similar. For more information, please see the Python section of the documentation for your database server.

Django

The two frameworks we've discussed so far, web.py and Flask, are very thin web development frameworks. Django, on the other hand, contains a full stack of features, including an out-of-the-box admin interface for your data, *search engine optimization* (SEO), built-in web security, web content *caching* and *content delivery network* (CDN) integration, and an *object relational mapping* (ORM) layer for easy database integration.

I've thrown out a lot of web development industry buzzwords, so let's step through them one by one and define them.

> » **Search engine optimization** is the science (and art) of optimizing web pages so that they rank well in search engine results.

» **Caching** in general is the process of preloading frequently accessed content from a slower storage mechanism (i.e., a database or disk) and keeping it in memory for fast retrieval. In the context of the web, this generally means loading it from a database and keeping it in memory.

» **Content delivery networks** are globally distributed media servers that distribute images and other website assets much more quickly than a normal web server. When we request a site using a CDN, the assets are retrieved from the CDN servers closest to us, accelerating the page load.

» An **object relational mapping** is an interface to the database that abstracts tables as classes and the rows of data as objects. The properties of the object are the columns of the row (figure 45). ORMs make it easier to interact with SQL databases.

OBJECT RELATIONAL MAPPING

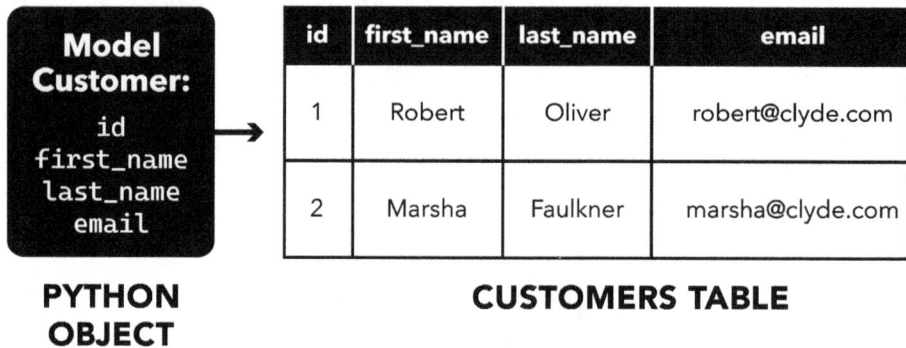

GRAPHIC

fig. 45

Model Customer:
id
first_name
last_name
email

id	first_name	last_name	email
1	Robert	Oliver	robert@clyde.com
2	Marsha	Faulkner	marsha@clyde.com

PYTHON OBJECT

CUSTOMERS TABLE

Now that you know its features, let's discuss Django in a bit more detail. I'd like to go over some of the data modeling and routing in Django that both set it apart from other Python-based web frameworks and illustrate more in-depth features of Python.

First, let's look at the folder structure of a basic Django site. In this example, I've called the site "coffeeshop."

```
coffeeshop/
    manage.py
    coffeeshop/
        __init__.py
        settings.py
        urls.py
        asgi.py
        wsgi.py
```

This structure may look familiar to you, because it contains a Python package. The `coffeeshop` folder is the main folder for the website. The `manage.py` file is a module that allows for command-line administration of the site. The `coffeeshop` folder inside this folder is the root of the Python package, and the `__init__.py` file defines the `coffeeshop` folder as a package. The `settings.py` file contains, as you might expect, settings that are specific to the website. The `urls.py` file contains the routing info to connect various URLs to functionality within the Django application. The `asgi.py` and `wsgi.py` files are there to interface with web servers.

Django uses a *model–view–controller* (MVC) architecture. The models are just classes that define the relationship to the data; in other words, the `Orders` class has `order` objects, where the table name is `orders` and each row represents a single `order`. The model can also handle interactions with other models and actions to perform upon certain events (like updating an `updated_at` column in the table whenever the row is updated).

The controllers normally contain the bulk of the *business logic*—that is, the code that performs the bulk of an application's unique workload. The controllers serve as the glue between models (which represent and process the data) and views.

Views are what the user sees. They can be pages to read or forms to fill out and POST back to the web server. The views are derived from the controller, and when a view page has a form to send back to the web server via a POST request, it is done through the controller.

Many benefits are conferred by this separation of concerns between the parts of the application the user can interact with and the internal logic and data handling; these benefits include a potential increase in security and performance. Most importantly, MVC makes it easier for you and others to work on your code. It encourages, by default, the don't repeat yourself (DRY) principle.

There are varying interpretations of the MVC paradigm. For example, Django calls the controller the view and the view the template. The theory behind this, as stated in the Django FAQs, is that the view is what gets presented to the user. Since the controller in the MVC pattern is responsible for this, Django considers it the view. And the Django template is the appearance of how that data is presented.

In my view, there isn't a particular right or wrong way to label the individual components of the paradigm. The key takeaway of MVC is the separation of concerns between data models, business logic, and presentation of data to the user.

A simple "Hello, World!" page could be rendered like this (in `coffeeshop/views.py`):

```python
from django.http import HttpResponse

def index(request):
    return HttpResponse("Hello, World!")
```

And the `urls.py` that connects this view to the index would look like this:

```python
from django.urls import path

from . import views

urlpatterns = [
    path('', views.index, name='index'),
]
```

A data model for the `Customer` class (stored in the `customers` table) would be similar to this:

```python
from django.db import models

class Customer(models.Model):
    first_name = models.CharField(max_length=64)
    last_name = models.CharField(max_length=64)
```

Objects derived from the `Customer` model would represent a row in the `customers` table and contain properties like `first_name`, `last_name`, and any others we added. This would let us access and update the data in these objects without having to write SQL or directly interact with the database.

This has been an extremely brief, whirlwind tour of Django. There are many more features I'd love to show you, but this would quickly become a book on Django if I did. Hopefully I've whetted your appetite for more, and if you're interested in writing web applications, I highly recommend you give the tutorial a try. You can learn more at https://docs.djangoproject.com.

JSON

JSON, or JavaScript Object Notation, is a way to serialize data structures (much like Pickle) for use with other programs or systems. While JSON was born from JavaScript, Python has functionality to import and export data using this format.

JSON is very popular, and most web APIs support it. Furthermore, when writing web applications, we can communicate directly with JavaScript code by using JSON.

SNIPPET

15-05.py

```
# Import the json module
import json

# Create a menu dictionary
menu = {"name": "Hot Chocolate", "price": 3.99}

# Convert to JSON
menu_json = json.dumps(menu)

# Display JSON
print(menu_json)
```

When we run this code, we'll see that the JSON object looks identical to the Python dictionary. In this simple example, they are interchangeable; however, this isn't always the case, as JavaScript Object Notation is quite different in many respects from Python data structures. That said, the Python `json` module contains the logic necessary to convert Python data to JSON and convert JSON to Python data. As long as the Python object is a dictionary, tuple, list, string, integer, float, True/False, or None, `json` can handle it. To load JSON, simply use the `json.loads` function.

```
# Import the json module
import json

# Sample JSON retrieved via API POST (note the single quotes)
sample_json = '{"name": "Hot Chocolate", "price": 3.99}'

# Convert from JSON into Python dictionary
menu = json.loads(sample_json)

# Display menu dictionary
print(menu)
```

You might be interested to know that with just the `json` module and a thin web framework like `web.py` or Flask, you can build an API server to respond to requests from a mobile app. In fact, I've built interfaces just like this. Pair it with a database server and you have the basic Python programming knowledge required to write the next great app!

ON YOUR OWN

Write out the sales data to a JSON file when the user quits the ClydeBank Coffee Shop Simulator game. Then you can use one of the web frameworks we've mentioned to make a website that reads this data and displays stats about the sales totals.

Chapter Recap

» For simple website projects, it's hard to beat the simplicity of `web.py` or Flask. These frameworks are often used for API servers or simple websites.

» Django is a better choice for more complex sites, especially if you need extensive, out-of-the-box functionality. The administration pages alone can save you a lot of time.

» Python can connect to many different relational and document-based databases.

» Python can read and write JSON, or JavaScript Object Notation, for interaction with JavaScript.

| 16 |
Interfacing with SQLite

Chapter Overview
» SQLite is a simple, cross-platform database engine
» A table is like a spreadsheet with columns and rows
» SQL statements can SELECT (read), INSERT (add), UPDATE, and DELETE data

SQLite is a lightweight, cross-platform SQL database that is self-contained, meaning it doesn't need a separate server process like most other database engines. For learning and demonstration purposes, this is ideal because we can avoid the complex setup, security, and reliability concerns that are often related to database servers. However, just because SQLite is lightweight and easy to use doesn't mean it's a slouch. Its ability to be embedded into other software is one of the reasons it's the most used database engine in the world.

The sTunes Database
To demonstrate SQLite and Python's connections to it, we'll use a sample database from the *SQL QuickStart Guide* by Walter Shields, published by ClydeBank Media. You don't need the book to work through this example, but if you want a deep dive into SQLite, consider checking out this marvelous SQL tutorial.

NOTE

Visit the Digital Asset URL to download the sTunes.db file.

Installation
Installing SQLite is simple, but the instructions differ depending on your operating system.

Windows

Navigate to the SQLite download page (www.sqlite.org/download.html) and download the SQLite tools bundle (titled `sqlite-tools-win32-x86` with a version number after it) under the "Precompiled Binaries for Windows" section.

NOTE If you're running Windows Subsystem for Linux (WSL or WSL2), the instructions to install SQLite will differ based on which Linux distribution you're using inside the WSL terminal. Follow the instructions below for the Linux distribution of your choosing.

This ZIP file will contain several binary programs. The one we're after is sqlite3.exe. It doesn't really matter where you put these files, but where you put them will impact how the program is run.

If you put them in your `Source` folder, as described in the introduction, then the full path will be similar to this:

```
C:\Users\You\Source\sqlite3.exe
```

In this case, `You` will be replaced with your username. And Windows provides an environment variable to easily reference your home directory, so the path will look like this:

```
%USERPROFILE%\Source\sqlite3.exe
```

If you choose to put `SQLite3` binaries (especially `sqlite3.exe`) in another folder, you'll need to adjust the command to match that location.

macOS

SQLite (available as the sqlite3 program via the terminal) is preinstalled on modern macOS systems.

Linux

SQLite is probably preinstalled on your distribution, but if not, try running these commands:

```
# Debian, Ubuntu, Linux Mint, and other Debian-based distros
apt install sqlite3
```

```
# Fedora, Red Hat Enterprise Linux, and related distros
yum install sqlite

# Arch, Manjaro, and other Arch-based distros
pacman -S sqlite
```

Running SQLite

On macOS, Linux, and Windows with WSL, simply run ...

```
sqlite3
```

... on the terminal / command line. To use `sqlite3.exe` on Windows, run:

```
%USERPROFILE%\Source\sqlite3.exe
```

If you put your binary elsewhere, you'll need to modify this location as discussed in the installation section of the chapter.

If you type the name of the database you want to open at the end of the command (followed by a space), you'll open that database, which will allow you to run SQL queries on that data. For example, if our database is named `sTunes.db` and we're running the command from the same folder, we'll see this:

```
sqlite3 sTunes.db
```

While fully exploring the database is beyond the scope of this chapter, we can use a few simple commands to browse the structure of the sTunes database. When we start SQLite, we'll see this:

```
sqlite3 sTunes.db
SQLite version 3.37.0 2021-12-09 01:34:53
Enter ".help" for usage hints.
sqlite>
```

The `sqlite>` is our prompt for commands.

DETOUR

The `sqlite>` prompt is a command loop. Let's imagine that we're writing it. In Python, it might look something like this:

```
running = True
while running:
    cmd = input("sqlite> ")
    # Use regular expressions to parse cmd
    # Check for matches against defined commands
    if cmd == ".quit":
        running = False
```

If we run this in Python, we'll notice that it asks for input over and over until we finally type `.quit`, which is the same command used to exit sqlite3.

The actual command loop of sqlite3 is quite a bit more complicated, but I wanted to show you the overall concept in Python.

If you were going to write something similar, what kind of code would you use to check for various commands?

A Brief Tour of sTunes

First, let's look at the tables, the structures that store rows of data. Think of tables like spreadsheets—collections of data rows separated by columns. To see a list of the tables, type …

```
.tables
```

… and hit ENTER.

If we want to see the structure of a table—that is, the definition of columns within the table—we can use the `.schema` command.

```
.schema tracks
```

In this example, `tracks` is the name of the table we want to see. When we run this, we'll see the following:

```
CREATE TABLE IF NOT EXISTS "tracks"
(
    [TrackId] INTEGER PRIMARY KEY AUTOINCREMENT NOT NULL,
    [Name] NVARCHAR(200)  NOT NULL,
    [AlbumId] INTEGER,
```

```
      [MediaTypeId] INTEGER  NOT NULL,
      [GenreId] INTEGER,
      [Composer] NVARCHAR(220),
      [Milliseconds] INTEGER  NOT NULL,
      [Bytes] INTEGER,
      [UnitPrice] NUMERIC(10,2)  NOT NULL,
      FOREIGN KEY ([AlbumId]) REFERENCES "albums" ([AlbumId])
        ON DELETE NO ACTION ON UPDATE NO ACTION,
      FOREIGN KEY ([GenreId]) REFERENCES "genres" ([GenreId])
        ON DELETE NO ACTION ON UPDATE NO ACTION,
      FOREIGN KEY ([MediaTypeId]) REFERENCES "media_types" ([MediaTypeId])
        ON DELETE NO ACTION ON UPDATE NO ACTION
      );
CREATE INDEX [IFK_TrackAlbumId] ON "tracks" ([AlbumId]);
CREATE INDEX [IFK_TrackGenreId] ON "tracks" ([GenreId]);
CREATE INDEX [IFK_TrackMediaTypeId] ON "tracks" ([MediaTypeId]);
```

Here we have the SQL statements necessary to generate the table structure for `tracks`. And, as we look through the output, we can see the names of the columns, like `TrackId`, `Name`, `AlbumId`, `MediaTypeId`, `GenreId`, `Composer`, `Milliseconds`, `Bytes`, and `UnitPrice`.

The FOREIGN KEYs basically tell SQLite that the `AlbumId`, `GenreId`, and `MediaTypeId` are references to other tables. This is where the term "relational database" comes from; these tables have columns that carry references to related data.

Now let's run an SQL query, which differs from a command like `.table` or `.schema` in that we're going to actually ask the database for data—in this case, the contents of the `tracks` table.

```
select * from tracks;
```

We put a semicolon at the end of our SQL commands in SQLite so the prompt knows we've finished entering data. When we run this command, a full listing of the tracks is displayed. The `tracks` table is too much to show here, so let's look at the first five rows of the `albums` table.

```
select * from albums limit 5;

1|For Those About To Rock We Salute You|1
2|Balls to the Wall|2
```

```
3|Restless and Wild|2
4|Let There Be Rock|1
5|Big Ones|3
```

These are the first five rows in the `albums` table, with each column separated by a pipe symbol (the key above the backslash on your keyboard). If you'd like a more user-friendly view, you can set the mode to "table."

```
.mode table
```

Then when you rerun the query, it will be displayed in an attractive format.

```
+-------------+--------------------------------------------+----------+
| AlbumId     |                   Title                    | ArtistId |
+-------------+--------------------------------------------+----------+
| 1           | For Those About To Rock We Salute You      | 1        |
| 2           | Balls to the Wall                          | 2        |
| 3           | Restless and Wild                          | 2        |
| 4           | Let There Be Rock                          | 1        |
| 5           | Big Ones                                   | 3        |
+-------------+--------------------------------------------+----------+
```

More SQL: Beyond SELECT

We can do more than view data, of course. By using INSERT and UPDATE SQL statements, we can add data, and with the DELETE statement we can delete rows. There are many other commands, including the CREATE TABLE command, but here's an overview of the basics.

Insert

To insert data into a table, run the following:

```
insert into table (column1, column2, column3) values (X, Y, Z);
```

In this example, replace `table` with the name of the table (e.g., `tracks`), columns 1 through 3 with column names (e.g., `AlbumId`, `Title`, and `ArtistId`), and X, Y, and Z with the appropriate data to add.

Update

To update an existing row:

```
update table set column1 = value1, column2 = value2 where id = X;
```

In the previous example, `table` is the name of the table, `column1` and `column2` are column names, `value1` and `value2` are the data to set, and `id` is the column to check for the value of `X` to limit the update to that particular row. We can specify a condition that will match multiple rows, and we can update as many columns at once as we like (separated by commas).

Be careful when running UPDATE statements. If you don't add a conditional, it will update every row in the table with the values you specify for each column. This could be disastrous on a live production database. There's no need to ask how I know this, but you can safely assume I had to immediately restore from backup after this unfortunate incident.

Delete

To delete an existing row, run this:

```
delete from table where id = X;
```

In the previous example, `table` is the name of the table, and `id` is the column to check for the value of `X` to limit the deletion to that row. We can specify a condition that will match multiple rows, and we can update as many columns at once as we like (separated by commas).

Be especially careful when running DELETE statements. If you don't add a conditional, it will delete every row in the table. This could be disastrous on a live production database. I haven't done this (thank goodness!) because the update snafu that I may or may not have been part of certainly drilled into my head the importance of triple-checking UPDATE and DELETE statements.

Querying Data with Python

Python includes SQLite support in its standard modules. Before we delve into an example, though, be sure you have `sTunes.db` downloaded and you know where it is located on your disk. For this code, I recommend creating a new folder in your `Source` folder called `sqlite`, and if you take this approach, you can put your `sTunes.db` file in that folder—keeping everything simple for this exercise. If you want to have your database in another location, that's fine, but you'll have to add the full path to its location to the name of the file.

```python
# Import the sqlite3 module
import sqlite3

# Create a db object by connecting to the sTunes.db database
db = sqlite3.connect("sTunes.db")

# Run a SELECT query, then loop through
# the results and display the row data

query = "select * from tracks"

for row in db.execute(query):
    print(row)
```

In this example, we import the `sqlite3` module and create a connection object named `db` that is returned from the `sqlite3.connect` function. This `db` object has an `execute` method that can process our SQL statements (specified in the `query` string). In this case, we can iterate over the results, placing the data in `row` so we can print it inside the loop. When we run this code, we'll see a listing of all the tracks stored in the database.

ON YOUR OWN

Use the sqlite3 `.tables` command to see a list of the tables, then modify your query string to select the contents from other tables.

Modifying Data with Python

We can run other statements, too, like INSERT, UPDATE, and even DELETE. If we run those commands, we don't need to iterate over the results.

```python
# Don't run this unless you really want
# to see how a delete query works

query = "delete from tracks where TrackId = 3500"
db.execute(query)
```

If we execute this code, it will delete the row matching `TrackId` with the number 3500. Goodbye, Franz Schubert's string quartet!

Further Ideas

This is just a small sample of what you can do with SQLite and Python. To get a better feel for the capabilities of SQLite, I recommend querying other tables, inserting your own songs, or perhaps even using a web framework like `web.py` or Flask to view the data. The possibilities are endless!

Chapter Recap

» SQLite is a lightweight, cross-platform database engine that can store a database in a single file. We can administer the data with the `sqlite3` executable program and interface with the database in Python via the standard `sqlite3` module.

» Databases are made up of one or more tables, and each table is much like a spreadsheet with columns (fields) and rows (entries) of data.

» Using SQL, we can SELECT (read), INSERT (add), UPDATE, and DELETE data. We can perform other SQL commands as well to modify the table and other database operations.

| 17 |

Test-Driven Development

Chapter Overview
 »   Test-driven development makes for better code
 »   Unit testing ensures proper operation of foundational components
 »   Strive for good test coverage

Test-driven development is a paradigm in programming that encourages developers to write a test first to make sure their code does what it is supposed to do, then write the function and run the test. They know when their code is working as intended when their test passes, and if they modify that code in the future, they'll be able to rerun the test to make sure their changes still provide the desired functionality.

By designing tests like this ahead of time—even before we write the original function—we know when the code is successfully run. Testing also detects *regression*, which occurs when code that was previously working breaks. When we add new features in our programs, we don't always think to test items that were already there. Testing each time we make a substantive change or a release of our code to the public ensures that everything is working properly.

Getting Started with Unit Testing

If your application is simple, it might be easy to construct a test that covers the entire application's purpose. For example, in our distance calculation code, simply feeding a question into the class's methods and testing against a known answer is sufficient for basic minimal testing. But in a more complex application, it is likely impossible to encompass all the functionality of the program in one long test.

This is where *unit testing* comes into play. Unit tests are individual checks on specific methods, functions, and other well-defined code blocks that ensure that the application is working as expected. I've worked on programs that had no tests at all (which is far from ideal, especially on big projects) and on code bases featuring thousands of tests. In all that time, I've never thought that there were too many tests. In fact, it's always been the opposite.

Let's construct a simple module (i.e., a Python program file) with a single function, then construct a test for the function. This will involve two different Python files, so let's first write the code for the main program. Let's call it greeting.py.

SNIPPET

17-01.py

```
def say_greeting(name = "World"):
    return("Hello, " + name + "!")
```

Simple enough, right? Now let's construct a test for it. Call this file greeting_tests.py.

SNIPPET

17-02.py

```
# Import the unittest module
import unittest

# Import our greeting module
import greeting

class GreetingTests(unittest.TestCase):
    def test_greeting_without_name(self):
        # Test without an argument
        self.assertEqual(greeting.say_greeting(), "Hello, World!")
    def test_greeting_with_name(self):
        # Test with an argument
        self.assertEqual(greeting.say_greeting("Robert"), "Hello, Robert!")

if __name__ == '__main__':
    unittest.main()
```

If we run this code (that is, the greeting_tests.py program), we'll see the following output:

```
..
----------------------------------------------------------------
Ran 2 tests in 0.001s
OK
```

The exact timing may vary, but see the two dots above the line? Those dots indicate that the two tests we created (test_greeting_without_name and test_greeting_with_name) both passed. Before we dig into the test code itself, let's make one small tweak to `greeting.py` and run the code again.

```python
def say_greeting(name = "World"):
    return("Well hello, " + name + "!")
```

Now switch back to `greeting_tests.py` and run it. The output will change.

```
FF
======================================================================
FAIL: test_greeting_with_name (__main__.GreetingTests)
----------------------------------------------------------------------
Traceback (most recent call last):
    File "/Users/rwoliver2/Source/python-book/greeting_tests.py", line 13, ↦
    ↳ in test_greeting_with_name
        self.assertEqual(greeting.say_greeting("Robert"), "Hello, Robert!")
AssertionError: 'Well hello, Robert!' != 'Hello, Robert!'
- Well hello, Robert!
? ^^^^^^
+ Hello, Robert!
? ^


======================================================================
FAIL: test_greeting_without_name (__main__.GreetingTests)
----------------------------------------------------------------------
Traceback (most recent call last):
    File "/Users/rwoliver2/Source/python-book/greeting_tests.py", line 10, ↦
    ↳ in test_greeting_without_name
        self.assertEqual(greeting.say_greeting(), "Hello, World!")
AssertionError: 'Well hello, World!' != 'Hello, World!'
- Well hello, World!
? ^^^^^^
+ Hello, World!
? ^


----------------------------------------------------------------------
Ran 2 tests in 0.000s
FAILED (failures=2)
```

At the top of the tests, you'll see `FF` where the two dots were previously. That means both tests failed. If just one had failed, it would have said `F.` (or `.F`, depending on which test failed). Additionally, for each test that fails, details are shown about what went wrong. The key line is the `AssertionError` line:

```
AssertionError: 'Well hello, World!' != 'Hello, World!'
```

Here we see that it was expecting "Hello, World!" (and "Hello, Robert!" for the second test), but we modified it to say "Well hello" in the first part of the return value, so that fails.

You can add as many tests as you like. Every method with a name beginning with `test` is executed in the `GreetingTests` class by this code:

```
if __name__ == '__main__':
    unittest.main()
```

You don't specifically have to name the class `GreetingTests`, but I find it a handy format. I use `ModuleTests`, where `Module` is replaced with the name of the module that I'm testing. The built-in behavior of this class comes from its parent class, `unittest.TestCase`. This provides the `main()` method that triggers our tests contained within the class.

Assertions

In our example test, we made two *assertions*, each in its own test method.

```
self.assertEqual(greeting.say_greeting(), "Hello, World!")
self.assertEqual(greeting.say_greeting("Robert"), "Hello, Robert!")
```

An assertion lets us test the output of our code (usually the return value of one of our functions or methods) against a known value. Individual tests can have more than one assertion, but it's better to break apart our code into its smallest testable components. This ensures that we follow the unit testing methodology.

In our previous example, the `assertEqual` method checks to see if the first value is equal to the second. This works much like an `if` comparison except that it comes bundled with all the test logic that produces the pass/fail and detailed testing displays.

That's not the only assertion, though. Let's step through a few of the most commonly used methods.

assertEqual

The `assertEqual` method checks whether the supplied values are equal.

```
# If greeting.say_greeting() returns "Hello, World!", it passes.
    self.assertEqual(greeting.say_greeting(), "Hello, World!")
```

assertNotEqual

The `assertNotEqual` method checks whether the supplied values are not equal.

```
# If greeting.say_greeting() returns "Hello, World!", it fails.
    self.assertNotEqual(greeting.say_greeting(), "Hello, World!")
```

assertTrue

The `assertTrue` method checks to see if the statement is `True`.

```
# These assertions pass
self.assertTrue(True)
self.assertTrue(1 == 1)


# These fail
self.assertTrue(False)
self.assertTrue(1 == 2)


# This passes because it will return True
self.assertTrue(greeting.say_greeting())
```

assertFalse

The `assertFalse` method checks to see if the statement is `False`.

```
# These pass
self.assertFalse(False)
self.assertFalse(1 == 2)


# These assertions fail
self.assertFalse(True)
self.assertFalse(1 == 1)


# This fails because it will return True
self.assertTrue(greeting.say_greeting())
```

Test Driven Design

Most of the time, I use `assertEqual` and `assertTrue`. When designing your tests, you may run into two common problems, both of which underscore design issues in your code that need addressing.

The most common issue uncovered by test-driven development is the lack of units within a program. Dividing your code into reusable building blocks with functions, classes, and methods will make it easier to read and easier to test. Rather than having a long collection of lines of code that do a complicated task, break it down into simpler functions.

Another common issue is that functions do not return values that are meaningful, or, at the least, a test on them wouldn't produce a correct pass or fail. If your functions do work but don't return values, or they return values that don't correlate with the success of the code inside that function (i.e., you just return `True` even if the code fails), you probably need to rework the function so that it checks the return values of the work you are performing.

```python
def write_file(data, filename):
    # Write the file
    return True
```

In the previous example, the function could return `True` even if something went wrong. Here's a better way to structure it:

```python
def write_file(data, filename):
    try:
        # Write the file
    except Exception as e:
        # Handle the exception, then return False
        return False
    # If we made it this far, it was successful, return True
    return True
```

In this case, the function returns `False` if an exception is raised. Otherwise, `True` is returned. You can then use `assertTrue` to make sure it works properly.

```python
self.assertTrue(write_file("Hello", "test.txt"))
```

Test Coverage

When I first learned of test-driven development, I tended to go a bit overboard with my tests. My *test coverage*, that is, how much of the total code is covered by tests (usually expressed in a ratio or percentage), was quite high. It is possible to spend more time writing your tests than writing your actual program code. In that case, excessive testing can be a productivity time sink.

So how much testing is appropriate? There's no easy answer. If you're writing a simple program for your own use, you may be able to get away with no testing, or just a handful of tests covering critical functionality. But if you're writing for work—that is, people are paying you to code, or your business or job depends on your program operating correctly, higher test coverage not only makes sense but helps you sleep better at night.

MY TAKE

Don't get too wrapped up in your test coverage percentages, especially if you feel you have adequate testing for your needs. In many cases, especially in business, time spent writing tests is never wasted. Worrying about whether you have too many tests is a good problem to have. If you write a test for most, if not all, of the functions or methods you use, your coverage is excellent. On the other hand, if you find regressions happening on a regular basis and you must do extensive manual checking to make sure your program worked as intended, you probably need to increase your test coverage by writing more tests.

ClydeBank Coffee Shop: Test-Driven Coffee Serving

Testing functionality in our coffee shop game would be incredibly useful—especially if we wanted to enhance the game in the future. By adding tests to certain key functions, we can ensure that if we do make modifications down the road, we won't break any of the core logic.

As an example, I've added a few simple tests to ensure that our static methods are functioning correctly.

SNIPPET

CCS-15.py

coffee_shop_simulator_tests.py

```python
import unittest
from coffee_shop_simulator import CoffeeShopSimulator


class CoffeeShopSimulatorTests(unittest.TestCase):
    def test_convert_to_float(self):
        # Test a string conversion to float
        test_float = 1.23
        test_string = "1.23"
```

```
self.assertEqual(CoffeeShopSimulator.convert_to_float(test_string), test_float)


    def test_x_of_y_with_numbers(self):
        # Test that x_of_y returns a list of x copies of a number y
        number_list = [1, 1, 1, 1, 1]
        self.assertEqual(CoffeeShopSimulator.x_of_y(5, 1), number_list)

    def test_x_of_y_with_strings(self):
        # Test that x_of_y returns a list of x copies of a string y
        string_list = ["a", "a", "a", "a"]
        self.assertEqual(CoffeeShopSimulator.x_of_y(4, "a"), string_list)



if __name__ == '__main__':
    unittest.main()
```

If you run these tests, you'll note that all three of them pass. And you might notice three other things about them. First, in testing a class, I use the `from x import y` construction.

```
from coffee_shop_simulator import CoffeeShopSimulator
```

This ensures that we have a version of the class for testing and lets me type `CoffeeShopSimulator` instead of the clunkier `coffee_shop_simulator.CoffeeShopSimulator`. Second, we test `x_of_y` in two ways: with numbers and with strings. We didn't design it to be used with strings, but I wanted to demonstrate that we can run multiple tests on a method or function—even testing it in ways that aren't currently used in the code. Either way, we know the code works as intended with these two tests, and we know that it's flexible enough to take different types of input.

Finally, you may have recalled that we removed the use of `x_of_y` entirely when we switched to numpy for weather generation. I'd love to tell you that I planned to leave this method in here to see if your now-keen programmer's eye would spot it. Or as a lesson in removing such vestigial code. Unfortunately, I can't make such a claim. I simply forgot to remove it. So I added two tests for code we don't even use in the game!

This will happen to you as you refactor. While removing unnecessary code is generally a good idea, in this case there isn't any harm in leaving it, because it isn't used and is a very simple function that doesn't take much code space. If you want to remove it, feel free, but if you do so, you'll need to remove the tests related to it or they'll fail.

Now that you know how to create tests, why not test other game functionality? I added a few tests to get you started, but nothing is stopping you from testing the entire game from start to finish. If you choose to go down this road, you'll need to know two things. First, you must instantiate a game object to test using the construction `game = CoffeeShopSimulator`. Second, parts of the game start a loop and ask for input, and when they do, your code will be playing the game, not running tests. To avoid this issue, you can test individual parts of the `CoffeeShopSimulator` class and avoid using the `run` method.

Chapter Recap

» Test-driven development helps us write better code and detect regressions.

» Unit testing involves testing individual parts of a program, usually testing the return value of functions or methods.

» We must ensure that functions and methods return meaningful results (e.g., returning `False` if something went wrong and `True` if everything was fine).

» It's difficult to write too many tests, but we should be mindful of our time and productivity by focusing on the essential functionality of the program.

| 18 |
Managing Your Code with Git

Chapter Overview
» Source code management eases collaboration
» Git is a popular source code management system
» GitHub is a popular Git repository hosting service

Until this point, our programs have simply existed as text files on our computer. Anytime we make a change, our previous content is overwritten. This doesn't sound like a problem until we make a change to a working program and break it at eleven o'clock at night, bringing down a website without a simple way to restore it. This may or may not be the voice of experience—but it is preventable.

Version tracking gives us a log of all the changes we make to our program, giving us the ability to reference or restore a previous version at any time. It also serves as a backup—provided we have synced with a remote location or provider. This process of tracking source code file versions and synchronizing for collaboration purposes is called *source code management*.

Before I was introduced to source code management, anytime I worked on a program with others I would make sure to work only on files that others weren't editing. That strategy was a Band-Aid at best, because eventually more than one person would want to work on the same file. Back in the Macromedia (now Adobe) Dreamweaver days of web development, you could check in and check out files, and this would advise other developers that you had that file and were making changes to it. But that system had numerous flaws and didn't carry over well to modern development methodologies.

In this chapter, we'll specifically be discussing the Git source code management system. Git was developed by Linus Torvalds and released to the public in 2005. Since its release it has enjoyed massive success, in part due to its excellent *branching* support and the ease of *merging* those branches. Branching is the process of copying code to a new, separate version in a software project. Unique branches move forward with new versions in parallel, and merging brings those versions back together, integrating the changes into a unified copy.

Software projects are stored in Git *repositories*. A repository is the container that stores source code. On a computer, a Git repository is simply a folder of code (and possibly subfolders) with a `.git` folder in the main folder. This `.git` folder stores the history of the changes to the code. A Git repository can be pushed to a remote copy of the repository for collaboration and backup purposes.

GitHub, GitLab, and Bitbucket are popular Git repository hosting companies, but anyone can host a repository themselves, because Git is open-source. This guide will focus on local repositories and syncing with GitHub, but the techniques used here should be compatible with other Git hosting.

Installing Git

Before you can use Git, you will need to install it on your computer. Visit https://git-scm.com and click the *Downloads* button to see instructions for your platform. Windows users will need to download the installer and run it. On macOS, you can install Homebrew (see https://brew.sh) to install Git. Once you've installed Homebrew, run `brew install git` to install Git.

Debian/Ubuntu/Linux Mint users need to run `apt install git`, and Linux Arch-based distributions such as Arch and Manjaro need to run `pacman -S git`. Red Hat-based distributions would run `yum install git`.

Once Git is installed, you should be able to open a terminal or console and run …

```
git version
```

… and you'll see the version of Git installed. If you get a message like "command not found," Git isn't installed properly, so you'll need to check the download/install instructions for your platform and try again.

Windows and macOS users can also install GitHub Desktop from https://desktop.github.com. It's an excellent Git management tool that allows you to graphically manage Git repositories. While it can be very useful, I am not covering it in this chapter because it isn't available for all platforms, and you may not have it on the system you're on—or on a remote system you've connected to. It's good to know how to use Git without it, but if you are running Windows or macOS and would prefer a graphical solution, it might be a good fit for you.

Forking and Cloning the ClydeBank Coffee Shop Game

The first step in making use of existing code on GitHub is to *fork* it to our own account. Forking a Git repository copies it to our account and lets us work with the code, including making changes of our own, without interfering with the original copy. We can later ask, via a ***pull request***, that the changes we made be integrated into the original project. A pull request asks the maintainer(s) of the original project for permission to merge our changes into the main project. They can review and ultimately accept or deny the merge.

Before you can fork the project, you'll need to make a free account on GitHub. Navigate to https://github.com and create the account, then go to https://github.com/clydebankmedia/Python-CoffeeShopSimulator and click the *fork* button at the top right of the screen. This will put a copy of the repository in your account. You can then ***clone***, or download, the repository to your computer, where you'll have access to the files.

When you click on the green *Code* button (figure 46) above the code listing in GitHub, you will see the commands for cloning the repository. I recommend using the HTTPS variant, as it is the simplest, but if you know how to use SSH keys, you can add your public SSH key to GitHub and use the command given in the SSH tab. Copy the HTTPS command to your clipboard and have it at the ready for your console or terminal. But first, we need to change into our source directory.

IMAGE

fig. 46

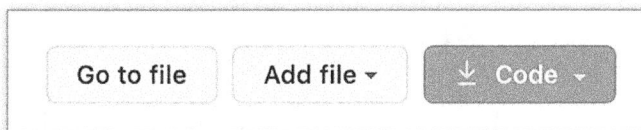

I make a folder called `Source` in my home directory, and I change into it with this on my Mac:

```
cd ~/Source
```

This works on Linux, too. The tilde (~) is short for home directory. If you're a Windows user, run this:

```
cd %HOMEPATH%\Source
```

NOTE

If you're running Windows Subsystem for Linux then you can run the Linux commands in this section. The `cd %HOMEPATH%` command works only on the Windows command prompt or PowerShell prompt and not the Bash terminal.

Now that you've changed directory (i.e., `cd`) into your Source directory, type `git clone`, press the spacebar, and then paste the command from the HTTPS tab of the Code pane in GitHub into the terminal and run it. The completed command will look something like this:

```
git clone https://github.com/rwoliver2/Python-CoffeeShopSimulator.git
```

IMPORTANT

When you fork a repository, a copy of it will be in *your* GitHub account. The previous command represents the repository name in my account (note the `rwoliver2`). Your command will have the `rwoliver2` substituted with your GitHub username, so be sure to use that copy instead of the exact link I have listed.

If all has gone well, you now have `Python-CoffeeShopSimulator` in `~/Source`, so the full path should be `~/Source/Python-CoffeeShopSimulator`.

You can now launch Visual Studio Code and open that folder to view and edit the code.

Committing Changes to Your Repository

If you make changes to the code and want to commit them to your fork, run this:

```
git add filename.py
```

In this case, substitute `filename.py` with the name of the file you want to add (e.g., `main.py`). By *adding* the file, you are basically staging it to be committed. You can run this command on any number of files you wish (including entire directories), or you can run …

```
git add .
```

… to add all the files (and files in folders within the current dictionary) to be staged for commit. You can run …

```
git status
```

... to see what changes are staged to be committed. If you run `git status` on a repository with no changes, you'll see this:

```
On branch main
Your branch is up to date with 'origin/main'.

nothing to commit, working tree clean
```

If you modify a file—say you add something to `main.py` and then run `git status`—you'll see this:

```
On branch main
Your branch is up to date with 'origin/main'.

Changes not staged for commit:
    (use "git add <file>..." to update what will be committed)
    (use "git restore <file>..." to discard changes in working directory)
        modified:   main.py

no changes added to commit (use "git add" and/or "git commit -a")
```

In this case, we can see that `main.py` has been modified.

To commit this change to your local repository, you would first stage (add) the file (as seen above), then run the following:

```
git commit -m "A note about your changes."
```

The message, specified by the `-m` argument (in this case, "A note about your changes.") can be any message, but it's helpful (to your future self and others) to be specific about what you changed.

You can commit multiple files at once, or you can tell Git to commit all modified files (skipping the need to add them) via:

```
git commit -a -m "A note about your changes."
```

The `-a` argument specifies "all," meaning all changed files should be included in the commit.

Use care when specifying the -a flag with `git commit`. You may include files that you aren't quite ready to commit.

Pushing to Remote

The `commit` command commits the changes to your local copy of Git, but to sync them to GitHub, you'll need to run this:

```
git push origin main
```

Let's dissect this command to see what each part does. First, `git push` is the actual command, telling Git we want to push our work to a remote repository. The `origin` part tells Git where to push the changes. If we clone a repository from GitHub, the origin will be set to GitHub, so it knows where to push these changes. The `main` portion indicates which branch to push.

Using Branches

Using branches is a way to separate sets of changes. For example, if you wanted to work on adding a particular feature, you could create a new branch for that.

```
git checkout -b branch_name
```

This new branch (named whatever you put in the previous command for `branch_name`) will now receive any changes you commit. If you want to push that branch, run the following:

```
git push origin branch_name
```

This keeps the changes separate from the main branch. To switch branches, use this:

```
git checkout branch_name
```

In the previous command, put the name of the branch you want to switch to in place of `branch_name`. For example, if you wanted to switch back to the main branch, you would use `git checkout main`.

If you want to create (and change to) a new branch, use the -b argument, as described in the original command `git checkout -b branch_name`.

Branches are independent sets of changes (i.e., commits), so the changes you make in one branch won't automatically carry over to the other.

Viewing Changes

To view the changes, or the differences between your current set of files and the last commit, run this:

```
git diff
```

This will show a `diff`, or difference summary, of the pending changes. For example, if I edit the `main.py` file and change the year 2023 to 2024 on the copyright line, the `diff` will reflect that.

```
diff --git a/main.py b/main.py
index df53dae..41f762b 100644
--- a/main.py
+++ b/main.py
@@ -1,5 +1,5 @@
 # ClydeBank Coffee Shop Simulator 4000
-# Copyright (C) 2023 ClydeBank Media, All Rights Reserved.
+# Copyright (C) 2024 ClydeBank Media, All Rights Reserved.
```

In this listing, you can see a minus sign in front of the line that was deleted and a plus sign in front of the line that was added. The line to be deleted will be shown in red, and the line added in green.

You can press the Q key to exit the diff viewer.

Viewing Your Commit Log

As your Git repository grows with changes, you can use ...

```
git log
```

... to see a listing of all the commits you've made. The results will look something like this:

```
commit 6dd258b5273bc4a13eee201fd6304efc61baef5a (HEAD -> main, origin/main, origin/HEAD)
Author: Robert W. Oliver II <118407+rwoliver2@users.noreply.github.com>
Date:   Sun Jul 3 23:11:07 2022 -0500
```

```
        Update README.md

commit a2af786f19023bd2ac2d023ce8b2f2ed664f733b
Author: Robert W. Oliver II <118407+rwoliver2@users.noreply.github.com>
Date:   Sun Jul 3 23:07:07 2022 -0500

        Initial commit.
```

As with the `diff` command, you can press Q to exit the viewer. If there are few commits, the results will be displayed, and you will be returned to the command prompt.

Alternatively, you can view a list of the commits that have been pushed to GitHub by navigating to the repository and clicking the "commits" icon (preceded by a clock icon and the number of commits) at the top of the file display.

Pull Requests

Now that you've committed changes to your repository and pushed them to your fork on GitHub, you can request that those changes be pulled into the official repository (i.e., https://github.com/clydebankmedia/Python-CoffeeShopSimulator) with a pull request.

To create a pull request, go to GitHub and navigate to your fork of the repository. Click the Pull Requests tab at the top and then click the green *New Pull Request* button. In the "comparing changes" section, you can specify the repository and branch to pull from (listed on the right), and the destination is listed on the left.

Once you select the destination and source branches and repositories, you'll be prompted to enter a note describing the request. Submitting the request doesn't automatically merge the changes—the maintainer of the official repository will have to make that decision.

Syncing with the Official Repository

Over time, your fork of the repository may (and likely will) differ from the official repository. It's a good idea to put them in sync as often as possible to prevent the two code bases from drifting so far apart that merging them requires manual intervention.

To do this, go to your fork of the repository in GitHub and click *Fetch Upstream*, then if it says it's behind, click *Fetch* and *Merge*. If all goes well, your repository will be automatically updated with changes from the official copy.

If you have altered your repository significantly, an automatic update may not be possible. In that case, you'll have to complete further steps—possibly including the manual editing of certain files to include changes that differ significantly from what you have added.

Watch over my shoulder as I clone the *Python QuickStart Guide* source code.

To watch the QuickClip, use the camera on your mobile phone to scan the QR code or visit the link below.

www.quickclips.io/python-7

SCAN ME   **VISIT URL**

Chapter Recap

» A Git repository is a collection of files that includes the changes made to those files over their lifetime in the repository.

» Forking a repository you plan to use is common practice, especially if you plan to make changes to its code. Optionally, you can create a pull request to ask the maintainer of the official project to incorporate your changes.

» Branches are independent sets of changes to the files in a repository. You can switch branches at any time and commit changes to those branches. You can also sync those branches with the repository hosted on GitHub via the `push` command.

| 19 |
The Junk Drawer

Chapter Overview
» Python has a built-in help system
» Environment variables and command line arguments can be used to pass data to a program
» Threading lets us do multiple tasks at once

Every culture across our beautiful blue planet shares three things in common—death, taxes, and a junk drawer. It's usually located in the kitchen (or dining room, in my case) and contains various power adapters to things we no longer own, several instruction manuals, various rubber bands and paper clips, an assortment of markers or crayons, a few clothespins (even if the nearest clothesline is several hundred miles away), and a spoon, ruler, or other such tool that keeps the drawer from opening all the way (but only sometimes).

This chapter is like a Python junk drawer. Except, rather than being a collection of things you'll never use, it contains things you will indeed use on a regular basis in Python—they just aren't big enough topics to warrant their own chapter.

Getting Help Inside Python

If you're inside the Python interpreter (executed via the command `python3` on the terminal or console), you can get instant help. To access the help system, simply run this:

```
help()
```

You'll enter an interactive help system that will allow you to access documentation on many different topics. For example, if you type `for` at the `help>` prompt, you'll get guidance on using `for` loops (figure 47). When viewing this help, use the arrow keys on your keyboard to navigate multipage content, and press the Q key to exit the help document and return to the `help>` prompt.

fig. 47

```
● ● ●                python-book — python3 — python3 — less • Python — 79x24
The "for" statement
*******************

The "for" statement is used to iterate over the elements of a sequence
(such as a string, tuple or list) or other iterable object:

   for_stmt ::= "for" target_list "in" expression_list ":" suite
               ["else" ":" suite]

The expression list is evaluated once; it should yield an iterable
object.  An iterator is created for the result of the
"expression_list".  The suite is then executed once for each item
provided by the iterator, in the order returned by the iterator.  Each
item in turn is assigned to the target list using the standard rules
for assignments (see Assignment statements), and then the suite is
executed.  When the items are exhausted (which is immediately when the
sequence is empty or an iterator raises a "StopIteration" exception),
the suite in the "else" clause, if present, is executed, and the loop
terminates.

A "break" statement executed in the first suite terminates the loop
without executing the "else" clause's suite.  A "continue" statement
executed in the first suite skips the rest of the suite and continues
:
```

The help documentation for the `for` statement.

To return to the main interpreter prompt, press CTRL+D (CTRL+Z on Windows).

As an added benefit, this help system is active even if you're not connected to the internet. I've been in situations where my internet access was down, or I wasn't near a hotspot and needed to quickly reference something. Just as we flip on light switches when our power goes out, I've instinctively reached for my web browser, assuming it would be there. In these cases, offline help is extremely useful.

Sorting Lists and Dictionaries

Sorting a list or dictionary in Python couldn't be simpler. Let's start with lists.

```python
# Create a shopping list
shopping_list = ["Eggs", "Butter", "Milk", "Sausage", "Apples"]


# Sort it
shopping_list.sort()


# Display the results
print(shopping_list)
```

When you run this code, you'll see this:

```
['Apples', 'Butter', 'Eggs', 'Milk', 'Sausage']
```

It's important to note that `sort` replaces the contents of the list with the sorted version. However, if you want to leave the original list unsorted and create a new, sorted list, use the `sorted` function.

SNIPPET

19-01.py

```
# Create a shopping list
shopping_list = ["Eggs", "Butter", "Milk", "Sausage", "Apples"]

# Sort it and store result in sorted_list
sorted_list = sorted(shopping_list)

# Display the results
print(sorted_list)
```

You can sort in reverse order by setting the `reverse` argument to `True`.

```
# Create a shopping list
shopping_list = ["Eggs", "Butter", "Milk", "Sausage", "Apples"]

# Sort it in reverse
shopping_list.sort(reverse = True)

# Display the results
print(shopping_list)
```

When you run the code, you'll see this:

```
['Sausage', 'Milk', 'Eggs', 'Butter', 'Apples']
```

Sorting dictionaries works much the same way, but you need to supply an index to `sort`.

SNIPPET

19-02.py

```
# Import pretty print
import pprint

# Create a menu dictionary
menu = [
    {"name": "Hot Chocolate", "price": 3.99},
```

```
        {"name": "Coffee", "price": 3.50},

        {"name": "Tea", "price": 2.99},

        {"name": "Orange Juice", "price": 1.99},

        {"name": "Soda", "price": 1.75},
]

# Create sort function
def sort_by(s):

        return s["name"]


# Sort by function
menu.sort(key = sort_by)


# Display results
pprint.pprint(menu)
```

This code displays:

```
[{'name': 'Coffee', 'price': 3.5},
 {'name': 'Hot Chocolate', 'price': 3.99},
 {'name': 'Orange Juice', 'price': 1.99},
 {'name': 'Soda', 'price': 1.75},
 {'name': 'Tea', 'price': 2.99}]
```

Environment Variables

We briefly touched on environment variables in chapter 15 when working with Flask, so let's expand on them a bit. Environment variables are useful for exchanging information (especially short strings) between the operating system and a program.

Sometimes environment variables directly control the behavior of the console shell or terminal. For example, the PROMPT variable controls the format of the prompt of some consoles or terminals. The username can be accessed on Windows with the USERNAME variable, while on macOS and Linux that information is stored in USER. Windows stores the home directory for the user in USERPROFILE, and macOS and Linux keep this location in HOME.

While there is some variation between operating systems, the behavior of environment variables is largely the same. When you're in bash or zsh, common shells (interactive command-line environments) on macOS and Linux, you can see a list of environment variables with the env command. In Windows, at the command prompt, the set command will display environment variables.

You can specify an environment variable on the command line when running a Python program (or any program).

```
VAR="Hello" python3 myprogram.py
```

Windows users will need to set the environment variable and then call Python. For example: `set VAR="Hello"` (new line) `python3 myprogram.py`.

In this example, the environment variable `VAR` will be set to `Hello` and the Python interpreter will be loaded with the `myprogram.py` program running. Using this method, the variable `VAR` is only available while the Python interpreter is running. You can access environment variables from within Python via the `os.environ` dictionary.

SNIPPET

19-03.py

```
# Import the os module
import os

# Iterate over environment variables and display the variable and its
value
for k, v in os.environ.items():
    print(k + " = " + v)
```

What displays with this code depends on your operating environment, but you should get a list of all the environment variables presently defined in your system. If you want to retrieve just one value, use this:

```
os.environ["VAR _ NAME"]
```

In the previous code, replace `VAR _ NAME` with the desired environment variable name. You can set an environment variable in the same manner, except that you specify a new value:

```
os.environ["VAR _ NAME"] = "Hello"
```

In this code, you would set `VAR _ NAME` to the value `"Hello"`.

Using Command Line Arguments

Command line arguments are variables that are passed to the program on start-up. As the name suggests, they are supplied to our program via the command line and they're accessible via a list named `sys.argv` (or, more specifically, the list `argv` from the `sys` module).

Before we look at how to read them, let's discuss how to supply them to your program. If you've been using Visual Studio Code, clicking *Run* executes something like this:

```
python3 yourprogram.py
```

Behind the scenes, it's a bit more complicated than that. It really runs something more like this:

```
/usr/bin/env /opt/homebrew/bin/python3
/Users/rwoliver2/.vscode/extensions/ms-python.python-
2022.4.1/pythonFiles/lib/python/debugpy/launcher 61829 --
/Users/rwoliver2/Source/python-book/yourprogram.py
```

Visual Studio Code adds all this fluff so that it can debug your Python program. It's handy to have, but it does make the command line absurd. Now you see why I simplified it. In any event, if you wanted to pass a command line argument, you would run your program like this:

```
python3 yourprogram.py help
```

In this case, "help" is the first argument. We can provide additional arguments, too.

```
python3 yourprogram.py infile.csv outfile.csv
```

Individual command line arguments are separated with a space. Fortunately, Python puts these arguments in a list and they're easy to access.

NOTE

If there is a space within your argument, you can surround the argument with quotes.

SNIPPET

19-04.py

```
# Import the sys module
import sys

input_file = sys.argv[1]
output_file = sys.argv[2]
```

```
print("Input file: " + input_file)
print("Output file: " + output_file)
```

If we save this file as `cmdlinetest.py` and run it like this in the terminal ...

```
python3 cmdlinetest.py infile.csv outfile.csv
```

... we'll see this:

```
Input file: infile.csv
Output file: outfile.csv
```

Did you notice something strange, though? Our `sys.argv` list begins at index 1. That's not quite right. Let's try it again, but this time display what's in the zero index position.

```
# Import the sys module
import sys

input_file = sys.argv[1]
output_file = sys.argv[2]

print("Input file: " + input_file)
print("Output file: " + output_file)
print("Zero index position: " + sys.argv[0])
```

Running this program like this ...

```
python3 infile.csv outfile.csv
```

... gives this:

```
Input file: infile.csv
Output file: outfile.csv
Zero index position: cmdlinetest.py
```

As you can see, indexes still start at 0. The Python law of indexes is still intact! The zero position stores the file name of the program, and actual command line arguments start at 1.

Actually, this is more of an embarrassing fact than a fun fact. While writing this sample program, I put 0 and 1 for the `input_file` and `output_file` command line argument positions, and the results looked like you might expect:

```
Input file: cmdlinetest.py
Output file: infile.csv
```

Only then did I realize I had forgotten that the name of the program is stored at the zero index. Enjoy this bit of trivia as you laugh at my silly mistake.

Lambda Expressions

A *lambda expression* is a short, nameless (sometimes called anonymous) inline function that is commonly used in sorting routines. The simplest way to explain a lambda is to see it in action.

```
# A very simple lambda
greet = lambda name: "Hello, " + name + "!"
```

The `lambda` statement tells Python that what follows is a lambda expression and, in this case, takes one argument, `name`. Then the value it returns is defined, in this case, `"Hello, " + name + "!"`. To use the lambda, we call it like any other function.

```
greet("Robert")
```

produces:

```
Hello, Robert!
```

I understand it's hard to tell the difference between a lambda expression and a regular function. They are anonymous, meaning they aren't formally defined as a function with `def`. They are best used when we need to define a quick, one-line function or for applying logic to a sorting routine.

Let's examine how you can use lambdas to define your own sorting logic. First, let's revisit the `sort()` method.

```
# A simple customer list
customers = ["Robert", "Bryan", "John", "Jo", "Brittney"]

# Sort list alphabetically
customers.sort()

# Display results
print(customers)
```

In this example, we'll see our `customer` list sorted as you might expect. But what if we want to sort by the last letter of the name instead of the first? An odd request, for sure; but lambdas to the rescue!

```
# A simple customer list
customers = ["Robert", "Bryan", "John", "Jo", "Brittney"]

# Sort by last letter in name
customers.sort(key = lambda name: list(name)[-1])

# Display the results
print(customers)
```

When we run this code, we get this:

```
['Bryan', 'John', 'Jo', 'Robert', 'Brittney']
```

Let's step through this line by line. First, we define the `customer` list, just as before. When we sort, though, we provide a key. The `key` argument's default value is the first character of every entry in the list, but with this lambda, we use the `list` function to break apart the name into a list of individual letters, then reference the -1 index, which returns the last letter in the list (which is also the last letter in each name). Armed with this key, the `sort` method can then sort by last letter.

By the way, lambdas can take more than one argument. Here's a simple example:

```
a = lambda x, y, z: x + y + z
print(a(1, 2, 3))
```

This code displays:

```
6
```

You don't have to give the lambda a name (like a in this case). I didn't in our sorting example. I did it in this example to demonstrate the concept more succinctly and clearly.

You may not use lambdas often in your Python programming, but they're incredibly useful for quick inline logic.

Threading

Python can walk and chew gum at the same time. Almost all computers today have multiple processor cores, so why not put them to good use? Doing multiple things at once not only improves performance but also provides a better user experience. Why have the user wait when you can process whatever you need to do in the background?

```python
# Import threading, datetime, and time modules
import threading
import datetime
import time

# Define the function for threading
def thread_loop(name):
    # Loop 10 times
    for i in range(10):
        # Get a string with the current time in ISO 8601 format
        now = datetime.datetime.now().isoformat()
        # Display the time
        print(name + " - current time: " + now)
        # Sleep 1 second
        time.sleep(1)

# Create several threads
thread1 = threading.Thread(target = thread_loop, args = ("thread1", ))
thread2 = threading.Thread(target = thread_loop, args = ("thread2", ))
thread3 = threading.Thread(target = thread_loop, args = ("thread3", ))

# Start each thread
thread1.start()
```

```
thread2.start()
thread3.start()

# Wait for threads to finish before exiting
thread3.join()
thread2.join()
thread1.join()
```

In this code, we start off by importing the `threading` module, which contains the logic necessary to process threads. We also import `datetime` and `time`: `datetime` to print the date, and `time` to sleep for 1 second. Then we define the function `thread_loop`. This is the function that will be the thread that executes in the background.

Inside the function, we loop ten times and grab the current date, using the ISO (International Organization for Standardization) 8601 standard for convenience. Next, we print the time and then sleep for 1 second, pausing execution before returning to the top of the loop again.

Back in the main execution of the program, we create three threads, `thread1`, `thread2`, and `thread3`. The `threading.Thread` call is given two arguments: the `target`, which in this case is the function `thread_loop`, and `args`, which are the arguments to supply to the function `thread_loop`. In our `thread_loop` function, it takes one argument, name, but `args` accepts a tuple and iterates over it, so to prevent it from separating out each individual letter of the name and passing that as a single variable, we use `("thread1", )`, creating an empty second entry, thus making the first (and only) argument sent to our function the name of the thread.

Once the threads are created, we `start` each one. The threads will loop and do their work, and the `join` method on each at the end will wait until the thread is finished before exiting the program. If we didn't use `join`, the threads would barely get started before the program ended.

> **IMPORTANT**
>
> If you use threading in your program, make sure that each thread is eventually joined. Otherwise, the thread can be inadvertently terminated when your program ends.

When you see the resulting display, you'll note that sometimes one thread starts to print in the middle of another one, or before the thread has a chance to enter a new line. This effect will vary depending on many factors, mainly the speed of your computer and what else is running on your machine at the time you run the program.

When you are threading, it is important to make sure that you don't have a ***race condition***. Informally, a race condition is a situation when one or more thread performs a task (updating a variable, displaying results to the screen, etc.) at the same time as another thread (or the main program) in a way that was unintended or is potentially harmful to the execution of the program. Race conditions are notoriously hard to debug, so when you use threads, be careful when modifying variables outside the function or performing tasks that can affect the entire program.

To help prevent race conditions, you can obtain a lock and use it around critical segments of code to prevent multiple threads from accessing the same variable, running the same function, or otherwise performing actions that would be problematic if they were run while other threads were doing the same thing.

```
lock = threading.Lock()

with lock:
    self.critical_variable += 1
```

Using this technique, we can be sure that only one thread at a time will run the code within the `with` block. When using locks, be sure to lock only the lines of code that require synchronization with other threads, or else you will tie up your other threads and potentially reduce or defeat the benefits of using multiple threads.

I don't want to give you the impression that that's all there is to threads. Multithreaded applications are inherently more complex, and thoughts and details on their design could easily fill a book. For more details, please reference the Python threading documentation located at https://docs.python.org/3/library/threading.html.

Cryptographic Hashing

Cryptographic *hashing* is the process of taking a string of any size and generating a fixed-length, shorter code that represents the original data. Unlike with compression, the hash cannot be used to recreate the original data. Instead, the hash code is used to compare two strings (or, more commonly, files—which are just long strings of data). You can also use the hash of a string to ensure that the provided data matches the original data (figure 48).

HASHING

fig. 48

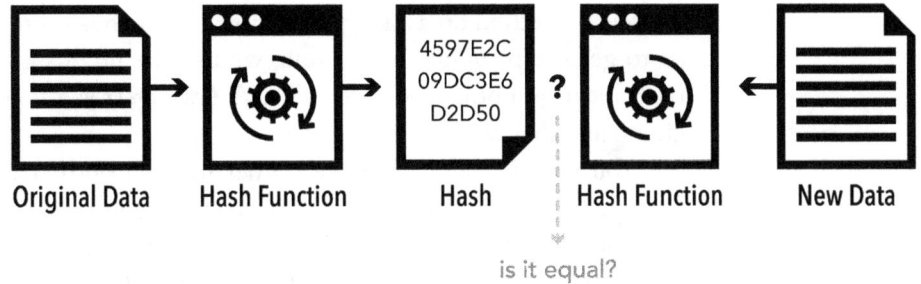

| Original Data | Hash Function | Hash | Hash Function | New Data |

is it equal?

Hashing can validate the contents of two sets of data. The hash function is run on both sets of data (the original and the new) and if the hashes match, the data are equal.

NOTE

Technically, two pieces of data can be completely different and have the same hash. This is extremely unlikely and, mathematically, a near impossibility, but it could happen. Nevertheless, for our purposes—and in virtually all situations you will run across—you can assume they are equal if they have the same hash.

Python makes hashing quite simple. Let's generate a hash of two strings and compare.

SNIPPET

19-07.py

```python
# Import the hashlib module
import hashlib

# Define two sets of data
original_data = "The quick brown fox jumped over the lazy red dog."
new_data = "The quick brown fox leaped over the spry orange cat."

# Hash them both
original_hash = hashlib.sha256(original_data.encode()).hexdigest()
new_hash = hashlib.sha256(new_data.encode()).hexdigest()

# Display the results
print("Original SHA256 hash: " + original_hash)
print("New SHA256 hash: " + new_hash)
```

When you run this code, you should get the following:

```
Original SHA256 hash: eba3f65217714021800aeae3c651cd4132800711078648dc117abc0a1b956fbc

New SHA256 hash: 407fa327c98cfdf8b42003bd4f7702b58f546239d33dd9c836df374da7054691
```

The `hashlib.sha256` does the heavy lifting, but first we encode the `original_data` string in UTF-8, which is the default when using the `encode()` method on a string. Additionally, the hash is returned as an object, so to get the printable hash value, we use the `hexdigest()` method on the hash result to obtain a usable value. A **hex digest** is a text string of printable characters that represents the hash.

You might wonder why we bother to hash both strings when we could have just compared them via the `==` comparison operator. Well, for a value this short—just a simple sentence—we could have. But hashing is typically performed on data that are quite large. Rather than hash it each time, a hash is performed once on the data and the result can be used to check whether one data set compares with another without having to rehash every single file involved.

When we download software, especially security-related software, the hash of the software download is often displayed as a string on the web page where we get the file. We can then compare that hash against the downloaded file. To generate the hash of a file, we can use the following console/terminal commands (in each example, replace `FILE` with the name of the file).

» Windows: `certutil -hashfile FILE SHA256`
» macOS: `openssl dgst -sha256 FILE`
» Linux: `sha256sum FILE`

FUN FACT

Hashing lies at the heart of cryptocurrency and blockchain technology. Essentially, the concept of blockchain is the hashing of each transaction and the previous transactions to form a chain of verification (figure 49).

GRAPHIC

fig. 49

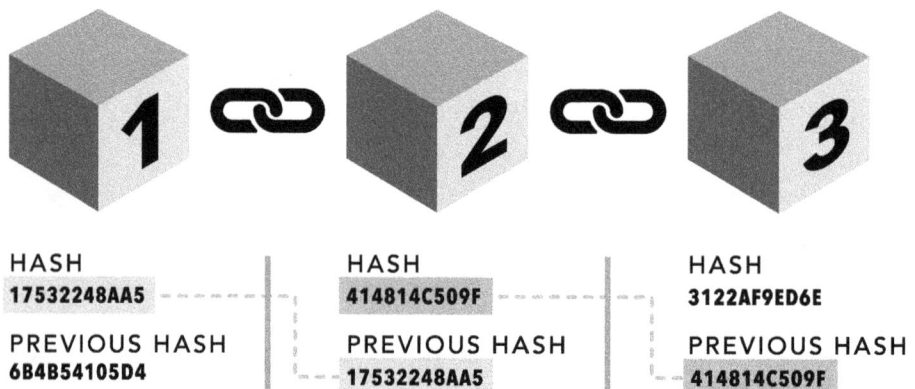

HASH
17532248AA5

PREVIOUS HASH
6B4B54105D4

HASH
414814C509F

PREVIOUS HASH
17532248AA5

HASH
3122AF9ED6E

PREVIOUS HASH
414814C509F

Working with CSV Files

Humans have invented a lot of different ***data exchange*** formats, yet few are as commonly used as comma-separated values files, or CSVs.

A data exchange format is a specified way of saving data to a file so that other programs can read them. Of course, plain text is readable by pretty much any program, but plain text isn't sufficient to store some nuanced data structures. So common formats were created to help different programs import and export data. JSON is now becoming a popular data exchange format over the web, but many programs have a CSV import and export function.

A comma-separated values (CSV) file is simply a text file in which the pieces of data are separated (delimited) by commas. Each "row" of data, that is, a line, can have one or more comma-separated values. CSV files are commonly used to import and export data to and from spreadsheets. Let's look at a simple sales report spreadsheet and then compare it to its CSV export (figure 50).

IMAGE

fig. 50

	A	B	C	D	E
1	Month	Coffee	Tea	Hot Chocolate	Espresso
2	Jan	523	301	507	332
3	Feb	621	339	501	339
4	Mar	512	218	497	401
5	Apr	511	401	324	385
6					

A simple sales report spreadsheet with delicious beverages.

A CSV export of this data would look like this:

```
Month,Coffee,Tea,Hot Chocolate,Espresso
Jan,523,301,507,332
Feb,621,339,501,339
Mar,512,218,497,401
Apr,511,401,324,385
```

As you can see, each row of the spreadsheet, including the header, is on its own line, and all the columns are separated by commas. Now let's read this CSV file in Python. If you want to run this example code, save the previous content as `sales.csv`.

SNIPPET

19-08.py

```python
# Import the csv module
import csv
```

```
# Import the pprint module
from pprint import pprint

# Create empty list
sales_data = []

with open("sales.csv", newline="") as csvfile:
    reader = csv.reader(csvfile)
    for row in reader:
        sales_data.append(row)

pprint(sales_data)
```

If the `sales.csv` file is in the same directory as this program, you'll see this:

```
[['Month', 'Coffee', 'Tea', 'Hot Chocolate', 'Espresso'],
    ['Jan', '523', '301', '507', '332'],
    ['Feb', '621', '339', '501', '339'],
    ['Mar', '512', '218', '497', '401'],
    ['Apr', '511', '401', '324', '385']]
```

I used the `pprint` module, called "pretty print", to better display the multidimensional list. But, ideally, I would like to see it this way:

```
[
    ['Month', 'Coffee', 'Tea', 'Hot Chocolate', 'Espresso'],
    ['Jan', '523', '301', '507', '332'],
    ['Feb', '621', '339', '501', '339'],
    ['Mar', '512', '218', '497', '401'],
    ['Apr', '511', '401', '324', '385']
]
```

In my mind, this makes the most sense, but the `pprint` version is nearly as illustrative. The `csv.reader` and subsequent `for` loop read each line as a comma-separated value line and append it as a list to the `sales_data` list, which is why the result is a multidimensional list—each row is its own list. This method makes it easier to access the data.

For example, if we want the third column of the second row, we use:

```
sales_data[1][2]
```

Indexes start at zero, not one.

The result would be `'301'`.
To write this data as a CSV, it's just as simple.

19-09.py

```
# Import the csv module
import csv

# Generate the data
sales_data = [
    ['Month', 'Coffee', 'Tea', 'Hot Chocolate', 'Espresso'],
    ['Jan', '523', '301', '507', '332'],
    ['Feb', '621', '339', '501', '339'],
    ['Mar', '512', '218', '497', '401'],
    ['Apr', '511', '401', '324', '385']
]

with open("sales-write.csv", "w", newline= '') as csvfile:
    writer = csv.writer(csvfile)
    for row in sales_data:
        writer.writerow(row)
```

When we run this code, the `for` loop will iterate over the writer, defining a temporary `row` list that `writer.writerow` uses to write to the `sales-write.csv` file. The `newline` argument serves to prevent a possible issue on Windows that might generate additional blank lines. We can examine the file and see that it looks like the original CSV file.

If you double-click on the `sales-write.csv` file, your operating system may try to open it in a spreadsheet program like Microsoft® Excel. If you want to see the actual CSV file contents, open it in a text editor instead. However, if you do open it in a spreadsheet program, you'll notice it will look much like our spreadsheet screenshot at the start of this section (figure 50).

Pip

Pip, which stands for "Pip Installs Packages" according to its creator, Ian Bicking, is a convenient tool for installing, managing, and updating Python packages. It allows us to utilize any package in the Python Package Index, or in other third-party repositories if they're compatibly configured.

To install a Python package, simply run the following:

```
pip install PACKAGE
```

Where `PACKAGE` is the name of the package you want to install. You can use the Python Package Index to search for Python packages. For more information on using it, please see chapter 21.

Compiled Modules

fig. 51

```
class Distance:
    def __init__(self, km):
        self._km = km
    @property
    def km(self):
        return self._km
    @km.setter
    def km(self, value):
        self._km = value
    @property
    def miles(self):
        return self._km / 1.609
    @miles.setter
    def miles(self, value):
        self._km = value * 1.609

distance2 = Distance(3)
print("3 kilometers is " + str(distance2.miles) + " miles.")
distance2.miles = 3
print(str(distance2.miles) + " miles is " + str(distance2.km) + " kilometers.")
```

The original `km-miles.py` file.

fig. 52

```
a
??+b?@sVGdd?d?Zed?Zedeej?d?de_eeej?deej?d?dSc@sHeZdZdd?Zedd??Zejdd??Zedd??Zejd??Zd          S)
DistancecCs
||_dS?N?Z_km)?self?km?r?
                        km-miles.py__init__szDistance.__init__cCs|jSrr?rrrrrsz
                                                                        Distance.kmcCs
||_dSrr?r?valuerrrrscCs
|jd?NgX9??v???rr          rrr?miles
szDistance.milescCs|d|_dSr
                        rr
sN__name__?
__module__?
rrrrs      __qualname__propertyr?setterr

r?z3 kilometers is z miles.z
 miles is z _
```

The bytecode `km-miles.pyc` file.

When Python imports a module in a Python program, it converts it to bytecode, an intermediate binary format that is closer to the type of code your computer executes behind the scenes. You will likely see a `distance.pyc` in your source code folder from when we made the `Distance` class into its own module. In figures 51 and 52, you can see the original `.py` file (our kilometers to meters example) and `.pyc` bytecode.

Bytecode isn't readable by humans, but that's fine because we don't edit it—instead we create and edit `.py` files. Bytecode is faster to load and is generally faster to execute. The resulting compiled file is saved in the same directory using the same file name but with a `.pyc` file extension.

You can force Python to bytecode compile any `.py` file by going into the interpreter (or writing a simple Python program) and using the following code:

```
import py_compile
py_compile.compile("file.py")
```

Replace `file.py` with the name of the file to import, and you'll see something like this:

```
'__pycache__/file.cpython-39.pyc'
```

Bytecode isn't readable by humans, but that's fine because we don't edit it—instead we create and edit `.py` files. Bytecode is faster to load and is generally faster to execute. The resulting compiled file is saved in the same directory using the same file name but with a `.pyc` file extension.

You can force Python to bytecode compile any `.py` file by going into the interpreter (or writing a simple Python program) and using the following code:

```
import py_compile
py_compile.compile("file.py")
```

Replace `file.py` with the name of the file to import, and you'll see something like this:

```
'__pycache__/file.cpython-39.pyc'
```

This creates a folder called `__pycache__` and places the file `.cpython-39.pyc` file within it. The 39 will vary based on your version of Python.

You can also compile all `.py` files in a directory by changing to that directory in your console or terminal (with the `cd directory` command, where `directory` is the name of the directory in question) and running this:

```
python -m compileall
```

If you're wanting to distribute a commercial program in bytecode (i.e., `.pyc` files), keep in mind that Python bytecode is easily reversed into Python source code (although the resulting file won't have comments). So you can't achieve total *obfuscation*—that is, the hiding of your source code—from the public with bytecode alone.

Chapter Recap

» We can access Python's built-in help system by typing `help()` at the interactive Python prompt and then entering the topic we'd like to reference at the `help>` prompt.

» Environment variables and command line arguments allow us to access data from the operating environment and command shell.

» Python's threading capability lets us do multiple things at once. It's important to join the threads at the end and to be careful of race conditions.

| 20 |
Optimizing Python

Chapter Overview
» The first optimization step is to profile your code
» Apparent speed is sometimes more important than actual speed
» Cache results and avoid doing the same thing twice

Much has been discussed, written, and shared about optimizing programs. And everyone has an opinion about how it should be done. Rather than strike out with some controversial or radical take on this, I think it best to distill down the common guidance I've been given (and have discovered) over the years into a concise checklist of things to do when your code is running slowly or using too many resources.

FUN FACT

The entire Super Mario Bros game for the Nintendo Entertainment System fit within the memory space of a 32 kilobyte (256 kilobit) cartridge. That's 32,000 characters. Back then, programmers were faced with enormous hardware limitations and yet still performed some amazing feats of engineering! How's that for inspiration for keeping your program's resource usage to a minimum?

Python may not be known as the fastest programming language, but it's certainly one of the most versatile. Nevertheless, the Python developers have spent a lot of time optimizing Python's performance, so you can expect generally good performance from the interpreter. Still, there are things you can do to help ensure your code runs as fast as possible.

These tips are in no specific order, and some may work better for you in some situations than others. However, you first need to know where to focus your efforts.

Profiling

The most effective way to optimize a program is to spend your time optimizing the slowest or most resource-consuming part. And profiling the application shows you what that part is, so it should be done first.

Python includes the cProfile module, which gives you a breakdown of the time spent in each part of a function or line of code.

SNIPPET

20-01.py

```python
import cProfile
import math


def myfunction(x):
    a = math.cos(x)
    b = math.pi
    c = math.e
    print(abs(a + b / c))


cProfile.run("for i in range(50000): myfunction(i)")
```

The `run` function takes a string containing the code to run (in this case, it executes `myfunction` 50,000 times). It also runs everything on one line, so the block that the `for` statement runs is actually after the colon and not indented.

```
200003 function calls in 0.161 seconds


Ordered by: standard name


Ncalls   tottime  percall  cumtime  percall  filename:lineno(function)
50000    0.015    0.000    0.155    0.000    <stdin>:1(myfunction)
1        0.006    0.006    0.161    0.161    <string>:1(<module>)
50000    0.002    0.000    0.002    0.000    {built-in method builtins.abs}
1        0.000    0.000    0.161    0.161    {built-in method builtins.exec}
50000    0.135    0.000    0.135    0.000    {built-in method builtins.print}
50000    0.003    0.000    0.003    0.000    {built-in method math.cos}
1        0.000    0.000    0.000    0.000    {method 'disable' of '_lsprof.Profiler' objects}
```

Here, you can see the number of calls (`ncalls`), total time (`tottime`), time per call (`percall`), cumulative time (`cumtime`), and the file name, line number, and function involved. You can ignore the `builtins.exec` line because `exec` is called internally by `cProfile.run` to execute the code to profile. Therefore, its cumulative time is 0.161, matching the total cumulative time.

Most important, of the built-in methods, `print` (represented by `builtins.print`) took the most time, followed by `cos` (`math.cos` – or cosine).

There's not a lot you can do to optimize `print`, but this serves to illustrate that profiling can help you focus on what's important. Since the proof is, as they say, in the pudding, I want you to see the results of each tip I give you. In this chapter, I'll profile each optimization with `cProfile` so you can see the difference.

Your performance journey should start with profiling. Once you have a baseline profiling report, then apply an optimization and profile again to see if what you did helped. Test only one thing at a time so you know what improved your code. If you test multiple items at once, you won't know which one made the most impact.

Apparent Speed Usually Matters More

There are two basic measures of performance in terms of programs: *wall clock time* and *apparent execution speed*. Wall clock time is the actual amount of time it takes for a task to be done. Apparent execution speed is the time it *appears* to take to do a given task and is largely a subjective measurement.

Sometimes the distinction is nonexistent or subtle, but a skilled programmer can make a long-executing task appear to take a shorter amount of time, in the eyes of the user. If that's not possible, at least providing a percentage of completion, or status messages as the task runs, can help the user feel more comfortable during the wait.

I'm sure you've wondered sometimes if a website or desktop application was locked up because it appeared to do nothing for a moment after you performed an action. In some ways, this kind of experience is worse than slowness, because it makes the user think that something is wrong or that your program is unreliable.

You can use threading to execute a long-running task in the background while you let the user perform other tasks. Or, if there's nothing else meaningful for the user to do during that period, use a thread to give an on-screen report of the task's status. Getting the progress of a task is simple if you are performing the work in a loop, which is most likely the case with long-running processes.

Here's a quick example of a function outputting the percentage complete during its execution.

```python
def percent(n):
    return(str(n * 100) + "%")

def long_task():
    # Start a long loop and do some string work
    for i in range(100000):
        a = "Hello, World!"
        b = a + " " + a
        c = len(b)
        for j in range(c):
            d = b[j]
            e = d
        progress = i / 100000
        print(percent(progress))

long_task()
```

Another example is an install program displaying interesting graphics or text for the user to read while the program is being set up on their computer. This is less common today than it was back when disks were slower and setup times were excessive, but the strategy is still used during operating system and office suite installs.

Another scenario you may have encountered is a *splash screen*: an attractive graphic displaying the name of a program, its author(s), and its version information while the program is being loaded. Adobe Photoshop and many other large programs use this technique. It is accomplished by quickly displaying the splash graphic before anything else is loaded or initialized and then using thread(s) in the background to get everything else set up and ready for the user. The eye is distracted by the colorful graphic or logo, and it gives the user the impression that work is being done, rather than leaving them wondering if the program actually started at all.

Don't Reinvent the Wheel

Unless you have a good reason to do differently, I advise using built-in functionality whenever possible. Sure, you can build your own list class and give more features, but smart programmers have written highly optimized code over the years to handle lists, and your implementation will likely not benefit from that expertise.

If you need functionality that isn't in the standard modules, try searching the Python Package Index (see chapter 19). You might find a module that does most or all of what you need. Even if it isn't the best or fastest code, you'll have a starting place to build from that can accelerate your development time.

Cache Results

When you are going to use the result of a function's output more than once, cache that result in a variable rather than invoking the function multiple times.

```
# Avoid this
for i in range(100):
    print(math.sin(math.pi / 3))


# Instead, do this
a = math.sin(math.pi / 3)
for i in range(100):
    print(a)
```

In the first example, the sine and division operation must be completed many times within the loop. But there's no need. If you know the data won't change, store it in a variable at the beginning and use it throughout your code.

Let's see the performance impact of this optimization.

SNIPPET

20-03.py

```
import cProfile
import math
import contextlib

# Avoid this
def slow_func():
    for i in range(100000):
        with contextlib.redirect_stdout(None):
            print(math.sin(math.pi / 3))

# Instead, do this
def fast_func():
    a = math.sin(math.pi / 3)
    for i in range(100000):
```

```
        with contextlib.redirect_stdout(None):
            print(a)

print("**** SLOW FUNCTION ****")
cProfile.run("slow_func()")

print("**** FAST FUNCTION ****")
cProfile.run("fast_func()")
```

I made two small differences in this code. First, I imported the
contextlib module and used it in a with block to redirect the standard
out that print uses to None, which prevents the loop from printing. I also
increased the range iteration count to 100000 to slow the function down and
make the performance impact more noticeable.

> If you find that this or any other loop code in this chapter takes too
> long on your computer, feel free to adjust the iteration count in range.

On my computer, when I run the previous code, the difference is clear.

```
**** SLOW FUNCTION ****
         1000004 function calls in 0.317 seconds


   Ordered by: standard name

   ncalls  tottime  percall  cumtime  percall filename:lineno(function)
        1    0.000    0.000    0.317    0.317 <string>:1(<module>)
        1    0.208    0.208    0.317    0.317 cache-results.py:6(slow_func)
   100000    0.013    0.000    0.013    0.000 contextlib.py:329(__init__)
   100000    0.039    0.000    0.051    0.000 contextlib.py:334(__enter__)
   100000    0.024    0.000    0.035    0.000 contextlib.py:339(__exit__)
        1    0.000    0.000    0.317    0.317 {built-in method builtins.exec}
   100000    0.004    0.000    0.004    0.000 {built-in method builtins.getattr}
   100000    0.004    0.000    0.004    0.000 {built-in method builtins.print}
   200000    0.010    0.000    0.010    0.000 {built-in method builtins.setattr}
   100000    0.005    0.000    0.005    0.000 {built-in method math.sin}
   100000    0.004    0.000    0.004    0.000 {method 'append' of 'list' objects}
        1    0.000    0.000    0.000    0.000 {method 'disable' of '_lsprof.Profiler' objects}
   100000    0.006    0.000    0.006    0.000 {method 'pop' of 'list' objects}


**** FAST FUNCTION ****
         900005 function calls in 0.285 seconds
```

```
Ordered by: standard name

ncalls  tottime  percall  cumtime  percall filename:lineno(function)
     1    0.000    0.000    0.285    0.285 <string>:1(<module>)
     1    0.188    0.188    0.285    0.285 cache-results.py:12(fast_func)
100000    0.013    0.000    0.013    0.000 contextlib.py:329(__init__)
100000    0.037    0.000    0.048    0.000 contextlib.py:334(__enter__)
100000    0.023    0.000    0.033    0.000 contextlib.py:339(__exit__)
     1    0.000    0.000    0.285    0.285 {built-in method builtins.exec}
100000    0.004    0.000    0.004    0.000 {built-in method builtins.getattr}
100000    0.003    0.000    0.003    0.000 {built-in method builtins.print}
200000    0.009    0.000    0.009    0.000 {built-in method builtins.setattr}
     1    0.000    0.000    0.000    0.000 {built-in method math.sin}
100000    0.003    0.000    0.003    0.000 {method 'append' of 'list' objects}
     1    0.000    0.000    0.000    0.000 {method 'disable' of '_lsprof.Profiler' objects}
100000    0.005    0.000    0.005    0.000 {method 'pop' of 'list' objects}
```

Not only is the `fast_func()` faster by 0.032 seconds, but the faster function makes almost 100,000 fewer function calls.

Just be careful that the cached data is always correct. If at some point the value could change (e.g., you alter it, or you need to change the way you get the data due to some condition in the code), run the function again to get a new value. Even if you must obtain the new value several times, that is better than having to run the same code hundreds or thousands of times in a loop.

Use Multiple Assignment

If you need to assign three or more variables in a row, use multiple assignment.

```
# Avoid this
a = 1
b = 2
c = 3
d = 4


# Instead, do this
a, b, c, d = 1, 2, 3, 4
```

This may give you a speed boost and lets the interpreter skip a few steps. To see it in action (and test the presence of a performance gain), we'll need to use a loop to extrapolate the results.

```
import cProfile

def slow_func():
    for i in range(100000):
        # Avoid this
        a = 1
        b = 2
        c = 3
        d = 4

def fast_func():
    for i in range(100000):
        # Instead, do this
        a, b, c, d = 1, 2, 3, 4

print("**** SLOW FUNCTION ****")
cProfile.run("slow_func()")

print("**** FAST FUNCTION ****")
cProfile.run("fast_func()")
```

And here are the results:

```
**** SLOW FUNCTION ****
        4 function calls in 0.010 seconds
    Ordered by: standard name
    ncalls  tottime  percall  cumtime  percall filename:lineno(function)
        1    0.000    0.000    0.010    0.010 <string>:1(<module>)
        1    0.010    0.010    0.010    0.010 assignment-results.py:3(slow_func)
        1    0.000    0.000    0.010    0.010 {built-in method builtins.exec}
        1    0.000    0.000    0.000    0.000 {method 'disable' of '_lsprof.Profiler' objects}
**** FAST FUNCTION ****
        4 function calls in 0.007 seconds
    Ordered by: standard name
    ncalls  tottime  percall  cumtime  percall filename:lineno(function)
        1    0.000    0.000    0.007    0.007 <string>:1(<module>)
```

```
   1    0.007    0.007    0.007    0.007 assignment-results.py:11(fast_func)
   1    0.000    0.000    0.007    0.007 {built-in method builtins.exec}
   1    0.000    0.000    0.000    0.000 {method 'disable' of '_lsprof.Profiler' objects}
```

It's not much, but every little bit helps. And, if you're doing this quite often, the time savings can really add up to a significant optimization.

Exit As Soon As Possible

If something goes wrong, or the function won't be able to do what it's supposed to do, raise an exception, or return a value that provides the calling code with a clue as to how to proceed. Oftentimes, I'll exit early with a `return False` or similar, and the calling code will check for `False` and interpret that to mean that something failed.

Depending on your case, this can be a huge timesaver. However, it's difficult to illustrate this in a code sample because the situation in your app will likely be dramatically different. Regardless, if you remember the mantra "exit early if you can't finish the block," you'll write faster, more efficient code.

Use Lazy Loading

Lazy loading is the process of importing modules and loading data that you need when you need it and not a moment before.

In our code samples, we've been importing the modules we need at the top of each program. There's nothing wrong with that approach, and for small programs it makes sense. But in larger programs, you can reduce memory usage and perhaps shave a few nanoseconds off your runtime by loading modules only when needed.

Use the Latest Python Version

With each release, the programmers of Python squash bugs and improve the security and performance of the interpreter. There have been many occasions when I've seen significant performance improvements by simply upgrading the version of Python I am using to the latest stable release.

Optimizing the Coffee Shop Simulator

I don't believe there's such a thing as perfect code, but it's certainly possible to optimize the coffee shop simulator game to be more efficient—

and possibly faster. Any potential performance gains should be discoverable through profiling.

Try using `cProfile` to benchmark the game and see if you can find the parts of code that are the slowest. Once you identify the bottlenecks, examine the code to determine if there is a better approach. There are undoubtedly some inefficiencies in the game that could be improved.

Chapter Recap

» Before doing anything else, profile your code with cProfile. This will save you time by pinpointing where you need to optimize your code.

» Sometimes apparent speed is more important than the actual time it takes to do something. Consider your users' workflow and enjoyment of the program.

» Cache results to avoid redundant code, exit a block of code as soon as you know you can't finish the block, try lazy loading modules, and use the latest version of Python for best results.

| 21 |
What's Next?

Chapter Overview
» Keeping up with Python
» Finding Python packages
» The open-source community of Python

You may not realize it yet, but you're a Python programmer.

And not just a beginner, either. If you've completed all the exercises in this book up until this point, you can safely say you have a fair bit of experience with programming in Python. Granted, writing your own program from scratch is something you've yet to do, but you have all the knowledge you need to get started on a project.

My hope is that I've given you the knowledge you'll need not only to write your own Python programs but to know how to ask the right questions when you get stuck. I've seen many a programming problem solved, by both colleagues and myself, when we knew exactly how to phrase the web search to find the right answer.

Don't feel bad if you find yourself constantly referencing things from this book even after you've read it from cover to cover. I've been programming for over twenty years, and I still look up things on a regular basis. You'll continue to do so, even as a master Python programmer. Maybe a bit less often, but it's impossible to know everything about Python. And even if you somehow managed that feat, new modules are released daily.

Keeping Up with Python
The Python web page, https://www.python.org, is an excellent resource for all things Python. Not only does it have good reference documentation, but the news section is updated often with announcements of new versions and important events in the Python ecosystem.

The Python Package Index

Are you looking for a package with certain functionality? The Python Package Index is the best place to start. At https://pypi.org, you can search for what you need, and it will show a list of matching packages.

For example, if you're needing to read a Microsoft® Excel spreadsheet, search for *excel* and you'll see a plethora of matches (figure 53).

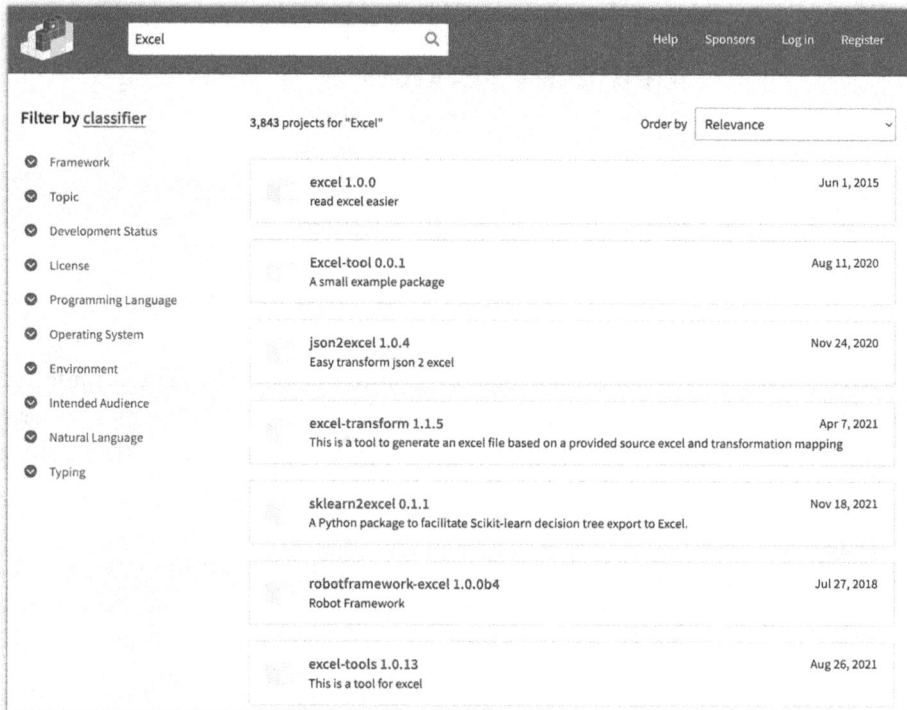

IMAGE

fig. 53

The Python Package Index list of packages relating to "Excel."

You can click on each result to see more details about it, and if you want to install it, you generally do so with the `pip` command.

NOTE

```
pip install package
```

Replace `package` with your package name.

Of course, not every package will suit your needs, and some have been abandoned. I would advise clicking on *Release history* on the left-hand side (figure 54) to see if there have been recent updates. If the last version was released eight years ago, that's probably a good indicator that the project is no longer supported.

fig. 54

A look at the release history of the drf-excel package.

Frequent updates are generally a good thing to see. Active development means you'll probably get quick security updates and bug fixes. Most projects have links to their GitHub page as well, where you can browse the code and see the history of the project. Additionally, a lot of packages will have instructions for use on their main page, and if not, you can usually find it on the project's home page (found under *Project links > Homepage*).

MY TAKE

If you're writing software that will be used long term or depended upon heavily for important tasks, it's a good idea to carefully consider using external packages. While they can provide extraordinary functionality with minimal effort, keep in mind that you are responsible for making sure the package is adequately maintained. And this doesn't just apply to the package itself, as it may have its own dependencies to consider.

I don't want to talk you out of using packages from the Python Package Index, but on important projects, I do advise performing due diligence on each dependency.

Python News through Google

For a broader view of all the news related to Python, you can use Google News. Visit https://news.google.com and type "Python" in the search bar at the top of the page (but don't yet hit ENTER). You'll see a dropdown of various options; click the one that says "Python" with *Topic* in italics right under it. The entry should have the Python logo.

When you select this item, Google will show a list of news articles in the media that pertain to Python. Choosing "Python *Topic*" rather than just blindly searching for "Python" will eliminate news stories about nonvenomous snakes. You can click the *follow* button at the top of the results to be alerted whenever there's a news story about Python.

Getting Help

If you get stuck on a Python problem, the programming Q&A forum Stack Overflow, located at https://stackoverflow.com, is a great place to get help. The search engine at the top of the page is pretty good at finding what you want, or you can use the `[python]` tag to limit your search to entries related to Python.

```
[python] converting string to integer
```

In this search, the `[python]` tag in brackets will ensure that the results are related to Python programming.

If you're looking for discussion, the Python subreddit at https://www.reddit.com/r/Python is a great place to start. The community is quite active, with almost a million members at time of publication.

The Python Education subreddit at https://www.reddit.com/r/learnpython is a great place for Python beginners and has over six hundred thousand members at time of publication. But you've read this book and you're an awesome Python programmer now, so you may not need this. Nevertheless, I've found that there's no greater teacher than the process of helping someone else learn. Discussing Python in either subreddit will sharpen your skills and keep you up to date on the language.

If conversing via Discord is your thing, check out the Python Discord at https://discord.gg/python.

Python Is Open-Source Software

The Python interpreter, as well as many of the packages that are available for it, is open-source. The project was developed with the hard work of many volunteers, and through their labors they have created not only an amazing programming language but a thriving ecosystem.

I encourage you to give back to the community if you can. You can submit bug fixes or patches, write documentation for Python, write a package, or even donate to the Python Software Foundation. Even if you're writing proprietary software for yourself or your company, you might still be able to release some small portion of it as an open-source package—perhaps some code that has a stand-alone function or integrates with another system.

Of course, if you're writing code for hire, check with your employer for their desired licensing terms. If they're leery of sharing any of their code, you can remind them that releasing part of their software will enlist the help of the broader open-source community to find bugs and submit patches that benefit everyone. Also, open-source projects can serve as free promotion for the company that releases them.

The ClydeBank Coffee Shop Simulator Game

Throughout this book we've built on the coffee shop simulator game. By chapter 16 it was complete, but that doesn't mean development has to stop there. I would encourage you to add your own features to the game or modify it as you see fit. I've made a few suggestions in the "On Your Own" callouts throughout the book, but feel free to implement your own enhancements. The sky's the limit!

Chapter Recap

» The official Python website contains news, great documentation, and a host of other resources.

» You can keep up with Python news via the Python website and through news alerts with Google News.

» Stack Overflow and Reddit are great places to get Python help.

» Python is open-source and has a large community of developers.

Conclusion

When my wife became a notary public, she received a little pamphlet titled "So, You're a Notary." I gave her a bit of undeserved teasing about this. However, after reading through it, I understood a deep philosophical truth about life. I'm sure the author of the pamphlet didn't intend it to be a life-changing publication, but what I realized from this gem was that so many of life's accomplishments don't come with a manual for mapping the rest of your path.

Your Python career began the second you picked up this book and committed yourself to learning Python. This was no small achievement, and here you are with some great experience under your belt. You've programmed a video game—granted, with some guidance, but how many people can say that? This process has given you a new way to think about computing problems. You have the power to make your computer do quite literally anything you want it to do. Dissatisfied with a piece of software you use? You can now write a replacement! Have an idea for the next killer application? Write it!

In chapter 21, (What's Next?), I tried to show you some next steps, but I could only speak in general terms because it is no understatement to say that the whole world of programming is in your hands. A new era of cloud computing was born when Dropbox was written with Python. YouTube uses Python to innovate with new features, letting you binge watch an endless stream of videos. And NASA uses Python to lead the next generation into space.

That leaves me with one final question for *you*—what awesome new software will you build with Python?

REMEMBER TO DOWNLOAD
YOUR FREE DIGITAL ASSETS!

All Source Code from Game and Examples

Regular Expression Cheat Sheet

List of Built-in Exceptions Cheat Sheet

TWO WAYS TO ACCESS YOUR FREE DIGITAL ASSETS

Use the camera app on your mobile phone to scan the QR code
or visit the link below and instantly access your digital assets.

SCAN ME

or

go.quickstartguides.com/python

VISIT URL

Appendix

On Your Own Answer Key

There's more than one way to solve a problem in programming. Some solutions are better than others, and specific approaches have the advantage of being faster, being easier to expand, or containing fewer lines of code. Nevertheless, don't feel bad if your code doesn't exactly match these examples. In fact, there may be even better solutions than these.

If you are stuck and need the solution, I encourage you to find the answer here and then expand on what you are trying to do. This will give you even more programming problem-solving experience.

Chapter 1: What's in a Name?

Here is the simplest approach to solving this exercise.

SNIPPET

```
name = input("What is your name? ")
print("The first letter of your name is " + name[:1] + ".")
```

CH01-01.py

Remember, if your example works but doesn't look like mine, don't worry. You still solved the problem!

Chapter 3: Number-Guessing Game

Here are several approaches to the number-guessing game.

Simplest Solution

SNIPPET

```
from random import seed
from random import randint


number = randint(1, 10)


guess = int(input("Please pick a number between 1 and 10: "))


if guess == number:
    print("You guessed the number correctly!")
```

CH03-01a.py

```
        else:
            print("Sorry, that's incorrect. The number was " + str(number))
```

Loop Solution

This solution actually takes one fewer line of code and is more interactive.

CH03-01b.py

```
from random import seed
from random import randint

number = randint(1, 10)

guess = int(input("Please pick a number between 1 and 10: "))

while guess != number:
    guess = int(input("Sorry, that's incorrect. Try again: "))

print("You guessed the number correctly!")
```

Chapter 5: More Bottles!

Here's a solution to reverse the flow of time and return the bottles to the wall.

CH05-01.py

```
# Define the bottles_song function with the start argument defaulting to 1
def bottles_song(start = 1):
    # Set the initial number of bottles to the start argument
    bottles = start
    # Loop through until bottles are restored
    while bottles <= 99:
        # Display the song
        this_verse = []
        this_verse.append(str(bottles) + " bottles of beer on the wall. ")
        this_verse.append(str(bottles) + " bottles of beer. ")
        this_verse.append("Take one down, pass it around, ")
        this_verse.append(str(bottles) + " bottles of beer on the wall. ")
        # Add a bottle
        bottles += 1
        # Yield to the calling function
        yield "".join(this_verse)
        # Pick back up here when we return
```

```
        return True

# Loop through the generator
for v in bottles _ song():
    print(v)
```

Chapter 6: Inches to Centimeters

Here's a way to construct the Length class and the sample code to use it.

CH06-01.py

```
class Length:
    def __ init __ (self, inches):
        self. _ inches = inches

    @property
    def inches(self):
        return self. _ inches

    @inches.setter
    def inches(self, value):
        self. _ inches = value

    @property
    def centimeters(self):
        return self. _ inches * 2.54

    @centimeters.setter
    def centimeters(self, value):
        self. _ inches = value / 2.54

l = Length(1)
print("1 inch is " + str(l.centimeters) + " centimeters.")
l.centimeters = 5
print(str(l.centimeters) + " centimeters is " + str(l.inches) + " inches.")
```

Chapter 7: A Fantasy World

Here's the class design I came up with for elements of a role-playing game. Your code may be simpler or more complex, depending on how far you went into the design detail.

```python
# A class of player (i.e., fighter, mage, rogue, etc.)
class PlayerClass:
    pass


# The brave fighter
class Fighter(PlayerClass):
    pass


# The wise mage
class Mage(PlayerClass):
    pass


# The sneaky rogue
class Rogue(PlayerClass):
    pass


# The powerful healer
class Healer(PlayerClass):
    pass


# Our player
class Player:
    pass


# Weapon base class
class Weapon:
    pass


# A short sword
class ShortSword(Weapon):
    pass


# A long sword
class LongSword(Weapon):
    pass


# A bow
class Bow(Weapon):
    pass
```

```python
# A dagger
class Dagger(Weapon):
    pass


# Armor base class
class Armor:
    pass


# Leather armor
class LeatherArmor(Armor):
    pass


# Plate armor
class PlateArmor(Armor):
    pass


# A shield
class Shield(Armor):
    pass


# Base spell class
class Spell:
    pass


# A fireball spell
class Fireball(Spell):
    pass


# A simple healing spell
class Heal(Spell):
    pass


# The monster
class Monster:
    pass


# A basilisk (don't look!)
class Basilisk(Monster):
    pass
```

Chapter 11: Counting the Days

Here's the simplest solution I can think of to find the difference between now and a future date. In this example, I used Halloween of 2023.

```python
import datetime

# The future date
future = datetime.datetime(2023, 10, 31, 0, 0)

# Now
now = datetime.datetime.now()

# Calculate difference
difference = future - now

# Display difference
print("It's " + str(difference) + " until " + str(future) + "!")
```

About
the Author

ROBERT OLIVER

Robert Oliver is the DevOps Manager at a leading learning management system provider and has consulted and developed software for leading firms across the globe for over two decades. He has been programming in Python for years and uses it in his daily systems management tasks.

In addition to writing technical books, Robert is the author of several fiction novels, including the successful Sign of Alchemy fantasy series.

Robert lives with his family in the beautiful Shoals Area of North Alabama.

QUICK CLIP

HOW I STARTED PROGRAMMING

- First learned the Logo programming language in fourth grade
- Started learning DOS and BASIC on the Tandy 1000
- Messed up DOS and the computer so badly I had to fix it
- Further programmed on my native
- Grandfather bought me a family 2000 on DOS 5 and Windows 3.1
- Programmed in QBasic, eventually older and wrote bits of assembly
- Moved on to C/C++
- Started with Python in mid-2000's

Meet the author of the *Python QuickStart Guide.*

To watch the Quick Clip, use the camera on your mobile phone to scan the QR code or visit the link below.

or

www.quickclips.io/python-8

SCAN ME   **VISIT URL**

About QuickStart Guides

QuickStart Guides are books for beginners, written by experts.

QuickStart Guides® are comprehensive learning companions tailored for the beginner experience. Our books are written by experts, subject matter authorities, and thought leaders within their respective areas of study.

For nearly a decade more than 850,000 readers have trusted QuickStart Guides® to help them get a handle on their finances, start their own business, invest in the stock market, find a new hobby, get a new job—the list is virtually endless.

The QuickStart Guides® series of books is published by ClydeBank Media, an independent publisher based in Albany, NY.

Connect with QuickStart Guides online at www.quickstartguides.com or follow us on Facebook, Instagram, and LinkedIn.

Follow us @quickstartguides

Glossary

Apparent execution speed
The speed at which a user perceives a program or process to run.

Argument
A value supplied to a function or method.

ASCII
Stands for American Standard Code for Information Interchange. The ASCII system defines human-readable characters from binary data. UTF-8 has largely replaced this format.

Assembly language
A human-readable version of machine code, the bare-metal programming language that computers natively understand.

Assertion
A test of the output of code against a known value.

Branching
The process of copying code to a new, independent version in a Git repository.

Breakpoint
A location in code where a debugger will break (pause) execution.

Buffer
A variable or data structure that stores data meant to be processed, usually during input and output operations.

Business logic
Code that contains unique and essential functionality within an application.

Caching
The process of loading frequently accessed data from a slower device (like a disk) to a faster device (like memory) for quick retrieval.

Case-sensitive
A condition in which uppercase and lowercase letters are considered distinct.

Casting
The act of converting one type of variable into another type.

Class
A structure that defines a reusable container that holds both data (variables) and logic (functions).

Class variable
A variable shared across all objects of the same class.

Cloning
In regard to Git repositories, the process of copying the repository to another location (usually from a provider like GitHub to a local computer).

Command line arguments
Options provided after the program name on the command line.

Compression
In regard to data, the act of eliminating redundancies and structuring data so that it takes up less space.

Concatenation
In Python, the act of joining one or more strings.

Constant
A read-only variable.

Content delivery network
A geographically distributed network of servers that serve assets (usually images, CSS, JavaScript, and HTML files) to visitors. The closest server is used, thus saving access time.

Data exchange
The act of transferring data in a standardized way.

Database
A software program that stores data in an organized manner and provides a mechanism to retrieve that data.

Decorator
In Python, a line of code placed above a function or method that declares additional scope or attributes.

Deduplication
The act of removing redundant data.

Delimiter
One or more characters that separate segments of data.

Delta
The change in value.

Design pattern
An established method or paradigm for approaching a problem.

Environment variables
Strings (usually short) that are available in the operating system and accessible to programs.

Escape sequence
A series of characters that represent something other than the characters themselves. Escape sequences provide special processing within a regular expression.

Evaluate
The act of executing the statement and converting it into a value.

Exception
An error that occurs during the regular execution of a program. Python can raise a wide variety of exception errors depending on the error condition encountered.

Flag
A variable, usually `True` or `False`, that denotes whether a certain status or state has been reached. Often used as a toggle switch or an indicator of an evaluation.

Floating-point number
A number that contains a decimal point.

Fork
A copy of a Git repository that is independent of the original repository. Can be merged back into the original repository via a pull request.

Function
A named, grouped set of commands that usually accepts arguments and returns one or more values.

Garbage collection
A feature of the Python interpreter that frees memory that was used by variables, objects, and other data structures that are no longer needed.

Generator
A block of code that runs until it reaches a `yield` statement, then returns control back to the caller. Subsequent calls to the generator will resume where it left off, continuing to the next `yield` statement.

GET request
An HTTP request that tells the web server that the browser would like the contents of a page.

Global variable
A variable that is within the scope of the main program.

Handle
The unique identifier of an open file or device.

Hashing
The process of taking a string and generating a shorter fixed-length code that represents the original data.

Hex digest
A string of hexadecimal digits produced by a hashing function.

Immutable
Not changeable; read-only.

Index
A pointer to a specific piece of data in a larger data structure. Lists, for example, contain multiple values, and an index allows a value to be specifically referenced by its position in the list.

Infinite loop
Any loop in execution that continues (or has the potential to continue) forever.

Inheritance
The process of a class deriving functionality or structure from an ancestor class.

Input
A term used to describe the data received from a user or storage device.

Input validation
The act of ensuring that input matches an expected format.

Instance variable
A variable defined within a class that is specific to that instance (in other words, specific to that object).

Integer
A variable that stores a whole number.

Interpreter
The core Python system that executes code.

IP address
A unique address referencing a network device.

Iteration
A single execution through a loop.

JSON
Stands for JavaScript Object Notation, a standard readable text format used to store and exchange data between processes.

Key-value pair
A pairing of a value with a named index to reference it.

Lambda expression
A short, nameless (sometimes called anonymous) function.

Lazy loading
The act of loading assets or modules when needed rather than at the beginning of execution.

Literal character
A character indicated to be the actual character and to have no special meaning beyond that.

Memory leak
A condition in which memory is used but not released. Over time, this grows to consume increased memory, possibly more than the system has available.

Merging
In regard to Git, the act of combining two separate branches.

Metacharacter
A special character or sequence of characters in a regular expression.

Method
A function within a class.

Model–view–controller
Abbreviated MVC, a paradigm that separates data, user interface, and logic into models, views, and controllers.

Module
Any Python code file.

Modulo
The value of the remainder when dividing two numbers.

Multilevel inheritance
A class possessing a chain of ancestors.

Multiple inheritance
A class possessing multiple ancestors.

Mutable
Changeable.

Namespace
A region of code that differentiates logic and data structures from other regions, preventing colliding names and providing organization to code.

Newline
A special character sequence that denotes a line break, moving the cursor position to the next line.

NOP
Stands for "no operation" and is a statement (such as `pass`) that tells Python to do nothing and move to the next operation.

Obfuscation
The act of hiding or obscuring the original source code of a program.

Object
An instance of a class.

Object relational mapping
Abbreviated as ORM, a paradigm aimed at making it easier to work with tables, data, and the relations between sets of data in a database.

Object-oriented programming
An approach to programming that involves objects that contain code and data, modeled from classes.

Operator
A character or symbol that assigns a value to a variable, logically compares values, or performs mathematical functions.

Output
A term used to describe data provided to a user.

Package
A collection of modules that can be imported and used in a program.

Port
A unique identifier more specific than an IP address, which can be opened for a specific program to transmit on the network.

Private variable
A variable that is accessible only to operations inside the class.

Property
A member of a class that acts like a variable but allows the execution of code when read or written.

Pull request
A request to the maintainer of a Git repository to accept a merge of code from another branch or a forked repository.

Race condition
A situation that occurs when two or more threads or processes are trying to access the same device or read/modify the same piece of data and inadvertently disrupt the other threads.

Refactor
Organize and reformat code to address previous design issues.

Regex anchor
A special symbol that describes a certain position or attribute within a string.

Regression
A flaw in software that was fixed but reappears later (usually due to further changes in the code).

Regular expressions
Sometimes called regex, a system of symbols that allow searching through strings to match specific patterns.

Repository
In regard to Git, a container where source code and its version history are stored.

Resources
A term encompassing one or more aspects of a system's used CPU, memory, and disk space.

Scalable
Able to grow and expand to meet increased demands.

Scope
The place where data structures and functions can be accessed.

Search engine optimization
The science and art of optimizing a website for better rankings in search engine results.

Serialization
The process of saving the state of an object and its data to a string (and later a file, if desired) so that it can be recreated later.

Setter
A method that sets a property of an object.

Source code management
The process of tracking source code file versions and synchronizing them for collaboration purposes.

Splash screen
A screen or window displayed to a user while the main program loads.

Standard in
Refers to the default device that receives input—usually the keyboard. Can be redirected if needed. Often abbreviated as stdin or STDIN.

Standard out
Refers to the default device that generates output—usually the screen. Can be redirected if needed. Often abbreviated as stdout or STDOUT.

String
A type of variable that contains text and numbers and is generally human-readable.

Test coverage
The ratio of lines tested to the total lines of code.

Test-driven development
A quality assurance paradigm in which programmers create tests based on the requirements of the program before writing any code and then regularly test that code to ensure proper operation.

Text file
A file containing readable characters.

Tuple
A read-only, ordered collection of data.

Unit testing
A testing method that focuses on ensuring that individual parts of code work as expected.

URL
Initialism for Uniform Resource Locator; the address of a page or resource on the web.

UTF-8
A method of character encoding that greatly expands the ASCII character set. It includes mostly letters, numbers, and glyphs from many international languages.

Variables
Locations to store data that are referenced by name.

Wall clock time
The actual time that a process takes to complete, not in terms of CPU time but measured from start to finish.

References

CHAPTER 8

https://peps.python.org/pep-0557/

CHAPTER 15

https://docs.djangoproject.com/en/4.0/faq/general/

CHAPTER 16

https://www.sqlite.org/mostdeployed.html

CONCLUSION

https://blog.dropbox.com/topics/company/thank-you--guido

https://www.python.org/about/quotes/

https://www.python.org/about/success/usa/

Index

math, 207–208, 208f
standard, 164
Modulo operator, 70
Multidimensional lists, 45–47
Multilevel inheritance, 140–142, 146–148
Multiple assignment, 337–339
Multiple inheritance, 142–144, 146–148
Multiplication, 205, 206f
Mutable, 40
MVC architecture. *See* Model–view–controller architecture
MySQL, 273

N

:n, 195
Names
  of modules, 161
  of variables, 25
Namespaces, 159–161
NASA, 2, 347
Nested comparisons, 57–59, 71
Nested loops, 71
Netflix, 2
Newlines, 33–34
No-operation statement, 106–107
NOP statement, 106–107
Notepad++, 7
Number(s)
  converting to strings, 31–32
  floating-point. *See* Floating-point numbers
  integers, 28–29
  in lists, 39–40
  `for` loops with, 63–64
  quotes around, 37
  strings converted to, 31
  true/false comparison using, 70–71
Number-guessing game, 72–73, 349–350
`numpy` module, 222, 298

O

Obfuscation, 330
Object(s)
  collection of, 146–148
  definition of, 114
  `__del__`, 123–124
  in dictionaries, 147–148
  `__enter__`, 122–123
  `__exit__`, 122–123
  `__init__`, 115–117, 121–122
  lifecycle of, 120–124
Object-oriented programming, 113–114, 137, 142
Object relational mapping, 275–276, 276f
Open-source software, 344–345
`open` statement, 227
Operators
  %, 70
  for comparisons, 56, 57f
  modulo, 70

Optimizing
  apparent execution speed, 333–334
  cache results, 335–337
  exiting, 339
  lazy loading, 339
  multiple assignment, 337–339
  profiling, 332–333
  wall clock time, 333–334
`order` argument, 156
Order of operations, 206
ORM. *See* Object relational mapping
Output. *See* Input/output
`OverflowError`, 83

P

Packages, 164–166, 327–328
Parent classes, 138–139
Parentheses, 40–41, 98, 138
Pascal, 1
`pass` statement, 106
Passing values, 93–96
Pattern counting, 177–178
Percentages, 211–212
pi, 208f
`pickle`, serialization with, 232–233
Pip, 327–328
Plus sign, 31
Port, 267
`print` function
  adding space to, 26
  definition of, 21–22
  description of, 93
  on dictionary, 44
  indenting of, 54
  on list, 44
  newline, 33
  passing string to, 25
  on set, 44
  on tuple, 44
Private variables, 124–127
Profiling, 332–333
Program file, 21–22
Program flow
  logical comparisons. *See* Logical comparisons
  nested comparisons, 57–59, 71
Programming
  definition of, 2–3
  description of, 19
  loops in. *See* Loops
  object-oriented, 113–114, 137, 142
  procedural, 113
  scope, 102
`prompt` argument, 97
Properties, 124–127
Pull requests, 303, 308
.py, 20
PyCharm, 7–8

Straight arrow, 13, 109
String(s)
    adding space to, 26
    capitalization using, 177
    converting to numbers, 31
    definition of, 25–26, 30
    F-strings, 195–196
    finding and replacing text, 175–177
    formatting, 193–196
    hashing of, 323
    as immutable, 107
    input validation, 180–182
    joining, 178–180
    in lists, 39–40
    `for` loop, 62
    multiline, 189
    numbers converted to, 31–32
    operations using, 175–181
    pattern counting, 177–178
    slicing, 27–28
    splitting, 178–180
    third, 26–27
Structured query language. *See* SQL
sTunes database, 281, 284–286
Sublime, 7
Substitution, 192
Subtraction, 205, 206*f*
`super()`, 138–139

T

`t_`, 198
Tab indentations, 54, 57–58
TAB key, 54–55
tan(n), 208*f*
Temporary variables, 60, 62, 83
`terminal`, 20
Test coverage, 297
Test-driven design, 296
Test-driven development
    assertions, 294–295
    definition of, 291
    unit testing, 291–294
Text, finding and replacing of, 175–177
Text files, 226
Themes, in Visual Studio Code, 10–11
Threading, 320–322, 333
Time, 213–216
`timedelta` function, 214, 216
TODO comment, 76
`True`, 44, 67, 95–96, 154
`try` statement, 81, 85
Tuples
    for arbitrary arguments, 101–102
    description of, 40–41, 44*f*
    lists of, 47
`TypeError`, 30

U

Underscore, 126
Uniform Resource Locator. *See* URL
Unit testing, 291–294
`UPDATE`, 286, 288
UPDATE statements, 287
URL, 243–244, 267–268
`urllib.request`, 244
`urlopen` function, 245
UTF-8, 197, 226–227, 246, 324
`utility` module, 240

V

Variables
    assigning value to, 54
    case application of, 35
    casting, 32
    class, 118–119
    definition of, 23–25
    environment, 271, 314–315
    global, 268
    immutable, 40
    instance. *See* Instance variables
    mutable, 40
    names of, 25
    private, 124–127
    strings, 25–32
    temporary, 60, 62, 83
    third, 26–27
    `TypeError` with, 30
`vars()` function, 142, 162
Vim, 7–8, 257
Visual Basic 6, 2
Visual Studio Code
    debugging in, 257–261
    formatted code in, 58*f*
    Git support, 303
    installing, 7–8
    overview of, 9–13
    themes in, 10–11
    walk-through, 9–13
    where to find, 9

W

Wall clock time, 333–334
Web pages
    fetching of, 243–246
    saving of, 246
`web.py`, 265–269, 275
Websites
    description of, 265
    Django, 275–279
    Flask, 269–272, 275
    `web.py`, 265–269, 275
`while` loop, 65–68, 70, 105, 229
`while not` loop, 88
Wikimedia, 246

Wikipedia, 244–246
Windows
  environment variables in, 314–315
  hashing in, 324
  installing Git on, 302
  installing Python on, 5
  installing SQLite on, 282
  installing Visual Studio Code on, 7
Windows Subsystem for Linux, 304
Writing data, 230, 272

Y
`yield` statement, 103, 105

Z
`ZeroDivisionError`, 82–83

GET YOUR NEXT
QuickStart Guide®
FOR FREE

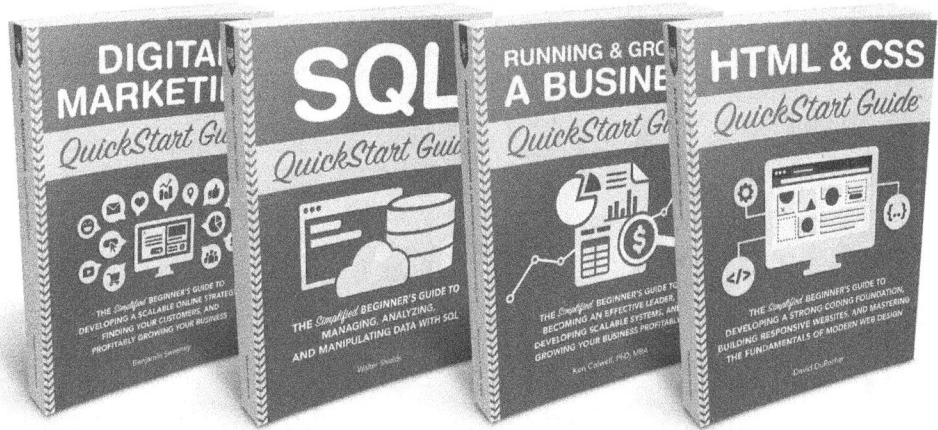

DIGITAL MARKETING QuickStart Guide

SQL QuickStart Guide

RUNNING & GROWING A BUSINESS QuickStart Guide

HTML & CSS QuickStart Guide

Leave us a quick video testimonial on our website and we will give you a **FREE QuickStart Guide** of your choice!

RECORD TESTIMONIAL

SUBMIT TO OUR WEBSITE

GET A FREE BOOK

TWO WAYS TO LEAVE A VIDEO TESTIMONIAL

Use the camera app on your mobile phone to scan the QR code or visit the link below to record your testimonial and get your free book.

or

go.quickstartguides.com/free-qsg

SCAN ME

VISIT URL

SAVE 10% ON YOUR NEXT
QuickStart Guide®

USE CODE: QSG10

www.quickstartguides.shop/sql

www.quickstartguides.shop/rungrow

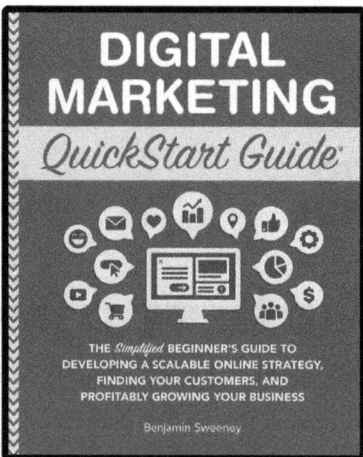

www.quickstartguides.shop/dmarketing

www.quickstartguides.shop/html-css

Use the camera app on your mobile phone to scan the QR code or visit the link below the cover to shop.
Get 10% off your entire order when you use code 'QSG10' at checkout at www.quickstartguides.com

LISTEN TO *QuickStart Guides* ON THE GO

NEW AUDIBLE MEMBERS
GET THEIR FIRST AUDIOBOOK

FREE!

DIGITAL MARKETING *QuickStart Guide*

FOREX TRADING *QuickStart Guide*

FLIPPING HOUSES *QuickStart Guide*

REAL ESTATE INVESTING *QuickStart Guide*

INVESTING *QuickStart Guide*

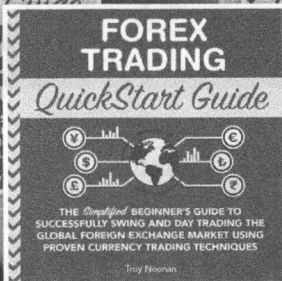

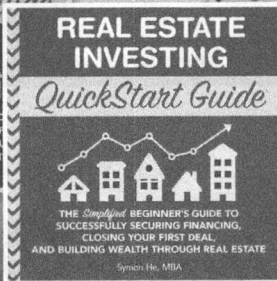

TWO WAYS TO SELECT A FREE AUDIOBOOK

Use the camera app on your mobile phone to scan the QR code or visit the link below to select your free audiobook from Audible.

or

www.quickstartguides.com/free-audiobook

SCAN ME　　　**VISIT URL**

CLYDEBANK MEDIA

QuickStart Guides®

PROUDLY SUPPORT ONE TREE PLANTED

One Tree Planted is a 501(c)(3) nonprofit organization focused on global reforestation, with millions of trees planted every year. ClydeBank Media is proud to support One Tree Planted as a reforestation partner.

Every dollar donated plants one tree and every tree makes a difference!

Learn more at www.clydebankmedia.com/charitable-giving or make a contribution at onetreeplanted.org.

www.ingramcontent.com/pod-product-compliance
Lightning Source LLC
Chambersburg PA
CBHW081107240326
41723CB00007B/397